FINLAND

BELARUS

D

2

UKRAINE

RUSSIA

KAZAKHSTAN

ROMANIA
•64

5• BULGARIA

1

TURKEY •66

60

CE

SYRIA

ISRAEL •69

68•

JORDAN

IRAQ

IRAN

EGYPT

SAUDI
ARABIA

UAE

OMAN

SUDAN

ERITREA

YEMEN

RAL
N REP

SOUTH
SUDAN

•70
ETHIOPIA

SOMALIA

UGANDA

KENYA

EM. REP
HE CONGO

•71

TANZANIA

ZAMBIA

MALAWI

•74 MOZAMBIQUE

ZIMBABWE

OTSWANA

MADAGASCAR

•72

SOUTH
AFRICA

UZBEKISTAN

KYRGYZSTAN

TURKMENISTAN •77

AFGHANISTAN

PAKISTAN •80

NEPAL •78

INDIA

BANGLADESH

•79

MYANMAR

LAOS

THAILAND

VIETNAM

•82

CAMBODIA

SRI
LANKA

•81

MALAYSIA

SINGAPORE

90•

MONGOLIA

CHINA

86•

•84

•83

•85 TAIWAN

PHILIPPINES

•89

INDONESIA

NORTH
KOREA

SOUTH
KOREA

JAPAN

•88 •87

TIMOR-
LESTE

PAPUA
NEW GUINEA

SOLOMON
ISLANDS

VANUATU

FIJI

AUSTRALIA

91•

96•

92•

94•

95•

93•

97•

99•

NEW ZEALAND

98• •100

RUN

RUN
RACES AND TRAILS
AROUND THE WORLD

CONTENTS

4

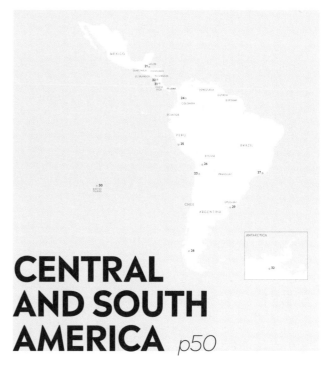

CENTRAL AND SOUTH AMERICA *p50*

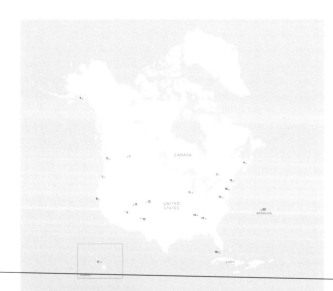

NORTH AMERICA *p12*

EUROPE *p74*

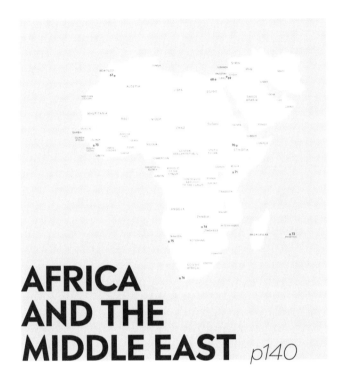

AFRICA AND THE MIDDLE EAST *p140*

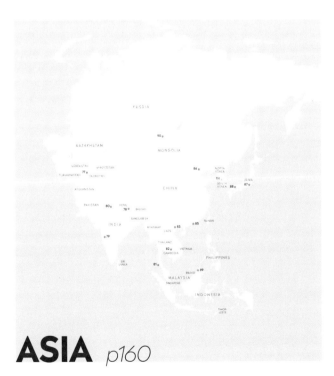

ASIA *p160*

AUSTRALASIA *p191*

Jogging through a
deep-green forest near
Vancouver in British
Columbia, Canada

INTRODUCTION

Running. Whether pounding the pavements with an encouraging running app, hitting the local parkrun with friends or signing up for a big city marathon, we're all doing it. But why? Well, for one thing, it's such a simple act – all that's needed is a pair of trainers and that all-important willpower. Then there's the challenge it brings, the feeling of pushing your body and testing your endurance – not to mention the sense of elation when you secure a personal best or cross a finish line. What's more, running can be a moving meditation, a way to let off steam, to find community and, wonderfully, a means to see the world around us. And that's where this book comes in.

Compiled by enthusiastic runners, sports journalists and travel writers, *Run* features 100 of the world's best running routes, from organized marathons to community-focused parkruns, tough trail runs to scenic city stretches. Here you'll find the big hitters – among them the world-famous Boston Marathon and the truly epic Ultra-Trail du Mont-Blanc – as well as some more unusual offerings. Race against a horse, try to beat the tides or lap 'til you drop: those up for a challenge will find it in these pages.

Each run has practical information to help you plan, including distance, total ascent and terrain, plus tips on the best sights to see on the way and snacks to devour post-run. We've also included elevation profiles, so you can – quite literally – see the ups and downs of the route, as well as advice on how to sign-up for official races. It's got everything you need to get started – so what are you waiting for? On your marks, get set, go!

PRACTICAL INFORMATION KEY

 DISTANCE    TOTAL ASCENT   TERRAIN

PREPARING FOR YOUR RUN

Whether running for fitness or fun, training for a marathon or planning to take on an epic ultra, it's important to do a bit of advance planning. To help you get ready for your run, we've put together some handy pointers.

Running Shoes

These are the most important piece of kit for any runner. The style you'll need will depend upon what type of running you're doing. For those tackling rougher terrain, for example, trail shoes offer more grip and support, while for those looking to compete in road races, fast and springy racing shoes work best. Getting the right fit and amount of support is also crucial – we recommend having your gait analysed at a specialist running store. This will match the degree of pronation (the way your foot rolls when you run) with your ideal shoe type. For instance, stability shoes are better for those who over-pronate (ankle rolls in), while neutral shoes are good for those who neither over- nor under-pronate.

LEAVE NO TRACE

Responsible Running

Protect the environment by keeping to the trail and closing all gates behind you (especially if you're in an area with grazing animals). Always take your rubbish with you and carry a refillable water bottle, bladder or flask to avoid using single-use plastic bottles.

Clothing

Choose clothes made with materials like polyester, nylon and bamboo, which help wick moisture away from the body. Short- or long-sleeved tops can be worn year round, depending on the weather conditions, with warmer base layers added to the mix in winter. Weatherproof gloves, a hat and a lightweight jacket are also important in cold or wet weather. On the bottom half, most runners choose shorts or running tights, many of which include handy pockets or linings to securely hold a phone or keys. Socks, meanwhile, should be made from breathable, wicking fabrics to help prevent blisters.

Heading up a mountain climb during the Ultra-Trail du Mont-Blanc in France

Nutrition

While nutrition is highly personal, there are some general rules that most runners follow. Make sure to consume carbohydrates (such as toast or a banana) roughly 30-60 minutes before running. For longer runs or races, eat simple carbs like rice, bread or pasta the evening before, which will help keep you fuelled the next day. Avoid foods high in fibre and fat, and dishes with chilli; they can cause stomach problems.

For half marathon distances and longer, you'll want to take in calories while you run: bananas, gels or energy drinks are most convenient. Water is also essential on most runs longer than 5–10 km (3.1–6.2 miles); add some electrolytes for longer distances or in warm weather. It's also a good idea to test out your food and drink regime before race day, to help avoid any issues with energy levels or your stomach.

Training Plans

Training plans vary widely and should be tailored to your own experience and aims. It's crucial to give yourself enough time to train: most 5-km (3.1-mile) to half marathon plans suggest at least 10 weeks' training,

Heading off on a training run along the riverside in Seoul, South Korea

while marathons and ultras need roughly 12–16 weeks' or more. Some runners schedule shorter practice races a few weeks before their main race to help them tweak their training plans and to test out kit and nutrition. Supplementary training, such as strength work and yoga, is also key to help keep your muscles healthy, as is factoring in regular rest days to avoid burnout.

Further Reading

The following websites are great resources when planning or training for a run.

www.runnersworld.com
Comprehensive resource covering kit, training plans, injury recovery and more.

www.runtastic.com
Great for keeping track of runs and following training plans, as well as wide-range content on things like nutrition tips and strength workouts.

www.strava.com
Exercise tracking website that helps plan routes and track training and progress.

www.trailrunnermag.com
Great advice and training tips for trail runners.

www.youtube.com/c/runningchannel
Training and advice from professional coaches and former Olympians for all levels of runner.

RUNNING SAFETY
Safety on Longer Runs

Always take a mobile phone with you – but don't rely on it for navigation.

Wear a running backpack filled with key kit like base layers, snacks and first aid supplies.

Stick to established routes that you can check in advance on platforms like Strava.

Take more food and water than you think you'll need.

In remote areas, try to avoid running alone.

ESSENTIAL KIT

Ready to start running but not sure what you need? Here's a handy overview of some of the essential kit you should always have with you, whether you're heading off on a quick jog or tackling a full marathon.

① **Socks** Comfort is key: look for moisture-wicking fabrics and make sure socks fit well. Some runners use compression socks or calf-sleeves on longer runs to help with blood flow and post-run recovery.

② **Water bottle** To keep hydrated on runs (and avoid single-use plastics), take a hand-held bottle or bring a soft-flask in a running belt.

③ **Mobile phone** Serves as a GPS tracking device and is useful for emergency calls (where signal is available).

④ **Sunglasses** Polarized sports sunglasses will protect eyes from glare – and flying bugs.

⑤ **Fitness earphones** Listen to playlists and podcasts on the go; just keep the volume low so you can hear what's happening around you.

⑥ **Sports armband** Essential for carrying keys, phone and bank card. Running belts are also an option, and include space for a drink and snacks.

⑦ **Road shoes** Most running shoes, unless specifically trail or track shoes, are designed for harder surfaces, like road, pavement and light trails.

⑧ **Trail shoes** With extra grip and support, trail running shoes are great for uneven and off-road terrain.

⑨ **Tracking watch** Track important details like time, distance and pace. Some can have training plans uploaded onto them or include maps.

⑩ **Running cap** In warm weather, a lightweight cap or visor keeps the sun off your face, while in bad weather it'll keep your head warm and dry.

EXTRA KIT

For longer runs, you'll require extra kit that's specific to the terrain and weather conditions. For trail races or ultra-marathons, the event organizer will also have a specific kit list, with many of the below items likely included.

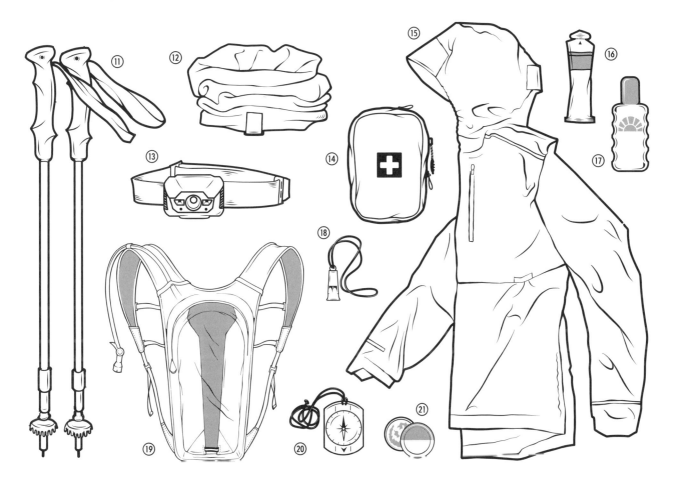

⑪ Lightweight poles Help with stability on hilly terrain – especially in wet conditions. Most can be attached to a belt or running vest when not in use.

⑫ Buff This versatile item can be used to warm your neck or head, or to protect from the sun.

⑬ Headtorch Essential on low-light runs and ultramarathons to help you navigate and stay safe. Use a lightweight option.

⑭ First aid kit A must have for ultras and longer runs. It should contain items to help treat blisters, cuts and sprains. Add a foil blanket, if possible.

⑮ Waterproof running jacket The best options will be light-weight and will pack down small into a running backpack, as well as being windproof and breathable. Bright colours help keep you visible, too.

⑯ Power snacks Gels, energy bars and dried fruit are great options; a drink with electro-lytes is also good on hot days.

⑰ Sunscreen Protect your skin with a high-SPF water-resistant sunscreen. You can also get sun-protective running clothing and hats.

⑱ Whistle Small, cheap and attracts attention in case of an emergency.

⑲ Hydration vest Perfect for carrying all the important kit, including drinks contained in bladders or soft flasks.

⑳ Compass This reliable piece of equipment will help you to navigate, without concerns about loss of battery or signal.

㉑ Anti-chafe protection Protect from chafing with something like Vaseline and use plasters to prevent blisters.

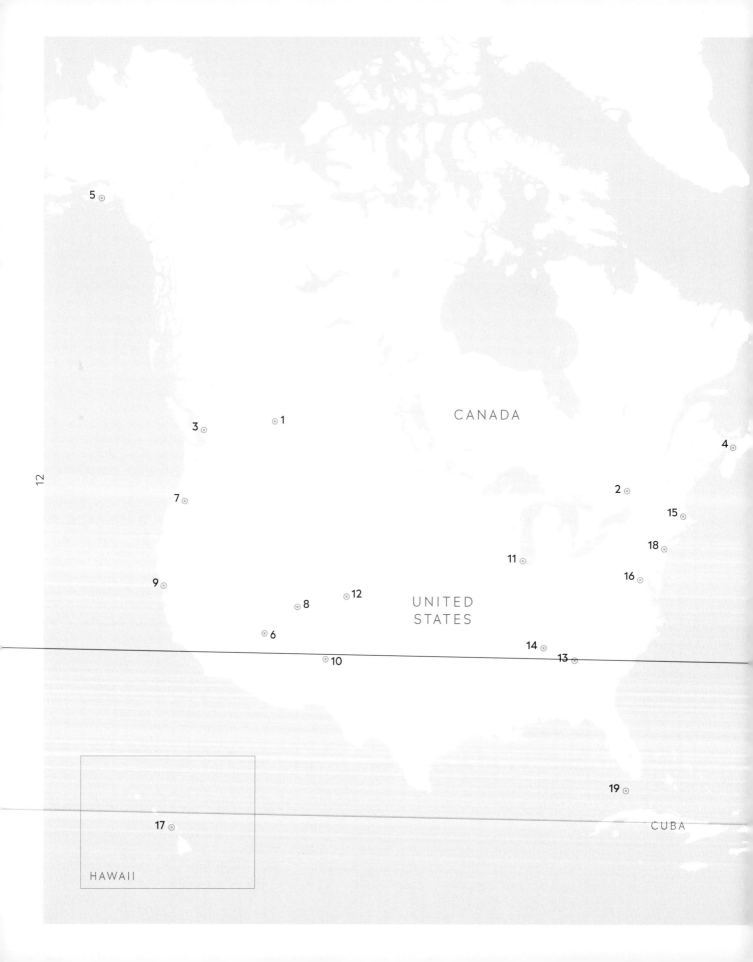

CANADA

UNITED
STATES

HAWAII

CUBA

5

3   1

4

12

2

15

7

18

11

16

9

8   12

6

14

10   13

19

17

⊙**20**
ERMUDA

NORTH AMERICA

1

Melissa's Road Race

BANFF, ALBERTA, CANADA

Majestic Rocky Mountain views and a supportive community vibe make the kilometres fly by at this sell-out running event in Canada's first national park.

Started in 1979 by the managers of Melissa's Missteak restaurant, Melissa's Road Race was an attempt to attract tourists to the mountain town of Banff in the off-season. Little did they know it, but this race would quickly become one of the most popular road races in Alberta.

A lot of the love for Melissa's comes from the locals, and the event is an annual tradition for many: one legend, Jim Fry, has completed every single race (over 40 so far), even the year he was on crutches. Non-runners line the streets to cheer participants on with clanging bells and high fives, to the upbeat strains of live music.

Besides the spirited atmosphere, the race offers staggering views of the Rocky Mountains. But you'll want to keep your eyes on the finish – Melissa's post-race party is legendary. Beer gardens, food trucks and even more live music keep the buzz going long into the evening.

SIGN-UP: *The race takes place in September and often sells out, so register early at* www.melissasroadrace.com.

⊖ 10 KM (6.2 MILES)

⊗ 207 M (679 FT)

⊖ PAVED/TRAIL

ELEVATION PROFILE

1,500 m
(4,920 ft)

1,000 m
(3,280 ft)

0   10 km (6.2 miles)

0 ········ metres ········ 500
0 ········ yards ········ 500

Around the 7.5 km (4.5 mile) mark, cross the Bow River for the last time, using a **FOOTBRIDGE** with stunning views of the rushing waters.

BANFF

Bow River Bridge

Finish

Start

Banff Pedestrian Bridge

Bow River

Surprise Corner

Crossing the century-old **BOW RIVER BRIDGE** brings views of Banff Avenue toward the base of Cascade Mountain.

As you descend on **BUFFALO STREET**, take a look at the Fairmont Banff Springs Hotel, a massive chateau-like structure built in 1888.

14

At the start of your run, pause to admire the eye-catching **SHAW CENTRE**, known for its curved glass-and-steel façade.

Start / Finish

Corktown Footbridge

Finish the route by crossing the **CORKTOWN FOOTBRIDGE**, named for the County Cork Irish labourers who built the structure.

OTTAWA

PATTERSON'S CREEK PARK is a pretty tree-dotted sliver of green found just off the canal.

Patterson's Creek Park

Lansdowne Park

TD Place Stadium

Bronson Bridge

15

Shortly after crossing to the western side of the canal, you'll spot **TD PLACE STADIUM** – it looks like a spaceship.

2

Ottawa Rideau Canal Loop

RIDEAU CANAL, OTTAWA, CANADA

Discover the different faces of Ottawa on this jog along the city's most historic waterway, which brilliantly showcases the beauty of the changing seasons.

Built in 1832, the Rideau Canal is the oldest continuously operated canal system in North America – and Ontario's only UNESCO World Heritage Site. Flowing through the Canadian capital, this historic ribbon of water is lined on each side by multiuse pathways that make a great spot for a casual afternoon jog.

You might think that running up and down the same stretch of path could be dull, but it never is here. Not only is this route home to some of Ottawa's best sights – including the leafy Confederation Park and tranquil Dow's Lake – it's also ever-changing, showing different sides to the city as the seasons turn. In spring, runners glide past the cheerful flowers that bloom along the canal in celebration of Ottawa's annual Tulip Festival; in summer, the heat sees the water dotted with kayakers and stand-up paddle boarders. And in autumn, the trees along the path burst into hues of orange and red. The most spectacular season, though, is winter, when Ottawa becomes a frozen wonderland. Then, runners get to look out onto the world's longest natural skating rink, while their breath puffs in front of them in frozen clouds.

SET OFF: *To get here, you can jump on a bus to the Rideau Centre bus stop; it's a short walk from the start of the run.*

⊖ 10 KM (6.2 MILES)

⬙ 56 M (184 FT)

⊖ PAVED

ELEVATION PROFILE

100 m (328 ft)

50 m (164 ft)

0   10 km (6.2 miles)

3

Stanley Park Seawall

STANLEY PARK, VANCOUVER, CANADA

Be prepared to stop in your tracks on this oceanside run. Snaking along the edge of Stanley Park, the seawall has stunning views of Vancouver and the natural beauty that surrounds it.

9.5 KM (5.9 MILES)

12 M (39 FT)

PAVED

16

Initially conceived in the early 20th century to prevent erosion, the Vancouver Seawall and its accompanying path quickly became a huge attraction. While the path continues 28 km (18.5 miles) around the city waterfront, the best section for running is this lush loop of Stanley Park. This leafy oasis is densely forested with old and new growth trees, and was once a First Nations ceremonial site, then a British military reserve, before finally being designated a public park in 1888. Today, it's the city's most popular recreation space.

The path along the seawall is paved, easily accessible and mostly flat, apart from a slight incline between Hallelujah Point and Brockton Point Lighthouse. Not surprisingly, this means it gets busy: you'll need to run early in the morning or out of season if you're after peace and quiet.

Even better than the smooth running path are the incredible views. From this route, the ocean is always in sight, whether it's lapping at the wall or far beyond the shore. Phenomenal panoramas encompass the glittering city skyline, the towering North Shore Mountains and the cobalt waters of Burrard Inlet, spanned by the arch of Lions Gate Bridge. Thankfully, there are plenty of scenic lookouts – complete with water fountains – where joggers can take a beat and admire the view.

ELEVATION PROFILE

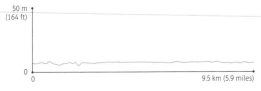

50 m
(164 ft)

0

0   9.5 km (5.9 miles)

Running along the Stanley Park Seawall, with views of Vancouver in the background

Said to be a young father turned to stone, **SIWASH ROCK** is important to Squamish First Nations culture as a symbol of selfless fatherhood.

Prospect Point

The most easterly point in the park, **BROCKTON POINT** is home to a lighthouse, nine totem poles and the Nine O'Clock Gun.

Siwash Rock

Backed by trees, the gorgeous **THIRD BEACH** has great views of West Van and the fjord and islands of Howe Sound.

Third Beach

STANLEY PARK

Ferguson Point

Brockton Point

Start / Finish

0 ········ metres ········ 500
0 ········ yards ········ 500

Lost Lagoon

Second Beach

LOST LAGOON was cut off from the ocean in the early 20th century, when the Stanley Park causeway (a highway to Lion's Gate Bridge) was built.

In between all the awe-inspiring vistas, you'll also see unique cultural landmarks, such as First Nations totem poles that honour British Columbia's Indigenous culture. And at the wall's edge, keep an eye out for the showpiece red-and-white 1914 Brockton Point Lighthouse and the bronze *Girl in the Wetsuit* sculpture (1972).

With so much to draw you from the trail, are you going to get your best time on this route? Probably not. But it's likely to be one of the most scenic routes you ever run.

SET OFF: *Take the bus to Stanley Park Drive at Pipeline Road, then enjoy a short warm-up walk to the start of the route, just past the park information booth.*

MAKE IT LONGER
False Creek Seawall

The seawall continues beyond the park. Instead of closing the loop at the information booth, strike out to Sunset Beach (4 km/2.5 miles) and continue as long as you like along the False Creek Seawall. From Science World, you can hop on the Expo Line back downtown.

4

Not Since Moses

FIVE ISLANDS PROVINCIAL PARK,
NOVA SCOTIA, CANADA

Prepare to get very dirty on this run across the exposed seabed of the Bay of Fundy, as you race the advance of the world's biggest tides.

10 KM (6.2 MILES) 3 M (10 FT) TRAIL

Every year, just off Canada's Nova Scotia province, enthusiastic runners attempt to dash 10 km (6 miles) over the ocean floor before the tides reclaim the land. It's a fast, fun-filled race – one whose name gives a nod to the Biblical story of Moses, who parted the Red Sea and led the ancient Israelites to the Promised Land.

The leviathan waters move lightning quick, but so long as you can complete the distance in less than 75 minutes you

Runners making their way across the gloopy seabed of the Bay of Fundy

can take part. (A team of volunteers also keep an eye on the rising tides.) The going is pretty sticky: expect a mix of shoe-sucking gloop, sandy bits, splashy bits and seaweed-slathered stone – but that's what makes this race such a blast. There's a strong chance of taking a tumble into the mud, but getting caked in salty sludge – and then helped up by your friendly fellow competitors – is all part of the fun.

SIGN-UP: *Space is limited; pre-register at* www.notsincemoses.ca.

18

ELEVATION PROFILE

50 m (164 ft)

0

0   10 km (6.2 miles)

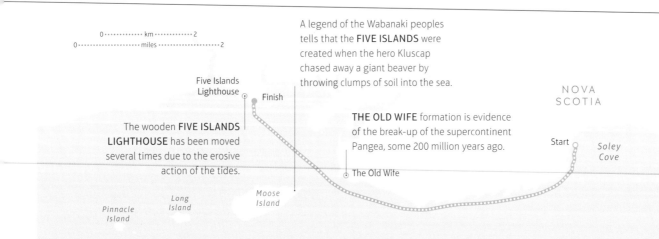

0 ·········· km ·········· 2
0 ·········· miles ·········· 2

A legend of the Wabanaki peoples tells that the **FIVE ISLANDS** were created when the hero Kluscap chased away a giant beaver by throwing clumps of soil into the sea.

Five Islands Lighthouse

Finish

NOVA SCOTIA

The wooden **FIVE ISLANDS LIGHTHOUSE** has been moved several times due to the erosive action of the tides.

THE OLD WIFE formation is evidence of the break-up of the supercontinent Pangea, some 200 million years ago.

Start

Soley Cove

The Old Wife

Moose Island

Long Island

Pinnacle Island

The steep **UPPER REACHES OF THE MOUNTAIN** reward runners with dizzying views over Seward and Resurrection Bay.

Race Point

0 ·········· metres ·········· 500
0 ·········· yards ·········· 500

There's a choice of routes near the beginning, before the path merges into one trail. Head straight up **THE CLIFFS** for the shortest – but trickiest – start.

The Chute

The Cliffs

The Gut

Start

Finish

ALASKA

The descent through **THE CHUTE** can be dusty, slippery, or on snow and ice; it's always perilously steep. Take your time.

5

Mount Marathon Race

SEWARD, ALASKA, US

What goes up, must come down on this zany there-and-back to the peak of a snow-capped mountain in Alaska.

5 KM (3.1 MILES)
881 M (2,890 FT)
TRAIL

Soaring above the port city of Seward in Alaska, Mount Marathon is the setting for what has been hailed as the "Toughest 5K on the Planet". This short yet punishing race takes runners on a scramble up the side of the mountain – all 920 m (3,000 ft) of it – over rock faces, up slippery mudbanks and then across a near-vertical slope of skittery scree. And that's just to reach the rock on its summit that marks the half-way point.

Coming back down is even harder. The seasoned advice is to keep a low centre of gravity, brace yourself against the slope and don't be afraid to "crab walk" down the

steepest bits if you have to. Once you've made it off the scree, you've just got the Chute to contend with – think dust clouds blurring your vision and probably a pocket or two of snow – and finally the Gut, complete with running water and loose rocks. The reward for finishing is priority entry to the next year's race – because you'll want to do it all again, of course.

SIGN-UP: *The race is held on 4 July. Places are limited, with priority going to those who have run before, but you can enter the lottery via www.mountmarathon.com.*

ELEVATION PROFILE

1,000 m
(3,280 ft)

0

0

5 km (3.1 miles)

19

REFUEL
Grab Supplies

There are water stops at the trailhead and Indian Garden all year round, plus extra seasonal ones from May to October, but take your own supplies to be safe. The supermarket next to Yavapai Lodge in Grand Canyon Village is a great place to stock up.

If you're after even more wow-factor, take the 2.5-km (1.5-mile) detour to **PLATEAU POINT**, where you'll get an excellent view of the Colorado River.

The **RIVER RESTHOUSE**, found on the banks of the winding Colorado River, marks the run's halfway point.

Colorado River

River Resthouse

Plateau Point

GRAND CANYON
NATIONAL PARK

Devil's Corkscrew

At **INDIAN GARDEN** you'll find a ranger station and useful facilities like self-rescue supplies and an emergency phone.

Indian Garden

The **DEVIL'S CORKSCREW** section of the trail winds through one of the oldest parts of the Grand Canyon.

THREE MILE RESTHOUSE provides shade, water, toilets and not much else. If you want to shorten your run to 10 km (6.2 miles), turn around here.

Three Mile
Resthouse

Start / Finish

0 ·········· km ·········· 1
0 ········· miles ········· 1

ELEVATION PROFILE

2,000 m
(6,560 ft)

0

0
24 km (15 miles)

20

6

Bright Angel Trail

BRIGHT ANGEL TRAILHEAD, GRAND CANYON
NATIONAL PARK, ARIZONA, US

*Delve into the heart of one of the most iconic landscapes in the US,
the Grand Canyon, on this rim-to-river trail. It takes in billions of years
of history and some truly spectacular views.*

24 KM (15 MILES) 1,340 M (4,396 FT) TRAIL

Twisting from the top of the Grand Canyon all the way to its floor, the Bright Angel Trail is one of the area's most popular hiking and running trails – and it's easy to see why. Magnificent views come thick and fast, from stunning vistas across the whole canyon to unexpected pools and pockets of green nestled amid the limestone.

The red-rock walls here are almost 2 billion years old, but it's the human history that makes this trail unique. The path follows one of the oldest routes into the canyon, used by the area's Native American communities for hundreds – if not thousands – of years. Up until the 1880s, the Havasupai and Hualapai made their way along this path each summer to the bottom of the canyon, where they'd use the waters of the Colorado River to grow crops. As you trace your way down the well-maintained path, you'll see ancient petroglyphs and the settlements of the Havasupai and Hualapai; the most striking of these is Indian Garden, an oasis in the middle of the dry, rocky terrain.

It's beautiful, but this out-and-back route can be tough. For one thing, it gets hot: it's a good idea to get going early, ideally around sunrise, to help you avoid the worst of the heat (as well as the crowds). For another, there's a lot of elevation involved – 1,340 m (4,396 ft), to be precise. Take it easy on the first half of the descent, which winds down for 6 km (4 miles) via a series of seemingly never-ending switchbacks; not only will your knees thank you, but you'll be saving your legs for the testing ascent on the way back.

SET OFF: *This route is best tackled in spring and autumn, when temperatures are generally milder.*

Switchbacks along the Bright
Angel Trail, as it winds its way
into the Grand Canyon

The **FROHNMAYER BRIDGE**, locally known as the Autzen Footbridge, connects Pre's Trail to Hayward Field and is used by the athletes to access the trail every day.

Start / Finish

The run begins by the University of Oregon's iconic **AUTZEN STADIUM**, where up to 54,000 football fans come to cheer on the Oregon Ducks.

EUGENE

Frohnmayer Bridge

Canoe Canal

0 ·········· metres ········· 500
0 ·········· yards ········· 500

Willamette River

Aspen Street Trailhead

The **ASPEN STREET TRAILHEAD**, in the neighbouring town of Springfield, makes a good alternative starting point for the route.

7

Pre's Trail

EUGENE, OREGON, US

Follow in the footsteps of legends on this famous route, the training ground of some of America's best distance runners.

8 KM (5 MILES)   25 M (82 FT)   TRAIL

Eugene is all about running. Nicknamed "Tracktown USA", this small town in the Pacific Northwest is the birthplace of Nike and the home of Hayward Field, the only venue in the US to host world-class track meets.

A hop, skip and a jump from Hayward Field is Pre's Trail, where elite athletes come to train every day. Yes, the riverside scenery is nice, but it's the trail's unique woodchip-and-bark surface that draws serious runners (it's supposed to be ideal for preventing injury). That and the history here. The route was pioneered by US distance running legend Steve "Pre" Prefontaine, who was inspired by European trails while racing on the international circuit in the 1970s. Suffice to say, a jog along this route follows in his iconic footsteps, and those of countless other running stars of the last 50 years.

SET OFF: *Park at the MLK Jr. Blvd trail-head, across from the Autzen Stadium.*

MAKE IT LONGER

Dorris Ranch

Follow the path along the river into the neighbouring town of Springfield and up 2nd Street to Dorris Ranch, a park with over 10 km (6 miles) of gravel roads and trails. The 6-km (4-mile) Middle Fork Path is a scenic option.

ELEVATION PROFILE

150 m (492 ft)

100 m (328 ft)

0   8 km (5 miles)

A group of athletes undertaking a training run on Pre's Trail

22

0 ·········· metres ·········· 400
0 ·········· yards ·········· 400

Mill Creek's **OLD POWER PLANT SPILLWAY** provides an excellent spot to cool down during the summer.

Mill Creek

Mill Creek
Waterfall

MILL CREEK WATERFALL is perfect for swimming, and has a small beach area where you can sit and relax.

Start / Finish

Old Power Plant Spillway

Mill Creek

Cowboys Jacuzzis

The waters of the **"COWBOY JACUZZIS"** are warmed by the desert stream flowing over a long section of slick rock.

8

Mill Creek

MILL CREEK NORTH FORK TRAILHEAD, MOAB, UTAH, US

This loop traces a path from arid desert to tree-dotted creek, passing by relaxing sun-warmed pools, a tumbling waterfall and ancient petroglyphs.

6.5 KM (4 MILES)   194 M (636 FT)   TRAIL

A stone's throw from the red-rock formations of Arches National Park, Mill Creek cuts through the desert landscape like a green ribbon. The first section of this run traces a path above this small canyon, giving expansive views over the sun-baked, sandy terrain, before dropping down a steep path into the creek itself.

It's like plunging into another world. Rough-trunked cottonwoods, silver leaf poplars and golden-yellow catalpas provide respite from the sun, while waterfalls and swimming holes cry out to joggers to take a refreshing dip. Only the most determined athletes can resist the "Cowboy Jacuzzis" – a series of shallow pools heated by the sun, offering blissful relief for tired legs.

Before you leave the gurgling streams and bright-green foliage behind, one last highlight remains: several panels of ancient petroglyphs. Carved by the Fremont Indians between 1,500 and 4,000 years ago, they're a poignant reminder of how long people have been treading this path.

SET OFF: *There is free parking at the Mill Creek North Fork Trailhead.*

ELEVATION PROFILE

1,500 m (4,920 ft)

1,000 m (3,280 ft)

0   6.5 km (4 miles)

You've made it; the Dipsea ends at gorgeous **STINSON BEACH**, a wide swathe of white sands framed by the Marin Hills.

The route briefly follows tiny Webb Creek down the aptly named **STEEP RAVINE**, a narrow gorge of giant rocks, roots and lush, dense foliage.

Finish

Steep
Ravine

9

Dipsea Race

MILL VALLEY TO STINSON BEACH, CALIFORNIA, US

Experience America's oldest trail race, an incredibly challenging but scenic route where anyone can be the winner.

12 KM (7.4 MILES) · 625 M (2,050 FT) · PAVED/TRAIL

First staged in 1905, the Dipsea Race remains a lovably small-scale, primarily local affair. The event was established after members of San Francisco's Olympic Club decided to run across the hills between Mill Valley and the Dipsea Inn, a hotel on the coast. The tough-but-beautiful terrain proved so inspiring they decided to make an annual race of it. It continues to be a major local event, with most of the participants hailing from the Bay Area.

Cutting through the woodlands of Mount Tamalpais State Park, just north

IN FOCUS
The Dipsea Demon

Californian Jack Kirk ran his first Dipsea Race in 1930 – little imagining he'd run it another 67 times, right up to 2003. Kirk's indefatigable determination to conquer the course quickly gained him the nickname the "Dipsea Demon". He won the race twice, in 1951 and again in 1967, at the age of 60. Jack died in 2007, at the fittingly ripe old age of 100.

of San Francisco's Golden Gate Bridge, the Dipsea is a real test of stamina and endurance, despite its relatively short length. Much of the dirt trail is steep and narrow, with the course pitching up and down like a giant rollercoaster. Runners are pushed to the limit, especially at the start. Beginning in Mill Valley, the course zig-zags up densely forested slopes via

ELEVATION PROFILE

500 m
(1,640 ft)

0

0   12 km (7.4 miles)

0 ·············· metres ·············· 800
0 ·············· yards ·············· 800

Start

Dipsea Stairs

Soak up the sensational views
of the Pacific coast from the
summit of **CARDIAC HILL**, the
highest point on the route.

Cardiac
Hill

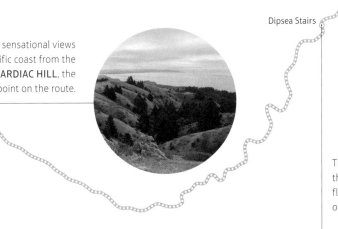

CALIFORNIA

The most notorious section is
the **DIPSEA STAIRS**: three steep
flights that climb to the height
of a 50-storey building.

three sets of stairs – some 675 gruelling
steps in the first mile. The trail then drops
down to Redwood Creek before another
long, punishing climb up the aptly named
Cardiac Hill. And not only is the terrain
hilly, it can be treacherous, too – in some
places, the route is littered with rocks
and roots that add extra obstacles for
aching legs.

Why do it? For the thrill, of course,
but also for the taste of the wild it brings.
Within minutes of the start it's like you're
in the arboreal forests of Alaska, a million
miles from civilization. Even more tantalizing, though, is the genuine possibility

of becoming the race winner. A unique
handicapping system allows the slowest
runners to go first – head starts of up to
25 minutes are based on age and gender –
which has led to some surprising victors
over the years. In 2010, a local 8-year-old
girl, Reilly Johnson, was the youngest
person to ever win the race, while in 2012,
72-year-old Hans Schmid became the
oldest person to claim first place. This
means that, whatever their age or running
ability, everyone has the chance to be the
next champion of the Dipsea.

SIGN-UP: *The application process favours
previous runners and local residents,
although places are open to other appli-
cants. See* www.dipsea.org *for details.*

A Dipsea participant making their way along the route
as it weaves above the Marin Headlands

10

Paseo del Bosque Trail

ALAMEDA TRAILHEAD TO RIO BRAVO
BOULEVARD, ALBUQUERQUE, NEW MEXICO, US

*Flanking the Rio Grande as it passes through the heart of
Albuquerque, this multiuse trail is dotted with natural wonders
and cultural sights that will lure you away from the path.*

Top Tip

There's lots of
information about the
trail on the City of
Albuquerque website
(*www.cabq.gov*).

28 KM (17 MILES)   40 M (131 FT)   PAVED/TRAIL

26

Slicing north-south through the sprawling capital of New Mexico, you might assume the Paseo del Bosque Trail serves up typical urban scenes of concrete and glass towers, roadways and traffic. But this agreeably flat, paved pathway reveals a more unexpected side to the city and the high desert country that surrounds it.

Running along the east bank of the Rio Grande, the path cuts through the great strands of cottonwoods, willows, olive trees and mesquite that border the river – known as "bosque" (Spanish for "woodland", pronounced "boss-key"), this habitat is a ribbon of life in an otherwise arid land. Commercial development here has been kept to a minimum, and though you're never far from the city, you'll see more of the reddish Sandia Mountains on the horizon than the urban skyline.

Nature lovers might want to combine their morning run with a few detours. The trail skirts Rio Grande Nature Center State Park, a wonderfully preserved section of bosque wetland that attracts a wide range of birdlife, as well as Tingley Beach, a series of ponds used for fishing and boating.

This run doesn't just take in the natural world, though – further south there's the National Hispanic Cultural Center, dedicated to Latinx art, culture and performance. Its distinctive Torreón building, which you can

ELEVATION PROFILE

1,600 m
(5,250 ft)

1,500 m
(4,920 ft)

0   28 km (17 miles)

Passing along a tree-lined section of the
Paseo del Bosque Trail

Check out the bird-rich wetlands of the **ALAMEDA & RIO GRANDE OPEN SPACE**, where you can glimpse ducks, geese and other wildlife.

Start

Alameda & Rio Grande Open Space

Leave your vehicle in the car park right next to the **ALAMEDA TRAILHEAD**, pull on your trainers and get ready to run.

Rio Grande

ALBUQUERQUE

Soak up the enchanting views of the Rio Grande from the **MIRADOR DEL RIO**, an observation deck just off the main trail.

As the trail skirts the **ABQ BIOPARK**, look out for the blue-green glass pavilions of the Botanical Gardens.

ABQ BioPark

Tingley Beach

Mirador del Rio

National Hispanic Cultural Center

Though there's very little sand, the series of ponds that make up **TINGLEY BEACH** are beautifully landscaped.

Rio Grande

Finish

see from the trail, was modelled on the circular watchtowers of colonial Spanish New Mexico. On the west bank of the river, a short run across the Montaño Road Bridge, the Pueblo Montaño Picnic Area holds a real surprise. Local artist Mark Chavez has created chainsaw sculptures from the cottonwood tree stumps left after the devastating bosque fires of 2003; they include vivid depictions of local fauna and flora and even a Mexican folklore character, La Llorona (aka "The Weeping Woman"). By the end of your morning jog, you'll have discovered sides to the New Mexico capital that few visitors see.

SET OFF: *Tackle the trail during autumn for cooler temperatures.*

REFUEL

A Latin Fusion Lunch

Eating options along the Bosque Trail itself are few, but towards the southern end of the route the National Hispanic Cultural Center offers an excellent pitstop for a post-run lunch. Helmed by Chef Stefani Mangrum, La Fonda del Bosque (*www.lafondadelbosqueabq.com*) showcases Latin fusion cooking and New Mexico inspired decor.

27

11

Chicago Marathon

GRANT PARK, CHICAGO, ILLINOIS, US

One of the largest, fastest, most renowned marathons in the world, this looping course round Chicago is great for personal bests – and for exploring some of the city's most diverse neighbourhoods.

42.2 KM (26.2 MILES)   48 M (157 FT)   PAVED

28

Maybe it's the fast, flat course. Maybe it's the iconic skyline. Or maybe it's the chance to get up close and personal with the diverse districts of one of America's greatest cities. Whatever the reason, the Chicago Marathon has become one of the most popular running events in the world, with over 45,000 participants each year.

It probably helps that the route is lined with around 1.7 million spectators, several people deep throughout, who descend on the city to lend their raucous support each year. Street parties also provide a boost, with some of the best taking place in Boystown, where costumed supporters blast music, and Chinatown, where dragon dancers help lift flagging spirits (and soles). And, of course, there's the route's smooth, level roads, which have carried multiple victors to the finish in record-breaking times – eight national records have been broken here, as have

Pounding the streets near mile 14, with the Willis Tower in the background

four world records. In fact, in 2019, Kenyan Brigid Kosgei completed the race in just 2 hours, 14 minutes and 4 seconds, which is still the fastest a woman has ever run any marathon; her compatriot, Dennis Kimetto, holds the men's record for this course (2 hours, 3 minutes and 45 seconds). While most runners won't make such super speedy progress, this is definitely a course where you can push yourself towards a new personal best.

It's all a far cry from when the first run was held in 1905. Just half a dozen competitors started the race that year and only ▶

ELEVATION PROFILE

200 m
(656 ft)

150 m
(492 ft)

0   42.2 km (26.2 miles)

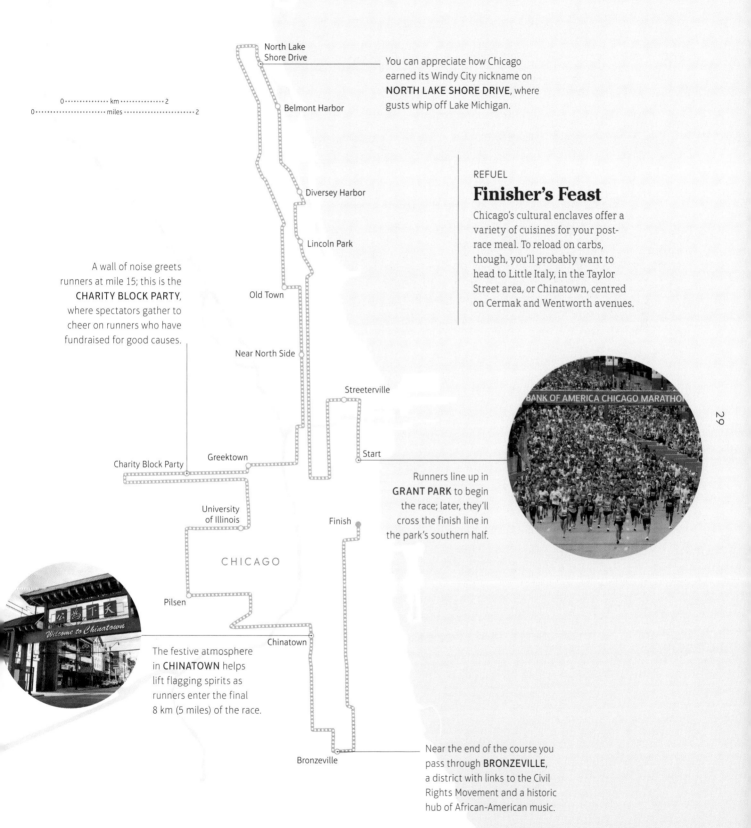

North Lake
Shore Drive

You can appreciate how Chicago
earned its Windy City nickname on
NORTH LAKE SHORE DRIVE, where
gusts whip off Lake Michigan.

0 ··········· km ··········· 2
0 ··········· miles ··········· 2

Belmont Harbor

Diversey Harbor

REFUEL
Finisher's Feast
Chicago's cultural enclaves offer a
variety of cuisines for your post-
race meal. To reload on carbs,
though, you'll probably want to
head to Little Italy, in the Taylor
Street area, or Chinatown, centred
on Cermak and Wentworth avenues.

Lincoln Park

A wall of noise greets
runners at mile 15; this is the
CHARITY BLOCK PARTY,
where spectators gather to
cheer on runners who have
fundraised for good causes.

Old Town

Near North Side

Streeterville

BANK OF AMERICA CHICAGO MARATHON

Charity Block Party   Greektown

Start

Runners line up in
GRANT PARK to begin
the race; later, they'll
cross the finish line in
the park's southern half.

University
of Illinois

Finish

CHICAGO

Pilsen

Welcome to Chinatown

The festive atmosphere
in **CHINATOWN** helps
lift flagging spirits as
runners enter the final
8 km (5 miles) of the race.

Chinatown

Bronzeville

Near the end of the course you
pass through **BRONZEVILLE**,
a district with links to the Civil
Rights Movement and a historic
hub of African-American music.

Running alongside Chicago's iconic skyscrapers

seven of those managed to finish it. The runners had to dodge traffic – hundreds of spectators followed them on bikes and in horsedrawn carriages and cars – and they were forced to stop at a railway crossing to wait for a passing train, then again at a drawbridge while a steamship chugged slowly through. Back then, the runners' routines were slightly more unorthodox, too. An American named John Lindquist built a healthy lead in the 1907 marathon fuelled by shots of whiskey. By mile 23 he could no longer keep his eyes open and

had to bow out before reaching the finish line. Frenchman Albert Corey fared better the following year, winning the event thanks to a drink regimen centred around champagne. Suffice to say, most participants today take a more health-conscious approach to fuelling en route.

The race had a fifty-year hiatus after falling out of favour in the 1920s (in part due to the Great Depression) but has been going strong since making its comeback in the late 1970s. Today's Chicago Marathon starts and ends in the grassy expanses of Grant Park and sees runners pounding their way through 29 of the city's neighbourhoods, taking in some of Chicago's most famous landmarks along the way. You'll pass Anish Kapoor's *Cloud Gate* sculpture, more affectionately known as "The Bean", cross the distinctively blue-green Chicago

> Runners pound their way through the city, taking in some of Chicago's most famous landmarks

River and run along the top of North Michigan Avenue, the city's main commercial district – and that's just in the first mile alone. From here the route provides a tour of Chicago, taking in many of the city's multicultural neighbourhoods as it goes: Little Italy, with its traditional trattorias; Chinatown's curved-roof temples; the colourful Mexican murals of Pilsen; and small but vibrant Greektown, where you'll pass by the Hellenic Museum and Cultural Center. After mile 23, it's onto the home straight, as you dig deep on the last section into Grant Park. There, the finish line – and a hefty silver finisher's medal – awaits.

SIGN-UP: *The race takes place in October. Registration for the following year is open from October to November at* www.chicagomarathon.com.

ANOTHER WAY
Shamrock Shuffle

The Shamrock Shuffle is an 8-km (5-mile) run that also starts and ends in Grant Park. Held in March, the high-spirited "race" is a continuation of the city's St Patrick's Day celebrations, with many runners turning up in Irish-themed fancy dress.

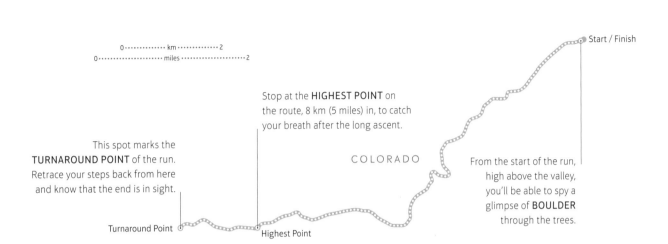

0 ···· km ···· 2
0 ···· miles ···· 2

Stop at the **HIGHEST POINT** on the route, 8 km (5 miles) in, to catch your breath after the long ascent.

This spot marks the **TURNAROUND POINT** of the run. Retrace your steps back from here and know that the end is in sight.

COLORADO

From the start of the run, high above the valley, you'll be able to spy a glimpse of **BOULDER** through the trees.

Start / Finish

Turnaround Point

Highest Point

12

Magnolia Road

BOULDER, COLORADO, US

Challenge yourself on this high-altitude out-and-back route. Found just outside of Boulder and situated at 2,470 m (8,100 ft), Magnolia Road is a regular training run for many professional US distance runners.

23 KM (14 MILES)   426 M (1,398 FT)   TRAIL

Runner tackling a morning training session along Magnolia Road

Come summer, the top runners of the NCAA (National Collegiate Athletic Association) head to Boulder, tucked in the foothills of the Rocky Mountains, to train at altitude. Rising early before it gets too hot, these athletes head out into the mountains to tackle Magnolia Road.

Nicknamed "Mags", this out-and-back run is gruelling. Starting at a high-altitude elevation of 2,470 m (8,100 ft), the route will have even the toughest runners gasping for breath. And while the overall elevation gain isn't that dramatic – 426 m (1,397 ft) in total – the rolling nature of the route means that you'll never really be running on flat ground. Passing through a mix of woodland and open fields, it's a calf-aching cycle of climbing and then descending, climbing then descending. By the end your legs will be throbbing, your heart pumping and your lungs heaving. But you'll have tackled one of the most famous training routes in the US – so make like the college kids and treat yourself to a celebratory beer.

SET OFF: *Do as the professionals do and tackle this run early in the morning.*

ELEVATION PROFILE

2,800 m
(9,186 ft)

2,400 m
(7,874 ft)

0   23 km (14 miles)

13

Amicalola Falls Loop

CHATTAHOOCHEE NATIONAL FOREST,
GEORGIA, US

*Head into wild, wooded backcountry on this challenging run,
which takes in the highest waterfall in Georgia.*

17 KM (10.5 MILES)   765 M (2,510 FT)   TRAIL

Traversing a small pocket of the Chattahoochee National Forest, this loop feels wonderfully remote. It starts with a bang near the Amicalola Falls, before winding deeper into the mossy forest, past towering oaks, red maples and tulip trees. Yellow-hued prairie warblers flit through the leaves, while pileated woodpeckers knock-knock-knock on tree trunks. These woods are wild and spotting black bears is a possibility; if you do, keep your distance.

Trail shoes are a necessity. The path is undulating, to say the least, with a couple of calf-biting ascents, including the rocky climb to the Len Foote Hike Inn. At this halfway pit-stop, the path breaks out of the trees to take in a sweeping panorama over the rolling, forest-covered hills. Pause to soak up the views before plunging back in for the return leg.

SET OFF: *Park at West Ridge Falls Access after entering the Amicalola Falls State Park; a fee of $5 applies.*

ELEVATION PROFILE

1,000 m
(3,280 ft)

500 m
(1,640 ft)

0   17 km (10.5 miles)

MAKE IT LONGER
Springer Mountain

Add on the 11-km (7-mile) round trip to Springer Mountain, the terminus of the Appalachian Trail, to give you some extra miles. It's accessed via the Appalachian Approach Trail, which leaves from the Len Foote Hike Inn – simply turn right, instead of going left back to the falls.

About 6 km (4 miles) into the run is an **UNNAMED OVERLOOK** with views over the Chattahoochee National Forest.

33

GEORGIA

Len Foote
Hike Inn

Unnamed
Overlook

Amicalola Creek

If you want to break up your run, stay the night at the eco-friendly **LEN FOOTE HIKE INN**, which has water-saving compost toilets and solar panels.

AMICALOLA FALLS is the tallest waterfall in Georgia; its name is a Cherokee term that translates to "Tumbling Water".

Amicalola Falls

Start / Finish

0 ·········· km ·········· 1
0 ········· miles ············· 1

NORTH AMERICA

14

Big Dog's Backyard Ultra

BELL BUCKLE, TENNESSEE, US

Run 'til you drop on a loop trail through the backwoods of rural Tennessee, on an ultra ultramarathon that is likely to last for days.

VARIES ⊖ VARIES ⊗ PAVED/TRAIL ⊘

34

Gruelling. Brutal. The weirdest, toughest race you've never heard of. Many descriptions have been hung on Big Dog's Backyard Ultra, but it's impossible to comprehend just how challenging this event is until you've lined up at the starting line. Again and again and again.

Big Dog's is the original backyard ultra. Organized by Gary Cantrell, better known as Lazarus Lake, it takes place on his sprawling farm in Bell Buckle, Tennessee. The idea is devilishly simple: run a loop measuring 4.16667 miles (6.7 km) within one hour. Then do it over and over again, starting each circuit on the hour – ideally finishing with enough time spare to eat, rest and maybe even catch a couple of minutes' sleep – until you can run no more. The winner is the last person standing. (The course record is an incredible 85 loops.)

You don't need to be the fastest or the strongest to succeed, you just need to keep dragging yourself to the start line until

A group of hardy runners competing in Big Dog's Backyard Ultra

you're the only one left – the challenge of Big Dog's lies in the mind rather than the muscles. Everyone bar the winner is classified as a Did Not Finish, so you either come first or you come nowhere. The fact that the second-placed runner is awarded an "assist", however, offers an insight into the kind of camaraderie that's built over the event. Lifelong friendships are formed in the attrition of Big Dog's backyard.

SIGN-UP: *Big Dog's takes place in October. You need to have won another Backyard Ultra to be eligible to enter; see* www.backyardultra.com *for a list of races.*

ELEVATION PROFILE

300 m (985 ft)

200 m (656 ft)

0   6.7 km (4.2 miles)

Barkley Marathons

Lazurus Lake is also the brains behind the Barkley Marathons, where runners have 60 hours to finish five 32-km (20-mile) loops of an unmarked course in Tennessee's Frozen Head State Park. Along the way, they need to collect pages from books that have been hidden in the woods – while trying not to get lost. The last time someone finished the course was in 2017.

Keep focused during the trail run(s) through the **WOODS**, where slippery leaf-litter and rocks can prove tricky to navigate.

TENNESSEE

0 ·········· metres ·········· 200
0 ·········· yards ·········· 200

Try to ignore the **FINISH LINE** that greets you at the end of each loop. It cruelly reads: "(There Is No) Finish".

Rest area

Millersburg Road

Start / Finish

In the **REST AREA** you can stretch, grab a bite to eat and enjoy a precious minute or two's sit-down – before heading back to the start line once again.

This map shows the day route, but for safety reasons runners switch to a simpler (and flatter) out-and-back stretch along **MILLERSBURG ROAD** at night.

Boston Marathon runners
nearing the finish line
on Boylston Street

Top Tip

The route's Cemetery
Mile section isn't too
crowded, making it
a good place for
supporters to stand.

15

Boston Marathon

HOPKINTON TO BOSTON,
MASSACHUSETTS, US

*Competing in the Boston Marathon is pretty much every
runner's dream. Each year, this prestigious race draws
fleet-footed athletes from around the globe, all looking
to take on the world's oldest marathon.*

42.2 KM (26.2 MILES)   252 M (827 FT)   PAVED

If there's one event that runners aspire
to do, it's the Boston Marathon. Set up
in 1897 by members of Boston Athletic
Association, it was inspired by the marathon
at the first modern Olympic games in
Athens, Greece. Fast forward almost 130
years and, today, Boston's version of this
race is the world's oldest annual marathon
and one that carries a lot of status – as
well as major bragging rights.

It's little surprise, then, that qualifying
for the marathon is notoriously difficult.
Most potential participants have to run
the tough qualifying time in another

marathon to gain entry. Over the years,
as the race has gained in popularity,
that time has become faster and faster –
and more and more difficult to achieve.
This isn't just a race that you train really
hard for, it's one that you have to train
really hard to even get into – simply
qualifying for the marathon is a massive
victory in itself. ▶

ELEVATION PROFILE

200 m
(656 ft)

0

0   42.2 km (26.2 miles)

REFUEL
Celebratory Beer

Once you've finished the marathon,
celebrate and rehydrate with a specially
crafted beer that's been brewed just for the
Boston Marathon weekend. The fittingly
named Samuel Adams 26.2 Brew is a refresh-
ingly crisp beer that will quench your post-
run thirst. Visit *www.samueladams.com*
to find on-tap and bottle purchase locations.

37

Running really fast isn't the only way to gain entry, though. Some runners decide to take on the marathon for a charitable cause. Places are more limited (around 2,500), but there's no taxing qualifying time to be met. Plus, there's the added bonus of doing a good turn.

However you enter, the race itself is no walk in the park. While at first blush the elevation map doesn't look too challenging – overall, the course actually runs downhill – it definitely doesn't take it easy on participants. The route starts with a descent, often tempting runners to push their pace in the hopes of conquering the first half of the marathon faster. But those in the know keep a check on their speed – run too fast to begin with and you'll find yourself with jelly legs before you've even hit the rolling hills that mark the rest of the course.

It's tough, but luckily for the entrants, this race has some of the best cheerleaders in the world. Folks here really get into the spirit of things: shouting constant encouragement to spur runners onward.

Runners will need all the support they can get by the time they reach the infamous Newton Hills.

Spirits are high – and not just because of the race itself. For Bostonians, the marathon is a way to say goodbye to the long winter (which can be toe-freezingly cold) and welcome in the much longed-for spring. Plus, the marathon is held on Patriots' Day, a public holiday, meaning there's often a festival-like vibe in the air.

Runners will need all the support they can get by the time they reach the infamous Newton Hills. Here, participants are forced to change gear and fight their way upwards, especially on the fourth and final climb. Known as Heartbreak Hill, this savage ascent near mile 20 sees the road rise 27 m (88 ft) in half a mile. The hill earned its name in 1936, after Johnny "Elder"

0 ············· km ············· 3
0 ················ miles ················ 3

Wellesley College
Scream Tunnel

At **HOPKINTON** is a statue of George V Brown, the athletic director for the Boston Athletic Association, who fired the starting pistol for the marathon from 1905 to 1937.

The **WELLESLEY COLLEGE SCREAM TUNNEL** is known for its cheeky signs and shrieking crowds.

Stylianos
Kyriakides statue

Start

Just after mile 3, runners pass a **STATUE OF STYLIANOS KYRIAKIDES**, a Greek runner who ran the 1946 Boston Marathon.

Wheelchair racers making their way past Wellesley College

Kelley caught up with Ellison Myers "Tarzan" Brown and patted his shoulder on the incline. Brown and Kelley battled it out over the next 10 km (6 miles) before Brown took the win. The loss was said to have broken Kelley's heart – hence the moniker.

That story has become a running legend, but it's not the only one associated with the Boston Marathon. Women weren't officially allowed to enter the race until 1972, but Kathrine Switzer became the first woman to officially run it back in 1967. (Roberta "Bobbi" Gibb, who ran in 1966, was technically the first, but she had been forced to run as a "bandit", without an official bib number; Switzer herself had to register as K V Switzer to secure a bib.)

For most runners, simply completing the marathon is an incredible achievement – and the final miles definitely have a triumphant air. Turning onto Boylston Street, the last stretch of the route, runners are kept going by the deafening roar of the crowds, whose cheers swell to a crescendo as they cross the finish line. After all, they've not only completed a marathon – they've completed the Boston Marathon.

SIGN-UP: *The marathon has qualifying times. See* www.baa.org/races/boston-marathon *for information and to register.*

BOSTON

Citgo Sign   Finish

Heartbreak Hill

On Marathon Sunday, the **OLD SOUTH CHURCH** near the finish line honors the race and its runners with a "Blessing of the Athletes".

Many argue that the real race begins after **HEARTBREAK HILL**, just outside Boston College.

IN FOCUS
2013 Bombing

In 2013, the historic race suffered a terrorist attack, in which three people were killed and hundreds more injured. The harrowing event caused an outpouring of grief – and of support. In fact, the following year more runners than ever signed up for the marathon, with an all-time high of 36,000 participants and a record-breaking 1 million spectators lining the course.

16
The National Mall

WASHINGTON, DC, US

Flowing along the National Mall, this run winds past mighty monuments, museums and memorials, in a grand tour of some of Washington, DC's most famous landmarks.

8.2 KM (5.1 MILES)   55 M (180 FT)   PAVED

A political and cultural powerhouse, Washington, DC is home to more than its fair share of nation-defining monuments. And what better way to take them in than with a run along the National Mall? Starting at the imposing white dome of the Capitol Building, this gentle route skirts the edge of the manicured lawns that form "America's front yard". Along the way are some truly tempting museums, including the National Museum of African American History and Culture and the National Museum of the American Indian. Further nods to US history emerge as the path continues onwards, including memorials for veterans of World War II and the Vietnam War.

The run's highlight, though, comes at the halfway point: by the great marble columns of the Lincoln Memorial. Run up the steps to see the statue of Abraham Lincoln, then turn for one of the US's most iconic views: the Washington Monument rising into the sky, its slender form perfectly mirrored in the Reflecting Pool.

40

SET OFF: *Run first thing in the morning to avoid busy crowds of visitors.*

ELEVATION PROFILE

50 m (164 ft)

0

0   8.2 km (5.1 miles)

Honouring the US's first president, the 169 m (555 ft) **WASHINGTON MONUMENT** is the world's tallest stone structure.

WASHINGTON, DC

Finish
Start

Lincoln Memorial

Reflecting Pool

World War II Memorial

Washington Monument

Smithsonian Castle

The red sandstone **SMITHSONIAN CASTLE** houses the visitor centre for the Smithsonian Institution.

The **UNITED STATES CAPITOL BUILDING** marks the start; it has housed the United States Congress for over 200 years.

Pay your respects at the **WORLD WAR II MEMORIAL,** honouring the 16 million troops who served in the US Armed Forces during the war.

0 ······ metres ······ 500
0 ······ yards ······ 500

The soft, palm-fringed sands of Wailea Beach on a sunny day

Mokapu Beach

ULUA BEACH is smaller than Wailea Beach and is popular with snorkelers and divers.

Ulua Beach

MAUI

WAILEA BEACH is a long stretch of pillow-soft sand, fronting a pair of luxurious resorts.

Wailea Beach

Stop at **WAILEA POINT**, where lava rocks extend into the ocean, and peek into the water for sea turtles.

Wailea Point

Start / Finish

0 ·········· metres ·········· 500
0 ·········· yards ·········· 500

17

Wailea Beach Path

WAILEA, MAUI, HAWAII, US

Follow the edge of the beautiful Hawaiian island of Maui on this palm-lined path, taking in stunning tropical vistas along the way.

5.6 KM (3.5 MILES) 60 M (197 FT) PAVED

This mostly flat oceanfront pathway curves along Maui's southwest coast, skirting the edge of Wailea, a luxurious resort and residential community. It's at its best first thing in the morning, when the air is cooler and the sunbathers are still asleep; time it right and you could be running with views of the sun rising over Haleakalā's soaring peak.

Don't expect any personal records here – the scenery is just too spectacular. The path traces a line past swaying palm trees, black lava outcrops and cream-coloured sandy beaches. There's even more to see in winter, when migrating humpbacks can be seen breaching near the shore. No matter the time of year, the deep-blue Pacific Ocean – dotted with the islands of Kaho'olawe and Molokini – is a constant companion, glittering and sparkling in the early morning sunshine.

SET OFF: *Multiple access points let you start and finish wherever you want.*

ELEVATION PROFILE

50 m
(164 ft)

0

0   5.6 km (3.5 miles)

MAKE IT LONGER

Beaches Galore

If you feel like extending your run, continue north along the sands to Keawakapu Beach; it adds about 1.6 km (1 mile) extra. Alternatively, head 1.3 km (0.8 miles) south along Makena Road, heading past Palauea Beach and luxury oceanfront homes to reach golden Po'olenalena Beach.

Runners jogging
alongside Central
Park South during the
New York City Marathon

18

New York City Marathon

STATEN ISLAND TO CENTRAL PARK,
NEW YORK CITY, NEW YORK, US

The world's largest marathon sees over 50,000 runners
pound their way along New York City's streets. Cheered
on by roaring crowds, participants pass through all five
boroughs on a whirlwind tour of this world-famous city.

42

42.2 KM (26.2 MILES)
246 M (810 FT)
PAVED

No one would deny it: the New York City
Marathon is one of the world's top races, a
rite of passage for long-distance runners
from all over the world. But for such a
renowned race, it had rather humble begin-
nings. Back in 1970, Fred Lebow and Vince
Chiapetta, presidents of the New York Road
Runners, organized a marathon around
Central Park. A smattering of spectators
turned up to see the 127 competitors (who
had paid just one dollar to enter) tackle
several laps of the park, dodging cyclists ▶

ELEVATION PROFILE

100 m
(328 ft)

0

0   42.2 km (26.2 miles)

Top Tip
Get your friends and family to download the TCS NYC Marathon app; they'll be able to track your live location.

IN FOCUS
Fred's Statue

Tucked away in a corner of Central Park (at 90th Street and East Drive) stands a curious statue of a man checking his watch. This is Fred Lebow, co-founder of the New York Marathon and one of its most vociferous supporters. Every year his statue is moved within view of the marathon's finish line.

and pedestrians as they went. In the end only 55 hardy runners crossed the finish line; they were handed recycled trophies and cheap wristwatches as prizes.

Over the next six years, the marathon lured more runners, yet it wasn't until 1976 that its popularity began to boom. This was thanks in part to George Spitz, a civil servant and keen runner, who suggested that the marathon should pass through all five of the city's boroughs, as a unique way of celebrating the US bicentennial. Over

2,000 entrants tackled the new route, which proved to be so popular that it was made a permanent feature. (Today, no matter the exact route, all New York City Marathons pass through each of the city's boroughs: Staten Island, Brooklyn, Queens, the Bronx and Manhattan.) Since then the marathon has continually set records, with a phenomenal 53,627 runners crossing the finish line in 2019 – a world first.

It's no wonder it's so popular: for the lucky participants, the marathon is a rare chance to see one of the most iconic cities in the world from a truly unique perspective. Highways and streets normally clogged with yellow taxis and public buses are filled only with runners. As the route weaves through the five boroughs, all of New York is on glorious display: soaring skyscrapers, glimmering waterways, gorgeous brownstones, and pretty parks shimmering with red and yellow fall colours.

There's no denying it's a legendary race – so it's little surprise there are so many legends associated with it. One of the most inspirational winners was Grete Waitz, a Norwegian teacher-turned pro runner who, starting in 1978, won the New York marathon a record nine times. She set several records on the way, too, including, in 1979, being the first ever woman to finish a marathon in under 2 hours 30 minutes. Then there's Mexican runner Germán Silva. During the 1994 race, with under a mile to go before the finish, he accidentally went the wrong way, taking him down to second place. Yet Silva retraced his steps and somehow still managed to win the race with an incredibly fast finish, beating his ▶

Marathon participants making their way through Manhattan during the race

Holding court at the northeast corner of Central Park, jazz legend **DUKE ELLINGTON** peers down at the runners from his piano as they exit the south side of Harlem.

Admire the iconic curves of Frank Lloyd Wright's **GUGGENHEIM MUSEUM** on Fifth Avenue, just before the route cuts into Central Park and heads towards the finish line. It's one of New York's most distinctive buildings, completed in 1959.

Duke Ellington statue

Guggenheim Museum

Finish

Enjoy one of your first uninterrupted views of Midtown Manhattan's iconic skyline – the Empire State Building included – as you cross from Brooklyn to Queens on the **PULASKI BRIDGE**.

NEW YORK CITY

Pulaski Bridge

The crowds of supporters lining **BEDFORD AVENUE** in Williamsburg create quite a party atmosphere as you slice through Brooklyn's most fashionable neighbourhood.

Bedford Avenue

For the incredibly lucky participants, the marathon is a rare chance to see one of the most iconic cities in the world from a truly unique perspective.

Traversing New York Harbor and connecting Staten Island with Brooklyn, the **VERRAZZANO-NARROWS BRIDGE** – America's longest suspension bridge – was opened in 1964. Soak up the spectacle as you and thousands of your fellow runners glide across it.

Start

Verrazzano-Narrows Bridge

0 ········ km ········ 3
0 ············ miles ············ 3

Left Crossing the Verrazzano-Narrows Bridge from Staten Island to Brooklyn

Below Handing out snacks to runners along the route

Locals host boisterous parties in apartments overlooking the route – people wave from open windows, while kids sit on fire escapes, their legs dangling as they cheer on the runners.

Right Crossing the street in Brooklyn during the New York City Marathon

compatriot Benjamín Paredes by two seconds. He was endearingly known as "Wrong Way Silva" thereafter.

One of the most heartwarming stories, though, revolves around marathon founder Fred Lebow. In 1992, while in remission from brain cancer, 60-year-old Lebow ran the marathon for the first and only time; all the other years he'd been too focused on organizing the event to participate. He finished the marathon in just over 5 and a half hours, accompanied the whole way by his good friend Grete Waitz and a cheering crowd.

It really is the joyous support of the spectators that makes this race so special. Runners often describe the phenomenon as "walls of sounds" – periods of eerie quiet, followed by astonishing bursts of noise, as throngs of well-wishers chant, clap and roar their support. To add to the mix, locals host boisterous parties in apartments overlooking the route – people wave from open windows, while kids sit on fire escapes, their legs dangling as they cheer on the runners. Restaurants and bars also open early and participants often find themselves serenaded by salsa and hip-hop.

This cacophony greets runners at several points on the route. On Lafayette Avenue, music pouring out of the windows accompanies the thump-thump of feet against the road. Along First Avenue, there's not so much a wall as a towering fortress of sound, as thousands of spectators roar their support, while in Harlem, gospel choirs serenade tired racers as they soldier on towards the finish. The noise builds to a crescendo along the stretch beside Central Park South – often the most densely packed section of the race – and then, with Midtown's skyscrapers looming above, the runners turn into Central Park. The final section is lined with international flags and packed grandstands, the cheers providing that final push as they cross the finish line, masters of the New York City Marathon.

SIGN-UP: *The marathon takes place in November. Register at* www.nyrr.org/ tcsnycmarathon *in March; there's often a two-week window. Entry is by lottery.*

Marathon runners making it across the finish line in Central Park

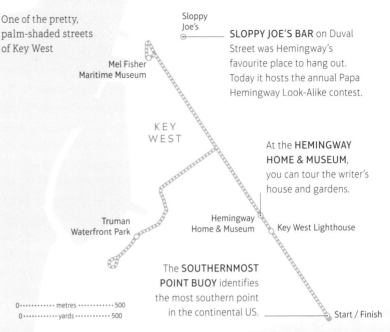

One of the pretty, palm-shaded streets of Key West

Sloppy Joe's

Mel Fisher Maritime Museum

KEY WEST

SLOPPY JOE'S BAR on Duval Street was Hemingway's favourite place to hang out. Today it hosts the annual Papa Hemingway Look-Alike contest.

At the **HEMINGWAY HOME & MUSEUM,** you can tour the writer's house and gardens.

Truman Waterfront Park

Hemingway Home & Museum

Key West Lighthouse

The **SOUTHERNMOST POINT BUOY** identifies the most southern point in the continental US.

Start / Finish

0 ·········· metres ·········· 500
0 ·········· yards ·········· 500

19

Hemingway 5K Sunset Run

KEY WEST, FLORIDA KEYS, FLORIDA, US

Jog along the sunny streets of Key West on this easygoing race that celebrates the island's most famous inhabitant, US author Ernest Hemingway.

48

Top Tip

From 11am head to Sea, Key West *(720B Caroline Street),* for a free Pre-Race Power Brunch.

5 KM (3.1 MILES)   7 M (23 FT)   PAVED

Ernest Hemingway spent most of the 1930s living on Key West, and every July his life and work is celebrated here with the week-long Hemingway Days festival. Its highlight? The ever-popular sunset run.

This laid-back 5-km (3.1-mile) race winds its way through Key West, passing Hemingway's magnificent former home (now a museum) and the bright-white Key West Lighthouse. At points you might find yourself running alongside the writer himself – or rather a bearded doppel-ganger from the festival's Hemingway look-alike contest.

For most participants, it's more of an amble than a race: runners chat to one another as they potter onwards, pausing here and there to admire the blues and pinks of the sunset. The easygoing vibe continues past the finish line, with runners gathering by the sea for a refreshing, ice-cold beer. Hemingway would approve.

SIGN-UP: *Register in advance at* www.keywesthalfmarathon.com.

ELEVATION PROFILE

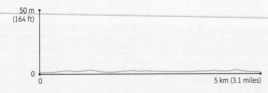

50 m (164 ft)

0

0   5 km (3.1 miles)

Bermuda Triangle Challenge

NATIONAL SPORTS CENTRE, BERMUDA

Run through paradise on this looping 10-km (6.2-mile) route, which takes you past brilliantly blue-hued waters and swaying palm trees.

Every year, the tiny North Atlantic island of Bermuda hosts the three-day Bermuda Triangle Challenge, involving a 1.6-km (1-mile) jog, a 10-km (6.2-mile) run and a marathon. While some runners tackle all three routes to "complete" the challenge, keep it simple and just do the 10-km (6-mile) race, soaking up the stunning island scenery on the way.

That said, you will have to work a little for the views – this loop is hilly, with runners hitting their first big ascent right after the start. Your calves might protest, but the landscape quickly quells any complaints. The first half of the route weaves through the island's leafy interior, while the second half takes in the soaring palms, cute waterfront houses and sparkling teal sea of the spectacular north shore. It's more than enough to power you to the end, where cheering crowds, beating drums and Gombeys (colourfully costumed dancers) encourage you across the finish line.

SIGN-UP: *The race is in January; registration opens the spring before at* www.bermudatrianglechallenge.com.

⊖ 10 KM (6.2 MILES)

⊘ 116 M (380 FT)

⊖ PAVED

ELEVATION PROFILE

100 m
(328 ft)

0

0   10 km (6.2 miles)

Sleepy little **FLATT'S VILLAGE** is known for its colourful houses, tranquil, boat-dotted inlet, and the Bermuda Aquarium, Museum and Zoo (BAMZ).

Also known as Gallows Island, **GIBBET ISLAND** has a dark history: executions were reportedly held here in the 1600 and 1700s.

49

Gibbet Island

Flatt's Village

km   1

0   miles   1

BERMUDA

Start / Finish

Bermuda Arboretum

The **BERMUDA ARBORETUM** is an expansive park with woodlands, meadows and walking trails.

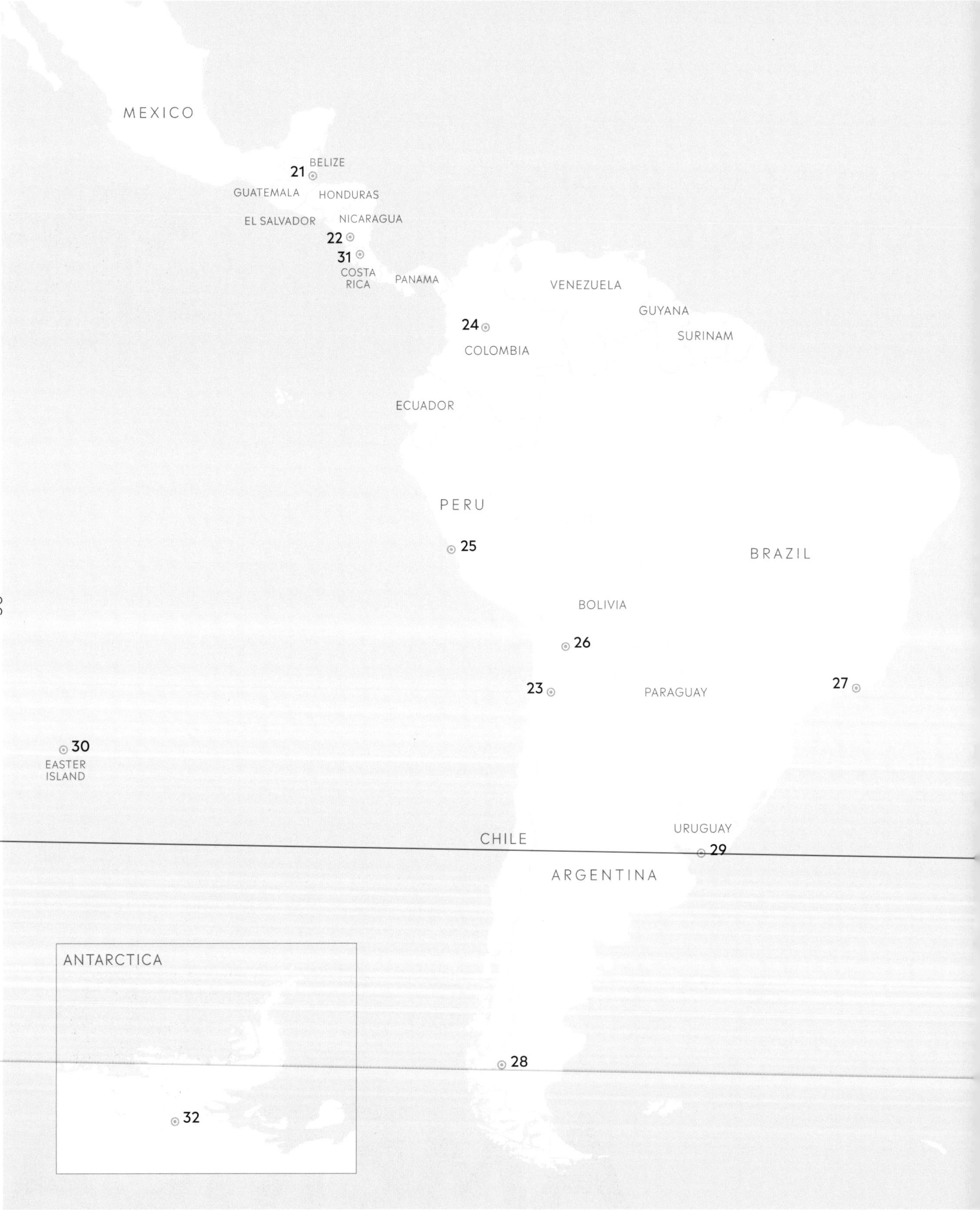

MEXICO

21 ⊙ BELIZE

GUATEMALA   HONDURAS

EL SALVADOR   NICARAGUA

22 ⊙

31 ⊙
COSTA
RICA   PANAMA   VENEZUELA

GUYANA

SURINAM

24 ⊙

COLOMBIA

ECUADOR

PERU

25 ⊙   BRAZIL

BOLIVIA

26 ⊙

23 ⊙   PARAGUAY   27 ⊙

30
⊙
EASTER
ISLAND

URUGUAY

CHILE   29 ⊙

ARGENTINA

ANTARCTICA

28 ⊙

32 ⊙

CENTRAL AND SOUTH AMERICA

Keeping up a steady pace during the
End of the World Marathon

21
End of the World Marathon

PLACENCIA VILLAGE, BELIZE

Despite its alarmist name, this marathon promises plenty of sun and fun as it traces some of the best beaches in Belize.

The first incarnation of this marathon in Placencia – a palm-fringed peninsula dangling off Belize's east coast – was held in December 2012, just days before the Mayan Calendar decreed the world would end. The earth kept spinning but the tongue-in-cheek name stuck, and runners still turn out each December to tackle the beautiful beachfront course.

The scenery is stunning – colourful Placencia Village, the Garifuna community of Seine Bight and the powdery white sands of Maya Beach – but the heat and humidity can be a challenge. Thankfully, there are plenty of water stations to provide much-needed hydration, as well as some light relief. Representing local businesses, each one features employees in fancy dress, who compete with each other to win the title of the Best Water Station. The NAIA Resort, around the 10.5-km (6.5-mile) mark, is a perennial winner thanks to its creative costumes, which have fittingly included apocalyptic zombies, complete with a "Thriller" dance routine.

SIGN-UP: *There are usually spaces available fairly close to the race date, but it doesn't hurt to register in advance via www.runbelize.org.*

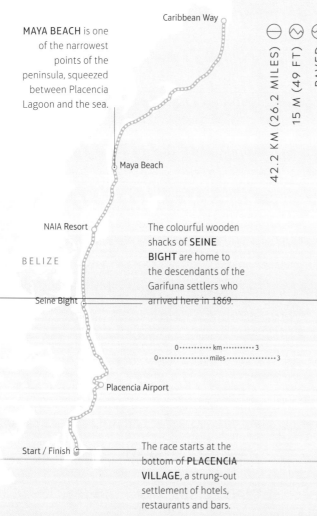

MAYA BEACH is one of the narrowest points of the peninsula, squeezed between Placencia Lagoon and the sea.

Caribbean Way

42.2 KM (26.2 MILES)

15 M (49 FT)

PAVED

Maya Beach

NAIA Resort

BELIZE

The colourful wooden shacks of **SEINE BIGHT** are home to the descendants of the Garifuna settlers who arrived here in 1869.

Seine Bight

0 ········· km ········· 3
0 ············· miles ················· 3

Placencia Airport

Start / Finish

The race starts at the bottom of **PLACENCIA VILLAGE**, a strung-out settlement of hotels, restaurants and bars.

ELEVATION PROFILE

50 m
(164 ft)

0

0

42.2 km (26.2 miles)

Top Tip

Avoid running during the wet season (roughly May–November), as the trail can be particularly muddy then.

22

Maderas Volcano

SANTA CRUZ, OMETEPE, NICARAGUA

Follow a challenging trail up and down the densely forested slopes of Maderas, one of a pair of volcanic peaks that rise like beacons above Lake Nicaragua.

14 KM (8.7 MILES)

1,353 M (4,439 FT)

TRAIL

Maderas may be the shorter of the two volcanoes on Ometepe – the largest fresh-water island in the world and a UNESCO Biosphere Reserve – but it still provides runners with a stern test. Starting and finishing in the village of Santa Cruz, this challenging loop trail snakes steeply up and down the 1,394-m (4,573-ft) peak. The route can be muddy and slippery, and clouds of fog often swirl around you at higher elevations. Yet the glorious scenery provides ample reward. The path to the summit passes through three types of forest – dry, tropical and cloud – each one rich in wildlife such as howler monkeys and

electric-blue morpho butterflies. When you finally reach the top, you're greeted not only with views of Maderas's crater lake, but also the nearby Concepción volcano and the shimmering waters of Lake Nicaragua, so vast it resembles an inland sea.

SET OFF: *To reach the island of Ometepe, take the ferry that runs from San Jorge, in west Nicaragua, to Moyogalpa.*

ELEVATION PROFILE

1,500 m
(4,920 ft)

0

0   14 km (8.7 miles)

Start / Finish

Look out for a series of prehistoric **PETROGLYPHS** depicting geometric shapes and creatures such as turtles.

Petroglyphs

OMETEPE

Cloud forest

The humid, misty **CLOUD FOREST** has shorter trees and plenty of mosses, ferns, lichens, bromeliads and orchids.

Volcán Maderas

The summit of Maderas looks down into a small **CRATER LAKE**, which emerged around 3,000 years ago.

0 ······· km ······· 1
0 ·········· miles ·········· 1

53

CENTRAL AND SOUTH AMERICA

23

Atacama Crossing Ultramarathon

VALLE ARCOIRIS TO SAN PEDRO DE ATACAMA, ATACAMA DESERT, CHILE

This challenging multiday ultra crosses a section of the Atacama Desert, traversing a Mars-like landscape of giant sand dunes and red, rocky hills.

Nestled between the coastal Cordillera de la Costa range and the soaring Andes Mountains, the Atacama Desert is a place of superlatives – the driest non-polar desert in the world and the oldest of all the deserts. It's fitting, then, that it's also the backdrop for the world's highest desert ultramarathon.

This race is no walk in the park. Runners have to tackle 250 km (155 miles) over six stages, all on tough terrain, including steep, sinking sand dunes and salt flats that are strewn here and there with ditches and rivets. The biggest challenge, however, is the extreme altitude: the race starts at 3,200 m (10,500 ft) and gradually descends to 2,400 m (7,900 ft). At such elevations, runners can struggle to get the oxygen their muscles so sorely need and there's a real risk of altitude sickness. Most competitors train at high elevations to prepare and spend several days acclimatizing in the region's main town, San Pedro de Atacama.

The physical demands are intense – but so is the beauty of the scenery. The race weaves through a stark yet stunning landscape of pale-rose sand and rust-red hills, as well as past over 40 rugged volcanoes. Among them is Licanabun, a conical peak that was once an Inca ceremonial site.

Running down a sand dune during the Atacama Crossing Ultramarathon

⊖ 250 KM (155 MILES)

⊗ 1,683 M (5,521 FT)

⊖ TRAIL/DESERT

ELEVATION PROFILE

3,500 m
(11,483 ft)

2,000 m
(6,562 ft)

0   250 km (155 miles)

54

Elsewhere, runners snake through the steep-walled slot canyons of Death Valley, whose crimson hills could easily belong on Mars, and across an eerily beautiful salt flat, its glimmering surface dotted with bright-pink flamingos. Then, each evening, they bed down in tents and watch as the star-strewn sky blazes above; the Atacama is one of the world's best stargazing spots, with several hi-tech observatories located here.

Eventually, after a sapping yet spectacular seven days crossing the desert, the adobe buildings of San Pedro appear on the horizon. Here, runners cross the finish line in tired triumph, their heads still filled with the Atacama's desolate beauty.

SIGN-UP: *Register at least four months in advance at www.racingtheplanet.com.*

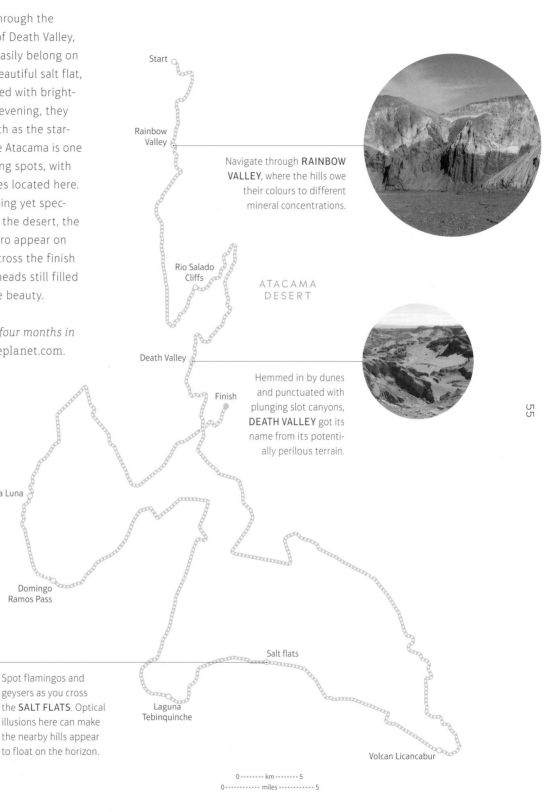

Start

Rainbow Valley

Navigate through **RAINBOW VALLEY**, where the hills owe their colours to different mineral concentrations.

Rio Salado Cliffs

ATACAMA DESERT

Death Valley

Finish

Hemmed in by dunes and punctuated with plunging slot canyons, **DEATH VALLEY** got its name from its potentially perilous terrain.

Valle de la Luna

Domingo Ramos Pass

Salt flats

Laguna Tebinquinche

Volcan Licancabur

Spot flamingos and geysers as you cross the **SALT FLATS**. Optical illusions here can make the nearby hills appear to float on the horizon.

0 ·········· km ·········· 5
0 ·········· miles ·········· 5

24

Bogotá Half Marathon

PARQUE SIMON BOLIVAR, BOGOTÁ, COLOMBIA

Explore Colombia's engaging capital on this challenging half marathon, which showcases the city's eye-catching architecture and beautiful green spaces.

21.1 KM (13.1 MILES)   145 M (475 FT)   PAVED

Bogotá's half marathon is not a fast race. While the route is fairly flat, the city's elevated Andean location – 2,640 m (8,661 ft) above sea level – means the altitude leaves participants gasping. Equally breathtaking? Bogotá's dynamic cityscape, beginning with tranquil Parque Simón Bolívar, the city's leafy lungs (and the race's start and end points).

Historic and modern buildings share the stage here, from stately 18th-century townhouses to concrete-and-glass skyscrapers, most notably the soaring Torre Colpatria. Green spaces lie dotted between them, including tree-lined Parque Nacional, as do examples of the city's ever-changing street art scene, especially in the trendy Chapinero neighbourhood. This whirlwind of sights will divert runners as they make their way round the course; take your time to enjoy the journey – this definitely isn't a race for PBs.

SIGN-UP: *Register in advance at* www.mediamaratonbogota.com.

ELEVATION PROFILE

2,700 m (8,858 ft)

2,500 m (8,202 ft)

0   21.1 km (13.1 miles)

0 ·········· km ·········· 2
0 ·········· miles ·········· 2

Finish

Start

BOGOTÁ

Bigger than Central Park in New York, **PARQUE SIMÓN BOLÍVAR** is a popular spot for sporting events.

Created in the 1930s, **PARQUE NACIONAL** is dotted with impressive monuments, including a ceremonial fountain.

Parque Nacional

Torre Colpatria

Once the tallest skyscraper in Colombia, the 196-m (643-ft) **TORRE COLPATRIA** dominates the horizon in the early stages.

Aerial view across the dynamic city of Bogotá

56

25
Malecón

FARO DE LA MARINA TO MIRADOR DE LA HERRADURA, LIMA, PERU

Escape the bustle of the Peruvian capital on this clifftop oceanside run, which passes through a series of art-dotted parks and offers stunning coastal views.

Lima's coast is undeniably dramatic: rugged cliffs, backed by sky-scraping apartment blocks, drop down towards the blue ocean. Running along a section of the clifftop is the Malecón, a flat, paved esplanade that's beloved by locals who come here to stroll, cycle and run.

This segment of the Malecón passes alongside glossy Miraflores and bohemian Barranco, two of Lima's trendiest neighbourhoods, and through eight stunning cliffside parks. Dotted with palm trees or colourful blooms, these patches of green are home to some intriguing artworks. In Parque del Amor sits *El Beso* ("The Kiss") by Victor Delfín, one of Peru's leading sculptors, while in Parque Intihuatana is Lima-born Fernando de Szyzslo's *Intihuatana*, inspired by the Incas' astronomical stone observatories. Nature paints a pretty picture, too: on a clear day, you'll haves views along the cliff-lined coast and across the shimmering Pacific.

SET OFF: *Take your phone with you to snap shots of the artwork dotting the esplanade.*

⊖ 9 KM (5.6 MILES)

⊘ 43 M (141 FT)

⊖ PAVED

ELEVATION PROFILE

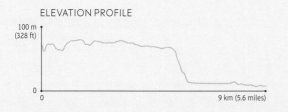

100 m (328 ft)

0

0   9 km (5.6 miles)

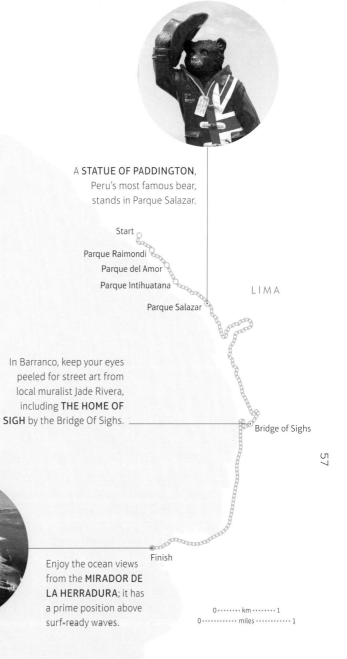

A **STATUE OF PADDINGTON**, Peru's most famous bear, stands in Parque Salazar.

Start
Parque Raimondi
Parque del Amor
Parque Intihuatana

LIMA

Parque Salazar

In Barranco, keep your eyes peeled for street art from local muralist Jade Rivera, including **THE HOME OF SIGH** by the Bridge Of Sighs.

Bridge of Sighs

57

Finish

Enjoy the ocean views from the **MIRADOR DE LA HERRADURA**; it has a prime position above surf-ready waves.

0 ········· km ········· 1
0 ········· miles ········· 1

REFUEL
Seafood Selections

Famed the world over for its cuisine, Lima promises the ultimate in seafood feasts. A dish cherished along South America's Pacific coast, *ceviche* is a light but divine post-run pick-me-up, combining white fish that is delicately "cooked" in lime juice and served with corn, sweet potato, red onion and a dash of chilli.

Traversing the Salar de Uyuni salt flat during the Ultra Bolivia Race

26

Ultra Bolivia Race

SALAR DE COIPASA TO SALAR DE UYUNI, BOLIVIA

Only hardcore runners need apply for this epic ultra, which heads across a pair of salt flats high in the Andes. The altitude, temperature and terrain provide a serious challenge, but the scenery is out of this world.

220 KM (137 MILES)   2,105 M (6,906 FT)   TRAIL

At the southern edge of Bolivia's *altiplano*, an inhospitable, high-altitude plain that stretches between two branches of the Andes, the Salar de Uyuni looks like a landscape from another planet. But it is, in fact, the world's largest salt flat. Flanked by towering mountains and volcanoes, this ancient lake bed sits at 3,656 m (11,995 ft) above sea level. It's pancake flat and dazzlingly white, with a striking pattern of geometric shapes formed by evaporation after the rainy season. Long a popular destination for backpackers, the salt flat is also the site of one of the world's most demanding runs: the Ultra Bolivia Race. ▶

ELEVATION PROFILE

4,000 m (13,123 ft)

3,500 m (11,483 ft)

0   220 km (137 miles)

CENTRAL AND SOUTH AMERICA

IN FOCUS
Continental Challenge

The Ultra Bolivia Race is part of the Continental Challenge, a series of five ultra marathons on five continents organized by Canal Aventure (*www. canal-aventure.com*) since 2014. The others are the Ultra Asia Race in northwest Vietnam; the Track in the Australian Outback, the Ultra Norway Race in the Lyngen Alps; and the Ultra Africa Race in southern Mozambique.

The second biggest salt flat in Bolivia, the **SALAR DE COIPASA** surrounds a large lake that's home to thousands of flamingos.

Located beside the village of the same name, the archaeological site of **ALCAYA** features a collection of ancient cave shrines and ruins.

On the northern edge of the Salar de Uyuni, the **TUNUPA VOLCANO** last erupted 1.36 to 1.56 million years ago.

One of a number of rocky outcrops that form "islands" in the middle of the salt flats, **ISLA PESCADO** vaguely resembles a fish (*pescado* in Spanish).

The village of **COLCHANI** is home to several small-scale salt-processing factories, a traditional industry in this region for millennia.

As well as giant cacti, **ISLA INCAHUASI** (Inca House Island) is covered with fossilized algae dating back 30,000–42,000 years.

NASA and the European Space Agency have taken advantage of the **SALAR DE UYUNI**'s remarkable flatness and reflectiveness to calibrate their satellites.

Start

Alcaya

Salinas

Tunupa Volcano

Jirira

Tahua

BOLIVIA

Salar de Uyuni

Isla Pescado

Isla Incahuasi

Colchani

Finish

0 ·········· km ·········· 20
0 ················ miles ················ 20

This 220-km (136.7-mile) epic is not to be taken lightly. It's broken into seven day-long stages, each one covering a distance between 26 and 42 km (16 and 26 miles). The most difficult stages are three and six: the former involves the greatest one-day ascent and descent – an arduous 850 m (2,789 ft) each way – while the latter is the longest daily stretch, an energy-sapping, seemingly never-ending slog of 42 km (26 miles).

To add to the challenge, there is a 10-hour time limit to finish each stage and runners must wear a backpack containing all their gear and supplies, including a sleeping bag, medical kit and sufficient food to last the whole week. High-factor sun cream and sunglasses are other essentials; on a clear day, the combination of the blazing sun and the dazzlingly white salt flats produces a blinding glare.

Overnight, runners sleep in tents under remarkably clear, star-filled skies. It's a magical experience, as long as you're able to ignore your aching muscles and the frigid nighttime temperatures, which quickly plunge to between -5° C (23° F) and -10° C (14° F) in September, when the race takes place. And that's before you take into account the wind, which often howls ferociously and can make it feel far colder.

The biggest physical test of the Ultra Run Bolivia, though, is the altitude. The route does not dip below 3,600 m (11,811 ft) and at this breathless elevation, running for a bus – let alone completing an ultra marathon – feels like a task of Herculean proportions. It's vital to take the time to properly acclimatize before the race – particularly if you normally reside at or close to sea level – and be fully aware of the signs of altitude ▶

Runners setting up camp for the night in the middle of the salt flat

Along the way, you pass through an otherworldly landscape that provides plenty of distractions from the demands on your body and mind.

sickness, which can carry a serious risk. In this oxygen-starved environment, runners also dehydrate far faster than normal, so taking on adequate fluids is crucial.

With all that in mind, why do the Ultra Bolivia Race at all? Because it's one of the most entrancing runs on the planet. The route starts at the Salar de Coipasa, a smaller salt flat, before arcing south through the larger and more formidable Salar de Uyuni. Along the way, you pass through an otherworldly landscape that provides plenty of distractions from the demands on your body and mind. In the distance rise stark massifs of soaring, snow-covered peaks, most notably Tunupa, a dormant volcano that is considered a mountain deity by many people in the surrounding area. The shimmering surface of the salt flats, meanwhile, are dotted with small "islands", the craggy summits of ancient volcanoes that poke above the surface. Once trading posts and meeting

points for communities across the region, they are now studded with clusters of looming cacti that are hundreds of years old, and populated by hummingbirds, finches and rabbit-like creatures known as vizcachas. Around the shores of the salt flats, the route winds past isolated villages and archaeological sites such as Alcaya, where ancient cave shrines are home to a number of mummified bodies, probably from the Quillacas-Azanaques culture (circa 900-1460 CE). They are open to visitors – if you can spare the time.

Beyond your fellow competitors and jeeps taking travellers on tours of the Salar de Uyuni and neighbouring Eduardo Avaroa reserve, people are few and far between in this hard-scrabble region. You may run past the odd llama herder or quinoa farmer, or perhaps a group of *saleros*. These salt harvesters hack away at the *salares* – which are 10 m (33 ft) deep in places – with pickaxes before piling up their wares in pyramids to dry in the sun. You might also

An encounter with a llama, one of the hardy creatures that lives on the *altiplano*

Above Making a careful ascent of a rocky slope

Above right Crossing the finish line after a gruelling week of racing

spy teams of more high-tech workers, attending to rectangular pools dotted around the salt flats. These are filled with a brine rich in lithium – a key component of the batteries in mobile phones, laptops and electric cars – which lies beneath the surface of this region in vast reserves. For the most part, however, it'll feel like you have this captivating place completely to yourself.

It's truly the beauty of the surroundings that keeps you going, even when you fall to the lowest of ebbs. In fact, running here has a meditative quality; for most of the route there are just two colours visible – the blinding white of the salt flats and the pale blue of the cloudless sky – a monotony that proves to be mesmerizing.

When you finally reach the end of the Ultra Bolivia Race – mind exhausted, throat parched and legs begging for mercy – the sense of satisfaction is immense. You've pushed yourself to the limit in a

race few runners would even contemplate, let alone attempt, and explored one of the most dramatic landscapes on earth along the way.

SIGN-UP: *Register in advance, as early as possible,* at www.canal-aventure.com. *You must provide a medical certificate and an electrocardiogram report.*

ANOTHER WAY

La Paz Marathon

For another high-altitude race in Bolivia, try the La Paz Marathon *(www.maratondelapaz.com),* which takes place in March. This hilly route reaches a testing elevation of 3,956 m (12,979 ft), before descending to the finish line. There's also a half marathon and a 10-km (6.2-mile) race.

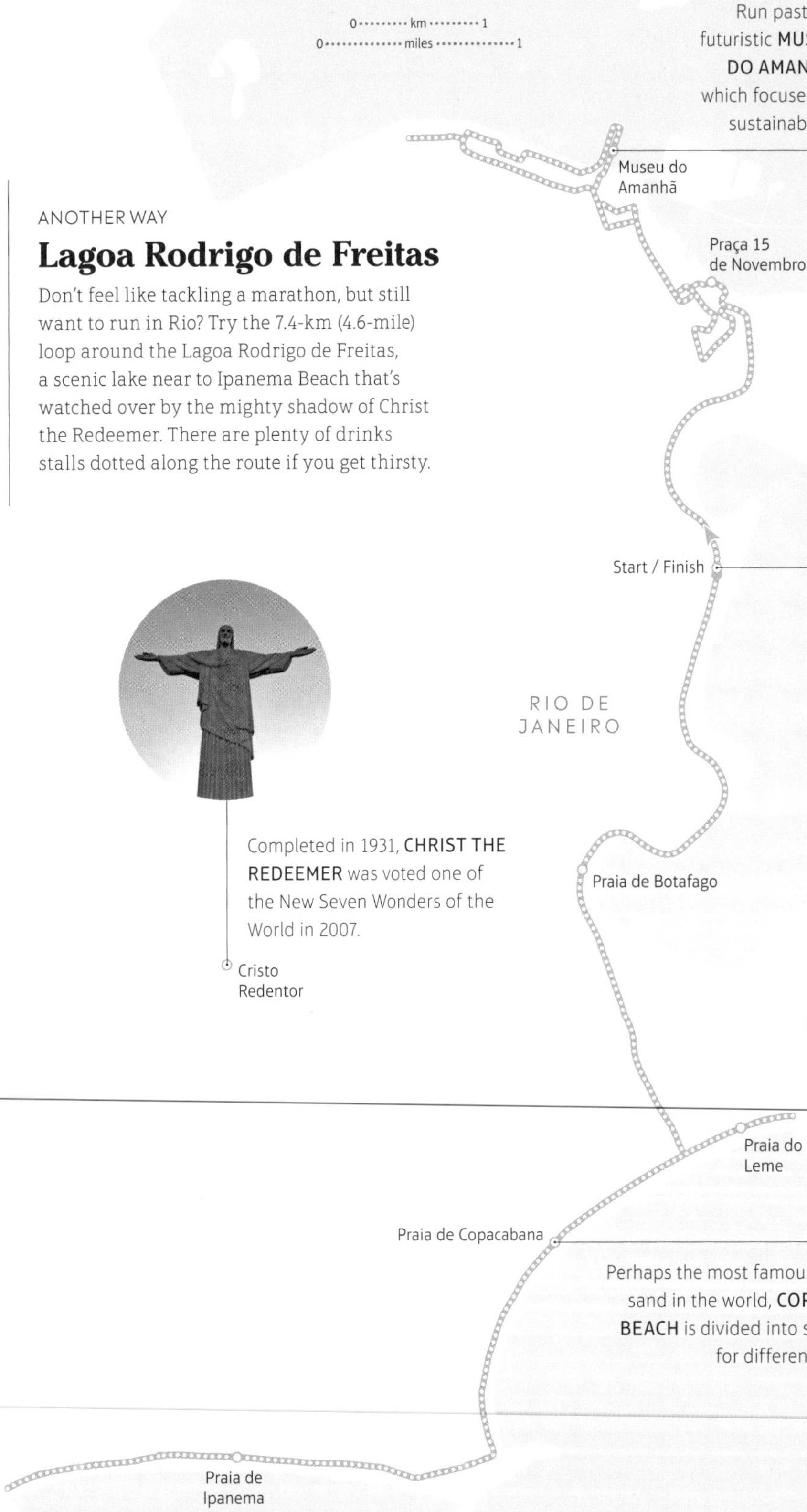

0 ······ km ····· 1
0 ······ miles ············ 1

Run past the futuristic **MUSEU DO AMANHÃ**, which focuses on sustainability.

Museu do Amanhã

Praça 15 de Novembro

ANOTHER WAY
Lagoa Rodrigo de Freitas

Don't feel like tackling a marathon, but still want to run in Rio? Try the 7.4-km (4.6-mile) loop around the Lagoa Rodrigo de Freitas, a scenic lake near to Ipanema Beach that's watched over by the mighty shadow of Christ the Redeemer. There are plenty of drinks stalls dotted along the route if you get thirsty.

Start / Finish

Built on reclaimed land, the popular **PARQUE ATERRO DO FLAMENGO** is a tree-dotted, landscaped park.

RIO DE JANEIRO

64

Completed in 1931, **CHRIST THE REDEEMER** was voted one of the New Seven Wonders of the World in 2007.

Cristo Redentor

Praia de Botafago

Praia do Leme

Praia de Copacabana

Perhaps the most famous stretch of sand in the world, **COPACABANA BEACH** is divided into six sections for different activities.

Praia de Ipanema

27

Rio Marathon

RIO DE JANEIRO, BRAZIL

Run one of the world's most beautiful marathons in the life-affirming city of Rio de Janeiro, taking in some of the city's best neighbourhoods as you go.

Runners jogging alongside Rio's glorious coastline during the city's marathon

42.2 KM (26.2 MILES)   95 M (312 FT)   PAVED

The Rio Marathon is the largest event of its kind in Latin America – and it's easy to see why. For one thing, the setting is spectacular: foliage-clad mountains line the city on one side, while on the other lies the sparkling Atlantic. For another, the race takes in some of the city's most vibrant neighbourhoods, many of them home to beautiful beaches.

Beginning and ending in Flamengo, an area best known for its leafy park, the route keeps close to the coast, with lively neighbourhoods thrown in as a matter of routine. There's Centro, the historic heart of the city, where modern office blocks sit alongside much older architecture, including the 18th-century Paço Imperial (Imperial Palace). Tiny Saúde, the birthplace of samba, also makes an appearance, as does Gloria, known for its Art-Deco buildings and yacht-dotted marina.

Unsurprisingly, the most iconic areas host the beaches. There's the golden crest of Copacabana, where football and volleyball players kick up joyous arcs of sand and the hawking cries of caipirinha vendors emanate from beach shacks. Then comes Ipanema, where socialites come to see and be seen, and counter-cultural types gather to discuss the prevailing winds of revolution.

As you run, you'll be watched over by some of Rio's major landmarks: the granite-and-quartz rump of Sugarloaf Mountain presides over the start and finish point, while to the west looms the mighty statue of Christ the Redeemer – conferring, hopefully, some divine favour on the runners below.

There's so much to take in here that, despite it being a largely flat course, you won't be breaking any records. But that's okay: it means that, once you finally cross the finish line, you'll still have energy to explore Rio's buzzing neighbourhoods.

SIGN-UP: *Register well in advance at www.maratonadorio.com.br.*

ELEVATION PROFILE

50 m (164 ft)

0

0   42.2 km (26.2 miles)

CENTRAL AND SOUTH AMERICA

On a clear day, the sharply serrated peaks of towering Monte Fitz Roy are reflected in the bewitching waters of **LAGUNA DE LOS TRES**.

Laguna de los Tres

Laguna Sucia

LOS GLACIARES NATIONAL PARK

Laguna Madre

Laguna Capri

0 ·····km····· 1
0 ····· miles ····· 1

Río de la Cascada

Keep your eyes peeled for torrent ducks in the sometimes glacier-filled **RÍO DE LA CASCADA**.

Mirador del Fitz Roy

Mirador Río de las Vueltas

Start / Finish

Pause for breath and tantalizing views of the mountains you're approaching at **MIRADOR DEL FITZ ROY**, 3.5 km (2.2 miles) in.

28

Laguna de Los Tres

EL CHALTÉN, LOS GLACIARES NATIONAL PARK, ARGENTINA

Escape into the wilds of Patagonia as you tackle a testing trail that takes in wildlife-rich beech forests, a tranquil glacial lake and – best of all – heavenly mountain vistas.

21 KM (13 MILES)

1,047 M (3,435 FT)

TRAIL

Traversing the lenga beech forests of Los Glaciares National Park, this out-and-back run is one of the region's most iconic trails. Starting from Argentina's capital of adventure, El Chaltén, it leads runners through leafy forest and across slippery scree, before leaving them, breathless but triumphant, at one of South America's most spectacular panoramic viewpoints.

The real challenge isn't the distance but the final 2 km (1.2 miles) to the Laguna de Los Tres, where a series of switchbacks harass your calves as you ascend a steep scree slope. At the top, the lake's turquoise waters reflect the snow-crowned Monte Fitz Roy, a multipronged hulk of granite that hits 3,405 m (11,171 ft) at its peak and dwarfs all those who stand beneath.

While the lure of such views will spur you on, be sure to pause and savour the silence on this run – something broken only by the burble of glacial rivers and the staccato tap of Magellanic woodpeckers tucked deep in the surrounding forest.

SET OFF: *This route can be tackled from October to April, but for a quieter path, run early or late in the season.*

ELEVATION PROFILE

2,000 m
(6,560 ft)

0

0   21 km (13 miles)

29

La Rambla de Montevideo

MONTEVIDEO, URUGUAY

Get to know Montevideo on a run along this bustling promenade, which winds along the city's sunny coastline.

23 KM (14.3 MILES)   42 M (138 FT)   PAVED

Running from Montevideo Bay to the affluent suburb of Carrasco, La Rambla is the longest continuous sidewalk in the world. The brick path, made up of 23 connected walkways, is flat, traffic-free and often caressed by a gentle South Atlantic breeze, making it the perfect place for a jog.

It's also a hotspot of culture and recreation. As you run along under clear-blue skies, you'll pass by fishers casting their lines from the seawall, while cyclists snake between folks out for a stroll. The melodies of the Spanish language cascade from the open-air cafés that line the path, as does the scent of *asado* (grilled meat accompanied by a salad and red wine).

The scenery doesn't disappoint either. To the left lies the city's eclectic skyline, made up of a mix of Art-Deco architecture and Neo-Classical spires. To the right, unobstructed views of white-sand beaches and the blue Atlantic, dotted with sail boats swaying on their moorings, stretch into the distance. It's Montevideo at its best.

SET OFF: *This is a great year-round run, thanks to temperatures ranging from 11° C (52° F) to 24° C (75° F).*

ELEVATION PROFILE

50 m (164 ft)

0

0   23 km (14.3 miles)

MONTEVIDEO

The **LAS LETRAS DE MONTEVIDEO** sign offers incredible views of the city and the sandy Playa de los Pocitos.

Start

Finish

Playa Malvin

Playa Verde

Las Letras de Montevideo

Plaza Trouville

Faro de Punta Carretas

The pier that sits next to the **FARO DE PUNTA CARRETAS**, a brick lighthouse dating from the 1800s, is a locally beloved fishing spot.

Near Plaza Trouville, look for the striking façade of **CASTILLO PITTAMIGLIO**, which is embellished with a replica Greek statue.

0 ·········· km ·········· 3
0 ·········· miles ·········· 3

30

Rapa Nui Marathon

HANGA ROA, RAPA NUI (EASTER ISLAND), CHILE

Taking you across Rapa Nui, this marathon gets you up close and personal with the otherworldly island, famed for its curious moai statues.

42.2 KM (26.2 MILES) 529 M (1,735 FT) PAVED

A mere speck in the Pacific Ocean some 3,700 km (2,300 miles) from mainland Chile, Rapa Nui (as Easter Island is known by its local inhabitants), is the setting for one of the world's most remote marathons. This out-and-back route takes you through a truly intriguing land, passing along the undulating spine of an island best known for its 887 stone moai. Carved from the soft volcanic tuff from which the island is formed, they date back to 1200 CE and were built to honour chiefs or significant community members when they died.

You'll see some of these famed figures right from the off. The race starts beside Ahu Tautira, a ceremonial platform hosting two moai. Despite erosion by the elements, there's no mistaking the intricately carved, quasi-human faces and truncated bodies that make these statues so iconic.

From there, the route winds from the island's southwest coast to its north,

Looking out over Hanga Roa, the start and end point of the Rapa Nui Marathon

passing alongside windswept meadows. These grassy blankets cover Rapa Nui's now extinct volcanoes, including Puna Pau, where the stones for the *pukao* (topknots) on many moai were sourced. Statues topped with these crimson headdresses are found at Anakena Beach, the turn-around point for the marathon. Lining the edge of the sand, these moai direct you back with their impassive gaze towards the interior.

While a glimpse of the maoi is guaranteed, one thing you can't be sure of is steady weather. The island's tropical conditions can go from heavy rain and

ELEVATION PROFILE

300 m
(984 ft)

0

0   42.2 km (26.2 miles)

MAKE IT SHORTER

Half the Distance

Both a half marathon and a 10-km (6.2-mile) race are held at the same time as the marathon. Taking a truncated stretch of the course, they give shorter-distance runners the opportunity to experience the thrill of Rapa Nui at their own pace.

ANAKENA BEACH is where the first inhabitants of Rapa Nui, led by supreme chief Hotu Matu'a, are believed to have landed around 1200 CE.

Anakena Beach

Ma'unga Terevaka

The island's highest point, **MA'UNGA TEREVAKA** (Terevaka Volcano) is worth a hike post-race (legs permitting).

RAPA NUI

Start / Finish

wind through to warm temperatures and 80 per cent humidity. The sun can be relentless, too; Rapa Nui is practically treeless, and so pockets of shade are few and far between. Add to this a fair few hills, and this can be a tough marathon.

Yet the effort is all worth it. Not only are participants members of an exclusive club – only 40 runners take part, due to limited accommodation options – but they get to experience Rapa Nui completely under their own steam. Such a unique experience is more than enough to keep your legs powering through the miles.

SIGN-UP: *As spaces are limited, enrol immediately after the end of the previous race via* www.maratonrapanui.cl.

Don't miss the **AHU TAUTIRA**, where two moai stand sentinel beside the fishing harbour of Caleta Hanga Roa.

0 ·········· km ·········· 3
0 ················ miles ················ 3

31

Moon Run Monteverde Adventure Trail

SANTA ELENA, COSTA RICA

Rise to the challenge as you clamber up into the pristine cloud forest of Costa Rica's Monteverde region, where steep, muddy trails and treetop hanging bridges take you through one of the most biodiverse places on earth.

22 KM (13.6 MILES) 1,385 M (4,544 FT) PAVED/TRAIL

It's safe to say that this route is definitely not for a first-time trail runner or casual half marathoner. Starting and ending in Santa Elena, and taking you deep into the cloud forest of nearby Selvatura Park, the Moon Run tackles extraordinarily arduous – yet beautiful – mountainous jungle terrain.

This 22-km (14-mile) Adventure Trail circuit is the middle of five distance options for the race, which also include a 6-km (3.7-mile) fun-run and an over 60-km (37-mile) ultra. Gaining 1,400 m (4,500 ft) of elevation, the route slips between stands of towering ficus trees and into the dense cloud forest of the Tilarán mountain range, home to 4 per cent of the world's total biodiversity. It's a far cry from the typical tourist paths. In fact, many of the trails on this route are off limits to all but the race participants, meaning you get to run through parts of the jungle seen by few other people. Various suspension bridges are slung high in the tree canopy; they're only crossable by walking (it's a

Jogging through hillside pastures on the outskirts of the cloud forest

disqualifiable offence to run), but you won't begrudge slowing down when the views over the forested landscape are this good.

The windy-misty December weather often adds to the fun, contributing to a quagmire of mud beneath your feet and bringing in rolling mists and powerful gusts of wind. Yet despite this, the experience is serene. With just 600 runners participating across all five distances, you'll likely find yourself alone except for the constant hum, buzz and chatter of the surrounding forest.

SIGN-UP: *Registration opens in July and closes in November of each year.*

ELEVATION PROFILE

2,000 m (6,562 ft)

1,000 m (3,280 ft)

0   22 km (13.6 miles)

ANOTHER WAY
Ultra Trail

If you're an experienced marathon runner and seeking an even greater challenge, take on the Ultra Trail, a 60-km (37-mile) ultramarathon. Starting at the same place as the other four distances, this strenuous run ventures even deeper into the dramatic depths of pristine cloud forest.

If the weather's clear, look northeast as you reach the second support station for the perfectly conical stratovolcano, **ARENAL**.

Mirador Arenal

Keep your eyes peeled for **CAPUCHIN MONKEYS** leaping between branches in the canopy above.

The pearly green **RESPLENDENT QUETZAL** is one of the most famous inhabitants of the cloud forest.

COSTA RICA

Selvatura Park

Slow to a gentle walk as you cross Selvatura Park's extraordinary 170-m (560-ft) **SUSPENSION BRIDGE**, which sits in the treetops.

Surrounded by lush forest, the tiny town of **SANTA ELENA** marks both the start and end of the race.

Start / Finish

0 ·········· km ·········· 1
0 ············ miles ················· 1

32

Antarctic Ice Marathon

UNION GLACIER CAMP, ANTARCTICA

Journey down to the icy expanse of Antarctica to take part in the southernmost marathon on earth. Prepare for sub-zero temperatures, energy-sapping conditions and the experience of a lifetime.

Looking for a serious challenge? This one is for you. Few runners dare to tackle this epic marathon across the "white continent", with only 60 or so participants running the course each year. The Antarctic Ice Marathon isn't just a race – it's an expedition.

The adventure begins long before you reach the starting line. From the isolated Chilean city of Punta Arenas, runners catch a flight south across the stark mountains and meandering waterways of Tierra del Fuego and the vast expanse of the choppy Southern Ocean. Eventually the plane touches down – gingerly – on a "blue ice" runway at Union Glacier Camp.

As you might expect, being so close to the South Pole, the cold and the terrain are the two biggest challenges at this event, which sees runners complete a 10.5-km (6.5-mile) loop four times. In December, the temperature here usually ranges between -10º C (14º F) and -20º C (4º F), while the wind is fierce and bitterly cold. These conditions demand the right clothing – thermals, windproof outer layers, goggles, woollen socks, sock liners and trail running shoes. Nevertheless, the cold will still sting your face, numb your extremities and chill your body to the core.

72

⊖ 42.2 KM (26.2 MILES)

⊗ 91 M (299 FT)

⊖ ICE

ELEVATION PROFILE

800 m
(2,625 ft)

600 m
(1,969 ft)

0   42.2 km (26.2 miles)

A competitor making
their way across the ice
on a loop of the course

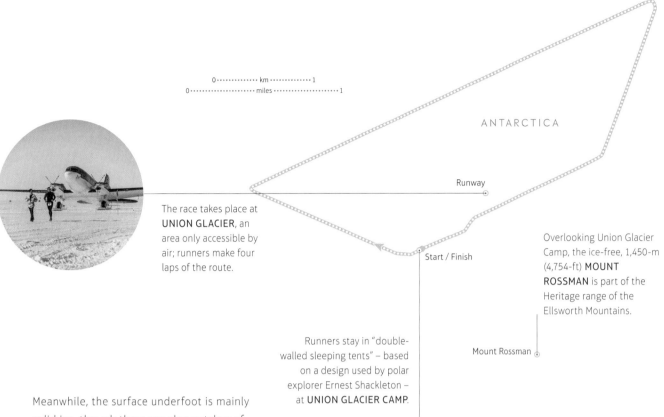

0 ············· km ·············· 1
0 ············· miles ·············· 1

ANTARCTICA

Runway

The race takes place at **UNION GLACIER**, an area only accessible by air; runners make four laps of the route.

Start / Finish

Overlooking Union Glacier Camp, the ice-free, 1,450-m (4,754-ft) **MOUNT ROSSMAN** is part of the Heritage range of the Ellsworth Mountains.

Mount Rossman

Runners stay in "double-walled sleeping tents" – based on a design used by polar explorer Ernest Shackleton – at **UNION GLACIER CAMP**.

Meanwhile, the surface underfoot is mainly solid ice, though there are also patches of soft and loose snow. With such harsh conditions, it's not surprising the route is far more tiring than a regular marathon. Although most competitors follow the same basic preparation routines, they generally extend their long runs and train in cold environments to get themselves ready – some even use treadmills in industrial freezers.

But nothing can quite prepare you for how it feels to be in Antarctica itself – an experience that is both humbling and awe-inspiring in equal measure. Beyond the camp and the fluttering route markers, there is a seemingly endless stretch of snow and ice, ridged with mountains, sculpted by the wind, and disappearing into the horizon. No matter how tired and cold you get during the final stages, it never feels anything less than a privilege to be in Antarctica, the greatest wilderness on earth.

SIGN-UP: *Register at least eight months in advance at* www.icemarathon.com.

IN FOCUS

7 Continents Marathon Club

Running the Antarctic Ice Marathon gets you one step closer to joining the exclusive 7 Continents Marathon Club *(www.icemarathon.com/7-continents)*. It currently has 389 members – 293 men and 96 women – who have each completed a marathon on every one of the planet's continents. New members recieve a medal, alongside serious bragging rights.

⊙ 36

⊙ 34

ICELAND

SWEDEN

FINLAND

⊙ 33

FAROE
ISLANDS

NORWAY

38 ⊙

ESTONIA

LATVIA

DENMARK

LITHUANIA

37 ⊙

35 ⊙

IRELAND

UNITED
KINGDOM

NETHER-
LANDS

44 ⊙

POLAND

BELARUS

39 ⊙

41⊙⊙ 40

⊙ 54

GERMANY

42 ⊙

BELGIUM

LUX.

CZECH
REPUBLIC

⊙ 62

SLOVAKIA

43 ⊙

FRANCE

45 ⊙

47 ⊙

AUSTRIA

HUNGARY

MOLDOVA

46 ⊙ SWITZ.

52 ⊙

63 ⊙

ROMANIA

53 ⊙

SLOVENIA

⊙ 64

59 ⊙

BOSNIA-
HERZ.

SERBIA

50 ⊙

⊙ 49

CROATIA

51 ⊙

ITALY

BULGARIA

56 ⊙

MONTE-
NEGRO

KOSOVO

⊙ 65

55 ⊙

⊙ 48

N. MAC.

ALBANIA

PORTUGAL

SPAIN

61 ⊙

GREECE

58 ⊙

60 ⊙

74

57 ⊙ CANARY
ISLANDS

66 ⊙

75

EUROPE

33

Atjan Wild Islands Festival

SAKSUN TO TJØRNUVÍK, STREYMOY,
FAROE ISLANDS, DENMARK

*Forging a path through a landscape of untamed, rugged hills,
this exhilirating yet challenging trail race shows off the wild
beauty of the Faroe Islands.*

22.7 KM (14 MILES) ◯ 1,170 M (3,839 FT) ◇ TRAIL ◇

76

An isolated archipelago found between Scotland and Iceland, the mountainous Faroes jut dramatically out of the harsh North Atlantic. These basalt islands have been sculpted by the elements into rocky peaks, plunging valleys and soaring sea cliffs, all cloaked in a layer of vibrant grassy green. It's an out-of-this-world landscape that makes a stunning canvas for the Atjan Wild Islands Festival, a five-day celebration of adventure held on Streymoy. This outdoorsy event includes kayaking, yoga, film screenings and, of course, running. There's everything from a 10-km (6.2-mile) race to an ultra, but the half marathon makes for the perfect blend of thigh-aching challenge and stunning scenery.

The route varies each year, but you can always expect tough mountain-running: there's around 1,100 m (3,600 ft) of climbing and the terrain is mixed, with participants tackling tussocks, felt-like grass and stony

slopes, plus the occasional rocky scramble for good measure. Previous experience of hill running is, suffice to say, essential. Coloured markers guide the way (paths are few), and runners are also given maps and digital coordinates before they set out, just in case the weather changes – a regular occurrence here. Participants need to be prepared for everything including heavy rain, strong winds and all-enveloping mist.

The race begins near Saksun in the north. A clutch of traditional grass-roofed houses surrounded by steep-sided

Treading carefully along a cloud-enveloped ridge on Streymoy

ELEVATION PROFILE

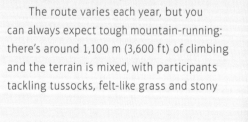

1,000 m
(3,280 ft)

0

0   22.7 km (14 miles)

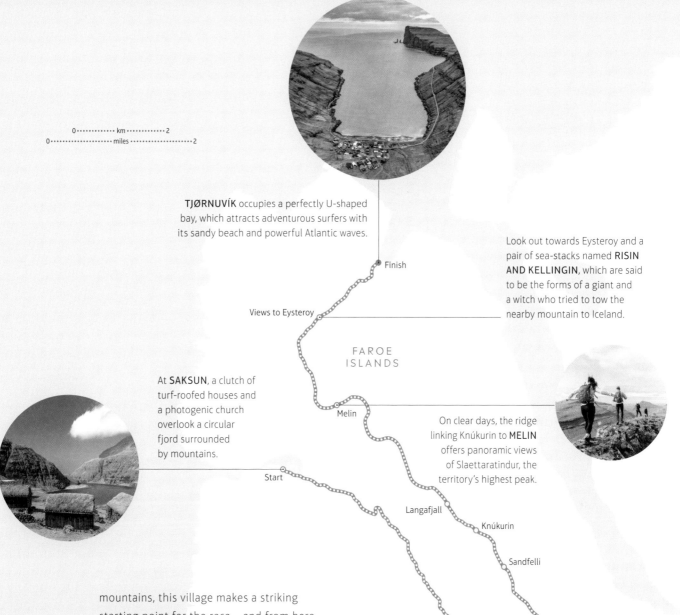

TJØRNUVÍK occupies a perfectly U-shaped bay, which attracts adventurous surfers with its sandy beach and powerful Atlantic waves.

Look out towards Eysteroy and a pair of sea-stacks named **RISIN AND KELLINGIN**, which are said to be the forms of a giant and a witch who tried to tow the nearby mountain to Iceland.

0 ········· km ········· 2
0 ········· miles ········· 2

Finish

Views to Eysteroy

FAROE ISLANDS

At **SAKSUN**, a clutch of turf-roofed houses and a photogenic church overlook a circular fjord surrounded by mountains.

Melin

On clear days, the ridge linking Knúkurin to **MELIN** offers panoramic views of Slaettaratindur, the territory's highest peak.

Start

Langafjall

Knúkurin

Sandfelli

mountains, this village makes a striking starting point for the race – and from here the scenery just keeps on getting better. Awe-inspiring views of rugged mountain-tops unfold across a string of brooding fells, with plunging cliffs and an iron-blue strait in the distance. The finish line lies in Tjørnuvík, a tiny colourful collection of houses set in a square sandy bay – it's the perfect scenic end for a truly stunning race.

SIGN-UP: *The trail race takes place on the first Saturday of September. Entry is open year-round, with participants limited to 500. Register at* www.atjanwildislands.com.

MAKE IT SHORTER
Less Climbing

The 10-km (6.2-mile) course offers a shorter option for those with less mountain experience, while still delivering jaw-dropping views. The start and finish points are the same, but the total climb is a more easygoing 500 m (1,640 ft).

Looking out over the expansive Ásbyrgi
Canyon from the top of Eyjan Hill

34

Eyjan Hill Trail

EYJAN HILL, ICELAND

*This literally epic run in the wilds of northeast Iceland
will see you scaling an ancient lava outcrop to gaze into
a canyon rooted in myth.*

4.7 KM (2.9 MILES)   76 M (249 FT)   PAVED/TRAIL

78

Eyjan Hill is a surreal sight. Marooned amid a sea of spruce
and pine, this rocky finger of land – whose name means
"the island" in Icelandic – stretches into the heart of the
horseshoe-shaped Ásbyrgi Canyon. It is all that remains
of a lava flow that swept through here about 9,000 years
ago, an unmoving reminder of Iceland's fiery nature.

The trail here is flat for the most part. Tracing the
hill's base, it cuts through the trees, passing blueberry and
juniper bushes along the way. You'll soon be panting on
the steep wooden steps that lead onto Eyjan itself,
though; it's best to walk up them, rather than run. At the
top, you can (carefully) continue to the cliff edge, where
stunning views of the chiselled walls of the Ásbyrgi Canyon
await. According to Norse mythology, the canyon is the
hoofprint of Sleipnir, the eight-legged horse of the Norse
god Óðinn, and Eyjan Hill is the untouched indent. It's
an epic legend for an equally epic run.

SET OFF: *Eyjan Hill can be accessed from dawn to dusk;
conditions are best between March and September.*

Make a pre-run stop at the **GLJÚFRASTOFA-
ÁSBYRGI VISITOR CENTRE** for an insight
into the area's dramatic geology.

⊙ Gljúfrastofa-Ásbyrgi
    Visitor Centre

● Start / Finish

Keep an eye out for the
varied birdlife that inhabit
the **ROCK FACES**, including
snow bunting and gyrfalcon.

ICELAND

Admire the views looking
deep into the **ÁSBYRGI
CANYON** from the trail's
turning point.

Eyjan Hill

0 ········· metres ········· 500
0 ········· yards ········· 500

IN FOCUS

Sleipnir

The offspring of the Norse god Loki,
Sleipnir appears in Old Norse poems
and stories from the 13th century.
Known for his strength, speed and
fearlessness, Sleipnir accompanied
Óðinn on numerous quests, and was
able to carry him in and out of Hel,
a realm of the afterlife.

ELEVATION PROFILE

200 m
(656 ft)

0

0   4.7 km (2.9 miles)

35

Archipelago Magic

SØBY TO ÆRØSKØBING, ÆRØ, DENMARK

Experience Denmark at its most postcard-perfect on this section of the Øhavsstien, which traces a path through vibrant fields and alongside sparkling coastline on the island of Ærø.

19.7 KM (12.2 MILES) 181 M (594 FT) PAVED/TRAIL

Running across Denmark's Southern Funen archipelago are over 220 km (135 miles) of scenic trails known as the Øhavsstien ("Archipelago Trail"). While it's possible to tackle the whole route on a multiday running holiday, hopping between the islands by ferry, this stretch on the idyllic island of Ærø makes a great afternoon run.

Starting in the small harbour of Søby, the easy-going route is a run of two scenic halves. The first passes by historic windmills and thatched farmhouses, flowing through patchwork fields of brilliant yellow and vibrant green. The second half, by contrast, contours along a glittering coastline lined with sandy shores, pebble beaches and a clutch of colourful beach huts. Almost too soon, fairytale Ærøskøbing materializes; here, you can put your feet up or catch another ferry to continue the runventure.

SET OFF: *Ærø is served by multiple ferry routes; see www.visitfyn.com for details.*

Top Tip

Be more eco-friendly by taking the electric ferry from Fynshav, on the island of Als, to Søby.

79

ELEVATION PROFILE

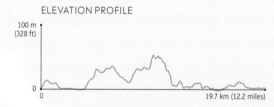

100 m (328 ft)

0

0   19.7 km (12.2 miles)

Teeming with birdlife the small lake of **VITSØ** attracts flocks of migratory ducks and geese.

Vitsø

Søbygaard

Circled by a moat with a drawbridge, **SØBYGAARD** is a 16th-century traditional manor house.

○ Start

0 ·········· km ·········· 2
0 ·········· miles ·········· 2

ÆRØ

Chocolate-box houses with red-tiled rooftops line **ÆRØSKØBING**'s pretty cobbled streets.

● Finish

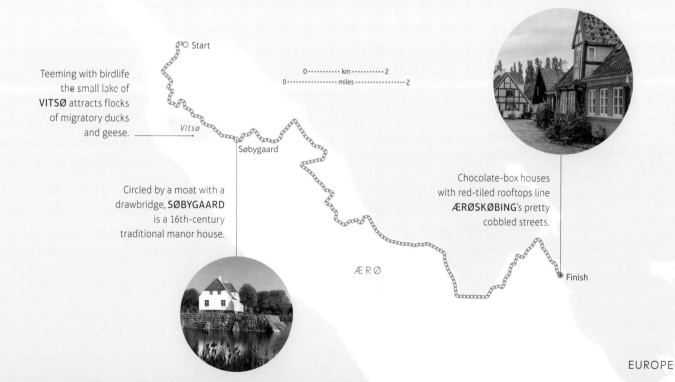

EUROPE

36

Midnight Sun Marathon

TROMSØ, NORWAY

The world's most northerly marathon is utterly unique. Here, surrounded by dramatic Arctic landscapes, participants run beneath the never-setting glow of the midnight sun.

Top Tip

Prepare for late-night running by training in the evening and timing your meals carefully.

42.2 KM (26.2 MILES)   202 M (663 FT)   PAVED

80

Blanketing the island of Tromsøya, nestled between rugged mountains and a narrow sea-strait, the small city of Tromsø is Norway's gateway to the Arctic. Lying 69 degrees north and 350 km (217 miles) north of the Arctic Circle, this part of the world sees round-the-clock daylight for several weeks each year during midsummer. Where better, then, to go for a midnight run?

ELEVATION PROFILE

100 m (328 ft)

0

0   42.2 km (26.2 miles)

As the name suggests, that's exactly what this race offers. Held at the height of midsummer, the Midnight Sun Marathon sees thousands of curious runners – some from as far afield as Kenya, the US and New Zealand – run under a sun that never sets. Marathon competitors cross the start line in downtown Tromsø at 8:30pm, with eager spectators shouting them on with cheers of "*heya!*" ("go!"). The route then strikes out to Tromsdalen on the mainland, before tracing the coastline of Tromsøya itself.

A string of sights captivates the attention of participants as they jog onwards. Within Tromsø, wonders include the snow-and-ice-inspired Arctic Cathedral – a modern show-stopper that consists of 11 triangular structures sandwiched together – and the Polaria Museum, its form reminiscent of toppling dominoes. But it's nature that gets the last word here. Outside the city, the route traces low-lying coastal roads, hemmed by windswept trees and bright wildflowers, serving up striking

Racing under the warm glow of the midnight sun

TROMSØ AIRPORT isn't so much a sight, but a mental pat on the back. Runners reaching this far are almost three-quarters of the way round.

Built in 1960, **TROMSØBRUA (TROMSØ BRIDGE)** links Tromsø to the Norwegian mainland. Runners cross the landmark twice during the marathon.

TROMSØ

Tromsø Airport

Start / Finish

Tromsøbrua

POLARIA is home to the world's northernmost aquarium and a panoramic cinema that screens polar-themed films.

Polaria

Arctic Cathedral

The **ARCTIC CATHEDRAL** is undoubtedly Tromsø's top sight. Inside, modern stained-glass windows imbue an ethereal ambiance.

Views across the water to distant snow-dusted mountains await runners at **TELEGRAPH BAY/ SOUTHERN POINT**.

Telegraph Bay

Gammelgård

Solligården

0 ·········· km ·········· 2
0 ·········· miles ·········· 2

vistas of the inky blue sea and raw, snowcapped mountains.

If you're lucky, clear skies will allow you to make the most of the views and the sunlight. As the sun sinks lower in the sky, the light shifts and the Arctic landscape is bathed in a golden hue. Even when its grey and cloudy, the neverending light still manages to imbue the scenery with a silvery glow. And, as you near the finish line, it's likely that the midnight sun will have begun to rise again – the almost-sunset merging seamlessly into the next day's sunrise.

SIGN-UP: *The marathon takes place on the closest Saturday to Midsummer's Day. Entry opens in early July the year before the race; to secure a spot, sign up by March.*

ANOTHER WAY

PolarNight Halfmarathon

Adventurous spirits should check out Tromsø's PolarNight Halfmarathon, which charts a course to Tromsøya island, heading out to the airport and back. Held during darkest January, it doesn't see daylight at all. Yes, it'll be bitterly cold, but you may be lucky enough to glimpse the spectacular Northern Lights.

The cliff top trail has stunning vistas of the **ORGAN PIPES**, vertical columns of rock that resemble the pipes of an organ.

Giant's Causeway

Shepherds Steps

Cliff top path

The **GIANT'S CAUSEWAY** was formed 50–60 million years ago following a period of intense volcanic activity.

NORTHERN IRELAND

Runkerry Beach

Start / Finish

Popular with surfers and geographers, **RUNKERRY BEACH** is pounded by more waves than any other beach in Northern Ireland.

37

Giant's Causeway

PORTBALLINTRAE, COUNTY ANTRIM, NORTHERN IRELAND, UK

Northern Ireland's rugged coastline provides a dramatic backdrop to this trail, which takes in wave-lashed sands, windswept clifftops and the world-famous Giant's Causeway.

9.2 KM (5.7 MILES) 255 M (837 FT) PAVED/TRAIL

This coastal jog is wonderfully scenic. Crossing the quiet waters of the Bush River, the route winds over grass-topped sand dunes to emerge onto golden Runkerry Beach, over-looked by the 19th-century Runkerry House. From here it's not far to the route's main event: Giant's Causeway. This UNESCO World Heritage Site is formed of 40,000 massive, black basalt columns, which tumble surreally down into the inky Atlantic Ocean. The run isn't over yet, though – and neither are the views. Breathe in the sea spray before tackling the Shepherd's Steps, 162 stone stairs once used by sheep and their sure-footed guides. The steep ascent leads to cliff-top panoramas of Causeway Coast, its ancient green headlands plunging into the wild Atlantic below.

SET OFF: *Waves on the beach can reach 3.7 m (12 ft) in stormy conditions; run on a low tide, good weather day.*

ELEVATION PROFILE

100 m (328 ft)

0

0   9.2 km (5.7 miles)

IN FOCUS
A Battle of Giants

According to legend, the giant Finn McCool built the Causeway as a crossing to confront his Scottish enemy, Benandonner. The much-larger foe, however, then used the path to attack Finn who, with the help of his wife, disguised himself as a baby. Fearing the size of the baby's father, the Scottish giant retreated, destroying the Causeway as he went.

38
Loch Affric Loop

LOCH AFFRIC, SCOTLAND, UK

Wildlife and wild scenery combine on this circuit run around Loch Affric, a stunning freshwater lake in the heart of the Highlands.

17.4 KM (10.8 MILES) 320 M (1,050 FT) PAVED/TRAIL

Loch Affric is one of Scotland's most beautiful lochs – making this trail one of the country's most beautiful runs. Head out along the northern side of the loch, where the trail gradually rises along potted singletrack, offering technical running with a side of spectacular mountain scenery – Càrn Eige and Mam Sodhail, the twin peaks at the top of Loch Affric, are the highest mountains north of the Great Glen. Keep an eye out, too, for solitary Scots pine trees, known as "Granny Pines". Over 200 years old, they are remnants of the endangered Caledonian Forest that once covered much of the Highlands. Crossing the River Affric marks the start of the return run and a switch to vehicle track. If anything, the views are even more impressive on this side, with the loch's waters backdropped by looming mountains all the way back.

SET OFF: *Run the trail from dawn to dusk; the car park is open 24 hours.*

Running along the stony roads that line the southern side of untamed Loch Affric

ELEVATION PROFILE

400 m
(1,312 ft)

200 m
(656 ft)

0   17.4 km (10.8 miles)

Get ready for the start of the climb above the loch's **NORTHERN SHORE**, as the trail leads up through thick bracken.

SCOTLAND

Start of climb

Start / Finish

Prepare to get your feet wet as you fjord several **BURNS** (mountain streams) along the way.

Mountain burns

Loch Affric

0 ·············· km ·············· 2
0 ·············· miles ·············· 2

Run past the old settlement at **ATHNAMULLOCH**, only abandoned in the 1950s when the last family left.

Athnamulloch

39

Man v Horse

LLANWRTYD WELLS, WALES, UK

Tracing a path through the rugged, rolling scenery of mid-Wales, this eccentric race pits hardy runners against horses and their riders.

33 KM (20.5 MILES) 1,215 M (3,986 FT) PAVED/TRAIL

A pub, a bet and a sleepy Welsh town were all it took to create Man v Horse. In 1980, some patrons of the Neuadd Arms Hotel in Llanwrtyd Wells were discussing the relative merits of men and horses as cross-country runners. The debate was overheard by Gordon Green, then the landlord of the pub, who decided to put the question to a test – with £1,000 worth of prize money for any human who could beat a horse. The ensuing wacky race was an instant hit, and has intrigued both runners and riders ever since.

For 24 years, it looked like the horses were unbeatable. With each equine victory, the pot of prize money accumulated and speculation grew more rife – would a human ever beat a horse? In 2004, however, when elite marathon runner Huw Lobb crossed the finish line in an impressive 2 hours and 5 minutes, that fabled day finally arrived. Not only could Lobb bask in his hard-earned victory as the first ever runner to win the race, but he also collected the £25,000 rollover prize money – one of the largest in the sport. There have been just two other human winners since.

On race day, runners leave from the town square outside the Neuadd Arms; 15 minutes later the horses set off in hot pursuit. It's a tough race – and not just because participants are competing against four-legged opponents. The trail loops its way along stony farm roads and narrow trails, winding up and down rich green hills that cause runners' chests to heave and their calves to ache. In places, the ground is turned into a carpet of thigh-splattering mud by the often rainy weather, while at other points there are gushing streams to ford.

For many runners, it's not long before they hear the thunder of their pursuers' hooves behind them. It's an unnerving experience to be on a narrow trail and hear "Horse coming through!", before a blur of

ELEVATION PROFILE

500 m (1,640 ft)

0

0   33 km (20.5 miles)

A horse and its rider dashing ahead of a line of runners during Man v Horse

For many runners,
it's not long before they
hear the thunder of
their pursuers' hooves
behind them.

0 ········· km ········· 1
0 ··········· miles ··········· 1

WALES

The churchyard of **EGLWYS OEN DUW** is a biodiversity hotspot, especially for birds such as sparrow hawks and tawny owls.

Eglwys Oen Duw Church

This spot marks the first **RIVER CROSSING** – one of many that runners have to tackle on the route.

River crossing

Crowds line the end of the course, cheering exhausted runners across the **FINISH LINE**.

Finish

Start

mane and tail powers past. The key rule? Stay on the right and keep your ears open.

On some of the trickier sections the horses and runners diverge, with the horses undertaking extra distance but on gentler terrain. It's enough to make hopeful runners think that they can steal the edge. Not so – by the two-thirds mark, when the race turns back towards Llanwrtyd Wells, all but the fastest runners have been overtaken.

SIGN-UP: *The race is held annually in June. Entries usually open in January at www.green-events.co.uk and sell out fast.*

The starting point for this race is the **NEUADD ARMS HOTEL**, a historic Grade-II listed building built during the Victorian era.

Runners making their
way across a crowd-lined
Tower Bridge

Top Tip
Spectators can watch
runners pass by at mile
15, then make a short
walk to see them again
around mile 18.

40

London Marathon

GREENWICH PARK TO THE MALL,
LONDON, ENGLAND, UK

*Energetic supporters cheer on thousands of runners as they
wind through the UK capital, taking in some of its most famous
landmarks and raising millions for charity along the way.*

42.2 KM (26.2 MILES) 135 M (443 FT) PAVED

Inspired by the success of the New York City
Marathon, the inaugural London Marathon
took place in March 1981. It was to be a
showcase of the UK capital, as well as a way
to provide "some happiness and sense of
achievement" for its participants. That year,
American Dick Beardsley and Norwegian
Inge Simonsen raced stride-by-stride all the
way to the finish line, where they crossed it
hand-in-hand as joint winners – an act that
would come to define the London Marathon's
supportive, community-focused spirit.

Today the race has boomed from fewer
than 8,000 runners to 45,000. Elite athletes

are drawn by its status as one of the World
Marathon Majors – and the knowledge that
it's a relatively flat course on which great
times can be run. For many people, though,
it's about getting a unique sight-seeing tour
of one of the world's most-visited cities.
Participants have the chance to run along
historic streets normally clogged with traffic,
all while enjoying a medley of London's
greatest sightseeing hits. Highlights include
the almost 1,000-year-old Tower of London,
the pyramidal Shard and the soaring skyscrapers of Canary Wharf. Close to the
finish, big hitters come one after another:
the London Eye and Big Ben, the Palace of
Westminster and Buckingham Palace.

Beyond the sights, the marathon is all
about helping others. In fact, it's the world's
largest annual fundraising event: to date,
participants have raised over £1 billion for
charity. Each year, more than 15,000 charity ▶

ELEVATION PROFILE

100 m
(328 ft)

0

0   42.2 km (26.2 miles)

87

With under 6 km (4 miles) to go, runners pass the famed **TOWER OF LONDON**, a nearly millennium-old castle that houses the Crown Jewels.

On the penultimate right turn runners reach stately **BUCKINGHAM PALACE**, the official residence of the King.

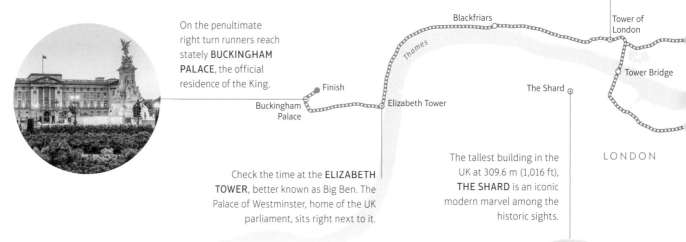

The tallest building in the UK at 309.6 m (1,016 ft), **THE SHARD** is an iconic modern marvel among the historic sights.

Check the time at the **ELIZABETH TOWER**, better known as Big Ben. The Palace of Westminster, home of the UK parliament, sits right next to it.

runners, the most of any major marathon, tackle the course. Hundreds of charities are represented: joggers wear the colourful vests and t-shirts of their chosen cause, many of which poignantly honour the memory of a loved one. The most eye-catching are those in fancy dress – and the marathon sure does have a reputation for elaborate costumes. There's everything under the sun here: look out for superheroes and movie characters, wild animals (gorillas tend to be popular), knights and dragons and, most dedicated of all, two-person horse costumes. Some runners cause a stir by dressing as London landmarks: in 2019, a runner attired as Big Ben set off alarm bells when they were too tall to cross under the finish line arch. Lloyd Scott, meanwhile, really went the extra mile in 2002 when he completed the marathon in a deep-sea diving outfit, which included a copper helmet and lead-lined boots. It took Scott five long days to complete the marathon, but he raised tens of thousands of pounds for the charity Cancer and Leukaemia In Childhood.

The crowd's support for every runner, whether in costume or not, makes the London Marathon an unforgettable experience. Most participants have their name on

Marathon participants passing the London Eye, found near the finish line

Limehouse

Canary Wharf

Rotherhithe

Thames

Woolwich

Cutty Sark

Greenwich

Charlton

Start

In Greenwich, runners head past the **CUTTY SARK.** Built in 1869, it was one of the fastest clipper ships of its era.

IN FOCUS
Deciding the Distance

International marathon distances varied until the 1908 London Olympic Games. Here, Queen Alexandra requested the race start at Windsor Castle and end at the White City Stadium – precisely 26 miles and 385 yards (or 42.195 km) away. The distance stuck.

their running top, so everyone can cheer them on, and at times it feels like the whole city has come out to support you. Certain stretches are famed for the roar of the crowd: there's the spine-tingling crescendo at Cutty Sark and the thrilling tunnel of whooping support on Tower Bridge, just before the halfway mark. There are also bands, orchestras and DJs playing, with the sound getting louder mile by mile. Then,

when everything starts to hurt, it's these cheers which carry you on to the final stretch along The Mall. Here, as over 1 million people have done before, runners cross the finish line grinning from ear to ear.

SIGN-UP: *Registration opens shortly after the previous marathon has finished; register via* www.tcslondonmarathon. com. *Entry is usually by ballot.*

Top Tip

Walk, cycle or use
public transport to get
to Bushy Park, as
parking for cars
is limited.

41

Bushy Park

BUSHY PARK, LONDON, ENGLAND, UK

*London's second-largest park will forever have a place in the
annals of running history. It was here, in this peaceful, deer-
dotted slice of green, that the world's very first parkrun was held.*

5 KM (3.1 MILES)   7 M (23 FT)   PAVED/TRAIL

Back in autumn 2004, keen runner Paul
Sinton-Hewitt had just lost his job and was
unable to run due to injury. Undaunted, he
took this as an opportunity to get started
on a plan he'd been brewing for a while: a
social time trial event open to everyone,
not just club runners and racers. So, on
2 October, thirteen runners laced up for
a 5-km (3.1-mile) morning run around
Bushy Park. From here the numbers began
to grow week on week – largely thanks
to word of mouth – with everyone from
hardcore runners to first-time joggers
turning up to take part. By the time the
event's second birthday rolled around,
almost 400 runners were attending the
event and demand was high enough for
Paul and his pals to set up a second
parkrun in Wimbledon. Over the next
couple of years, parkrun began to spread
across the UK, with six separate events
and over 800 participants by early 2008.

From there, this Saturday morning event has
become a global phenomenon – there are
now over 2,000 parkruns taking place in
20 countries across five continents. And no
wonder: parkrun's appeal is simple, after all.
It's completely free, covers a manageable
distance (always 5 km/3.1 miles), and is
open to everyone, whatever their running
ability. Plus, there's usually a real community feel: marathon runners jog alongside
retirees and families with pushchairs, while
friends egg each other towards the finish.

The route through Bushy Park remains
one of the most popular parkruns. Each

ELEVATION PROFILE

50 m
(164 ft)

0

0   5 km (3.1 miles)

parkrun participants jogging past deer
as they make their way through Bushy Park

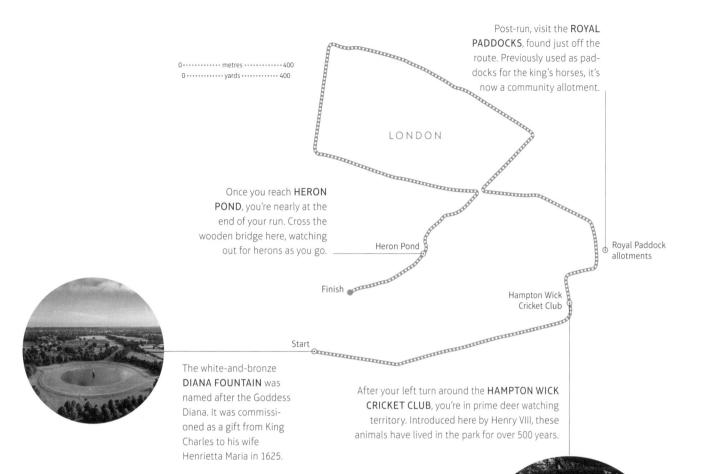

Post-run, visit the **ROYAL PADDOCKS**, found just off the route. Previously used as paddocks for the king's horses, it's now a community allotment.

LONDON

0 ·········· metres ·········· 400
0 ·········· yards ·········· 400

Once you reach **HERON POND**, you're nearly at the end of your run. Cross the wooden bridge here, watching out for herons as you go.

Heron Pond

Royal Paddock allotments

Finish

Hampton Wick Cricket Club

Start

The white-and-bronze **DIANA FOUNTAIN** was named after the Goddess Diana. It was commissioned as a gift from King Charles to his wife Henrietta Maria in 1625.

After your left turn around the **HAMPTON WICK CRICKET CLUB**, you're in prime deer watching territory. Introduced here by Henry VIII, these animals have lived in the park for over 500 years.

week, hundreds of participants turn up to tackle the largely flat trail, which winds through pretty parkland, complete with leafy trees and tranquil ponds. In fact, on Christmas Day in 2019, a staggering 2,545 people braved the cold to jog through Bushy, setting the record for the most runners ever. The course also holds the record for the fastest parkrun (13 minutes 48 seconds), thanks to former Olympian Andrew Baddeley. That's another couple for the history books, then.

SIGN-UP: *parkrun is held at 9am every Saturday. Register once at* www.parkrun.org.uk/bushy *to be allocated a barcode, then simply bring it to the event each week.*

REFUEL

A Bushy Park Brunch

Hungry after your morning run? Head over to the Pheasantry Cafe in the Woodland Gardens part of the park, where there's everything you need to revive yourself post jog. Put your feet up and enjoy an ever-popular avocado toast or a reviving English breakfast; there's great coffee, too.

0 ·········· metres ·········· 800
0 ·········· yards ·········· 800

BERE ISLAND

Viewpoint to
Hungry Hill ○ Lonehart Battery

From this spot, you'll
get great views of the
brooding **HUNGRY HILL**
on the mainland.

LONEHART BATTERY
looks out over the main-
land's Sheep's Head
and Beara peninsulas.

A downhill brings you to **RERRIN
VILLAGE** with glorious views
across to the sheltered Laurence's
Cove and its yachting marina.

Rerrin

Start / Finish

42

Bere Island parkrun

RERRIN, BERE ISLAND, COUNTY CORK, IRELAND

This off-the-beaten-track parkrun takes in rugged scenery as it winds around the hilly country roads of Bere Island.

⊖ 5 KM (3.1 MILES) ⊗ 76 M (249 FT) ⊗ PAVED/TRAIL

This parkrun is an adventure from start to finish. To just reach the start line, joggers have to take a ferry to the island from the fishing town of Castletownbere, then catch a ride with a friendly local runner to Rerrin village (lifts are readily offered).

Snaking down rolling country roads, the route itself winds around the eastern end of the island. There's no need to worry about traffic as island life pauses during the run, leaving you able to dedicate all

Jogging along country roads during
the Bere Island parkrun

your attention to the views: lush-green fields dotted with cows and sheep; craggy bays filled with turquoise water (on sunny days, at least); and the mainland's gorse- and heather-clad hills in the distance. Soak it all up, because before you know it you'll be back in Rerrin, where locals will undoubtedly invite you to the local café for a cuppa and a freshly baked scone.

ELEVATION PROFILE

100 m
(328 ft)

0
0   5 km (3.1 miles)

SIGN-UP: *As with all parkruns, register (once) on the website to get a barcode, then simply bring it to the event.*

43
Englischer Garten

EISBACHWALLE, MUNICH, GERMANY

Enjoy a gentle jog around Munich's most expansive park, rolling from its lively south to its tranquil north.

Resembling an English park, the vast Englischer Garten is larger than both New York's Central Park and London's Hyde Park. It's really two gardens in one – as is showcased by this looping route. The run starts next to the artificial waves of the Eisbachwelle, before weaving alongside the crowds lounging beneath Monopteros, a Greek-style temple. Passing Kleinhesseloher Lake, the route makes its way into the quieter north section; here, bustle gives way to tranquillity thanks to the shady forests and meadows grazed by sheep. Eventually, the tranquil flow of the Isar River leads you south again, and soon the sound of birdsong is replaced by blasts of Bavarian music and clinking glasses as the Chinesischen Turm (Chinese Tower) and its beer garden comes into view – a great spot for a post-run pick-me-up.

SET OFF: *With the park's paths totalling 78 km (48 miles) in length, it's easy to extend your run or make your own route.*

- ⊖ 13 KM (8 MILES)
- ⊗ 18 M (59 FT)
- ⊖ PAVED/TRAIL

ELEVATION PROFILE

600 m
(1,969 ft)

500 m
(1,640 ft)

0   13 km (8 miles)

REFUEL
Grab a Cold One

At the Chinesischen Turm's beer garden, you can kick back in the shade of old chestnut trees and drink refreshing golden Helles lager from Munich's Hofbräu brewery. There's also alcohol-free beer and traditional Bavarian beer-garden food like sausages, cheese and pretzels.

93

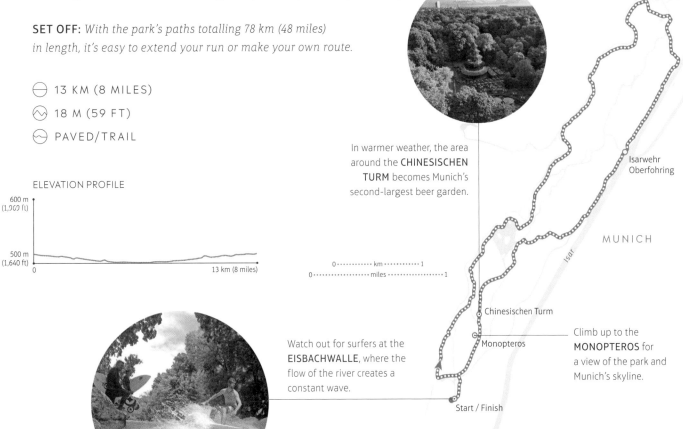

In warmer weather, the area around the **CHINESISCHEN TURM** becomes Munich's second-largest beer garden.

Isarwehr Oberfohring

MUNICH

0 ········· km ·········· 1
0 ········· miles ·········· 1

Chinesischen Turm

Monopteros

Climb up to the **MONOPTEROS** for a view of the park and Munich's skyline.

Watch out for surfers at the **EISBACHWALLE**, where the flow of the river creates a constant wave.

Start / Finish

EUROPE

Runners streaming
through the Tiergarten
Park, with the Victory
Column behind

44

Berlin Marathon

TIERGARTEN PARK, BERLIN, GERMANY

One of the world's most famous marathons, this race through the centre of Berlin has a storied history, playing an important role in both the reunification of Germany and in record-breaking runs.

42.2 KM (26.2 MILES) · 57 M (187 FT) · PAVED

Every year on the last Sunday of September, over 40,000 people line up in Berlin's leafy Tiergarten Park ready to tackle the Berlin Marathon, one of the World Marathon Majors. Looping through the city, the race passes through numerous neighbourhoods, from elegant Mitte with its grand government buildings, to creative Kreuzberg, home to cutting-edge galleries and colourful street art. Countless sights flash past on the way, including the imposing Rathaus Schöneberg and the musical Konzerthaus Berlin. Yet for many the highlight of this race is passing beneath the Brandenburger Tor (Brandenburg Gate) – and not just because it's near the end of the race.

Built at the end of the 18th century, the 15-m- (50-ft-) tall Greek-revival-style monument was a symbol of division during the Cold War, when both Germany and Berlin itself were split into two. During this time, the gate was a de facto part of the Berlin Wall, being located in a restricted zone inaccessible to either East or West Berliners. However, this symbolism was flipped on its head in 1989, when thousands of inhabitants from both sides of the city joyously celebrated the fall of the wall here. Ever since, the Brandenburg Gate has become an emblem of freedom and unity. ▶

REFUEL
Energize on the Go

From 5 km (3.1 miles) on, there are refreshment points every 2–4 km (1.2–2.4 miles). Some have water, others offer energy drinks, sweet tea and fruit, with energy gels available at one station after the halfway mark. Post-run, more sweet tea, salted pretzels and alcohol-free beer are on offer.

ELEVATION PROFILE

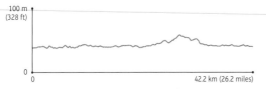

100 m (328 ft)

0

0 — 42.2 km (26.2 miles)

Top Tip

Get supporters to grab a
seat in the stands at the
finish line; they'll need
to get there early.

Many participants paused beneath
the Brandenburg Gate to take in
the significance of the moment,
stopping to touch the columns and
hug their fellow competitors.

This very fact was celebrated a year later at the 1990 Berlin Marathon. Founded in 1974 during the height of the Cold War, the race had up until then only taken place in West Germany. Shortly following the fall of the wall, the then race director Horst Milde reached out to the mayors of both sides of the city to request a new route for the marathon, one that would take in 8 km (5 miles) of East Berlin and pass beneath the iconic Brandenburg Gate. His proposal was accepted and so on 30 September 1990, just three days before the official reunification of Germany, thousands of runners – from both East and West Berlin – took to the course, becoming some of the first people to cross the previously divided city. Many participants paused beneath the Brandenburg Gate to take in the significance of the moment, stopping to touch the columns and hug their fellow competitors. Around them, crowds filled the once-deserted square surrounding the gate – a place that had been desolate and empty for almost 30 years – cheering jubilantly as the runners passed by. This marathon was all about coming together – in fact, the race was dubbed "Das Lauf der Einheit" ("The Run of Unity").

The 1990 race would have another significance: the new route marked it as one of the fastest world marathon courses, thanks to its flat elevation, wide boulevards and often good weather. Since then the Berlin Marathon has continued to make history with multiple world records set on its course. It's currently the fastest marathon in the world thanks to Kenyan athlete Eliud Kipchoge; here, in 2022, he broke the world record by completing the route in a staggering 2 hours, 1 minute and 9 seconds. The women's world record has also been broken in Berlin several times.

And yet at its heart, this race will always be more about unity than competition. The atmosphere is exuberant as over 1 million people from across the city pour onto the streets: om-pah-pah bands play bright tunes and spectators wave

Spree

Group of runners
jogging past the soaring
Victory Column in
Tiergarten Park

IN FOCUS

Warming Up

The day before the marathon there's a Frühstückslauf (Breakfast Run). Thousands of participants take part in this gentle 6-km (4-mile) jog (there are pacemakers at the front to slow everyone down), often wearing costumes and carrying their national flags. It ends in the Olympic Stadium with a free breakfast.

Enjoy some calmness in **TIERGARTEN PARK**, Berlin's largest green space, before the race begins.

Run through the historic **BRANDENBURG GATE**; from here, the finish line is only 400 m (1,310 ft) away.

At around 6.5 km (4 miles), the striking form of the **BERLIN TV TOWER** pops up above the building line.

Berlin TV Tower

Siegessäule

Start

Finish

Brandenburg Gate

Follow the flat tree-lined Straße des 17 Juni towards Berlin's imposing **VICTORY COLUMN** (Siegessäule).

Kaiser Wilhelm-Gedächtniskirche

BERLIN

Kurfüstendamm

Kreuzberg

Neukölln

Spree

0 ········· km ········ 1
0 ·········· miles ········· 1

The middle section takes you through the cool and creative districts of **KREUZBERG** and **NEUKÖLLN**. Look out for great street art.

signs and roar their support. Nowhere is this atmosphere more joyful than at the historic Brandenburg Gate, where runners pass beneath this symbol of peace and unity as they make their final strides towards the finish line.

SIGN-UP: *Registration opens shortly after the previous marathon has been run; register at* www.bmw-berlin-marathon. com/en. *Entry is usually by lottery.*

MAKE IT SHORTER
Take a Lift on the Cable Car

Several of the mountain summits found along the Königsroute have cable cars linking them to the valleys below, making it easy to shorten the length of this route. For a 15-km (9.3-mile) challenge, run the section from Weissbad to Kronberg, where a cable car awaits to whisk you all the way back down to the valley floor – no leg work necessary.

Stop off at **BERGGASTHAUS AESCHER**, an almost impossibly beautiful medieval hut that clings to the side of an abrupt rockface.

THE RIDGE from Hoher Kasten to Staubern mountain inn is largely flat, with glimpses of the Alpstein's peaks through the pines.

Hoher Hirschberg

Eggli

Start / Finish

Brülisau

Hoher Kasten

Kronberg

Berggasthaus Aescher

Berggasthaus Schäfler

Seealpsee

Stauberenkanzel

SWITZERLAND

Säntis

Berggasthaus Bollenwees

Rotsteinpass

The vertiginous 2,124-m (6,968-ft) **ROTSTEINPASS** is only accessible by steel cables and knee-crunching staircases hewn directly into the rocky cliffs.

Spend the night at **BERGGASTHAUS BOLLENWEES**, a mountain inn overlooking the iridescent Lake Fälensee.

0 ·········· km ·········· 2
0 ·········· miles ·········· 2

45

Königsroute

WEISSBAD, SWITZERLAND

Head off on an epic trail-running adventure through the little-visited Alpstein mountains, complete with stunning alpine scenery and medieval mountain inns.

86 KM (53 MILES)

6,651 M (21,821 FT)

TRAIL

Forming a natural border between Switzerland and Liechtenstein, the Alpstein mountain range is a trail runner's dream. Not only is this land of jagged stone peaks and forested valleys off the tourist radar, it's also crisscrossed with trails, chief among them the Königsroute (Royal Tour). This epic multiday running (and hiking) route tackles 86 km (53 miles) of trails, numerous peaks, and lots of up and down.

This route is definitely not one for the uninitiated. There are narrow paths, steep ascents and rocky ridges to negotiate, as well as technical terrain, including sections of ladders, cables and staircases that cling to the mountainside. Yet for those ready to take on the challenge, the effort is well rewarded. Jaw-dropping views open up at every turn: bright-green valleys dotted with mirror-like lakes; limestone ridges edged by banks of multicoloured wildflowers; pinnacled peaks reaching out of the clouds towards the clear blue sky. The route also weaves in and out of a handful of pretty

Running along dramatic rocky ridges in the Alpstein mountains

alpine settlements, including diminutive Brülisau and chocolate-box Weissbad.

These sights provide an excuse to stop for a breather, as do the spectacular guesthouses that line the trail. Often perched atop rocky summits, these rustic mountain inns offer hearty food to hungry runners, as well as offering a cosy bed for the night. Many also offer local whiskeys – there's no better way to end the day than by toasting to the next as you take in sunset views over the ragged peaks of the Alpstein.

SET OFF: *The route is off-limits in winter and spring; run it from May to October.*

ELEVATION PROFILE

3,000 m (9,843 ft)

0

0   86 km (53 miles)

Enjoy unforgettable views of the **LAUTERBRUNNEN VALLEY** on the cable car to Männlichen from either Wengen or Grindelwald.

Start

Pause to enjoy views of green meadows rising up to **TSCHUGGEN**'s rocky peak.

Views of Tschuggen

SWITZERLAND

Restaurant Grindelwaldblick

It's a short detour to the viewing platform at **RESTAURANT GRINDELWALDBLICK** for commanding views.

Finish

In **KLEINE SCHEIDEGG**, ride the cable car back down to the valley, taking in more beautiful alpine views.

0 ········· metres ········· 800
0 ········· yards ········· 800

46
Panorama Trail

MÄNNLICHEN TO KLEINE SCHEIDEGG, SWITZERLAND

Fill your lungs with fresh mountain air and confront the imposing north face of the Eiger on this laid-back alpine run in the Swiss Alps.

In a country famed for its dizzying mountain paths, this trail gives runners of all levels a more accessible taste of the Alps. The short, mostly downhill route spares you from the steady climbs and rocky terrain common to the area, but it certainly doesn't skimp on epic vistas. From the moment you step off the cable car in Männlichen, you find yourself with a clear view of the Eiger's north face. Infamously known as the most dangerous climbing route in the Alps, this near-vertical sheet of rock has awed adventurers for centuries. Even when the peak itself is shrouded in clouds, the panoramic vistas of the surrounding valley make this trail worth the effort regardless.

Heading gently downwards, the dirt trail serves up green alpine meadows, sprinkled here and there with splashes of brightly coloured wildflowers, while soaring peaks encircle the scene. It's almost a shame to arrive at Kleine Scheidegg, but the views from the cable car, which will whisk you back down to the valley below, aren't bad either.

SET OFF: *The trail is open mid-June to October; due to the altitude and unpredictable weather, bring water and layers.*

⊖ 8.7 KM (5.4 MILES)

⬳ 215 M (705 FT)

⊖ TRAIL

ELEVATION PROFILE

2,500 m (8,202 ft)

2,000 m (6,560 ft)

0

8.7 km (5.4 miles)

A jogger making their way around the edge of the tranquil Zeller See

At **PRIELAU**, gaze south towards the Grossglockner, the highest mountain in Austria at 3,798 m (12,460 ft) high.

With a historic centre and lots of restaurants, **ZELL AM SEE** is the perfect place to relax post-run.

Prielau

Einöd

Thumersbach

Start / Finish

Zeller See

Erlberg

Seespitz

AUSTRIA

Near **ERLBERG**, the loop starts to undulate and the terrain changes to packed mud paths.

47

Zeller See Loop

ZELL AM SEE, AUSTRIA

This easygoing run around the sapphire-blue Zeller See takes in pretty meadows, shadow-draped forest and beautiful mountain views.

11.2 KM (6.9 MILES)   46 M (151 FT)   PAVED/TRAIL

Nestled in the heart of the Austrian Alps, Zeller See is stunning. This deep-blue lake is encircled by forested mountains, whose peaks play host to skiers and snowboarders come winter, and whose lower slopes brim with wildflowers in spring and summer.

    This gentle run makes the most of the scenery. Starting in the resort town of Zell Am See on the lake's western side, weave south, looking out over bobbing boats and across to emerald mountains. The path then leaves the shore to pass through meadows brimming with wildflowers: buttercups, daisies and forget-me-nots pop with colour against the green grass and the air hums with insect chatter. The dappled light of the canopied woods lining the eastern bank comes next, before the route bursts back into sunshine to trace the lake's northern edge, serving up even more views of picture-postcard peaks.

SET OFF: *Run anticlockwise, saving views of the epic Grossglockner until last.*

ELEVATION PROFILE

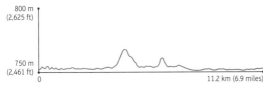

800 m (2,625 ft)

750 m (2,461 ft)

0   11.2 km (6.9 miles)

0 •••••• metres •••••• 500
0 •••••• yards •••••• 500

Look west from the Castel Sant'Angelo to glimpse **ST PETER'S BASILICA**, presiding over Vatican City. Its dome dominates the city's skyline.

St Peter's Basilica

Ponte Vittorio Emanuele II

Finish

ROME

The imposing **CASTEL SANT'ANGELO** was built for the tomb of Emperor Hadrian; today it's a museum.

Tiber

Run beneath the statue-lined **PONTE VITTORIO EMANUELE II**; it connects Vatican City with Rome's historic heart.

Ponte Sisto

Trastevere

Start

Take a detour through **TRASTEVERE**, a trendy neighbourhood known for its pretty cobbled streets and buzzing nightlife.

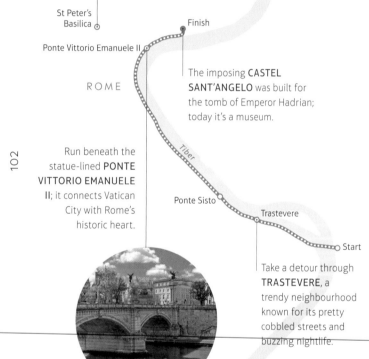

MAKE IT LONGER
Visit the Vatican

From the Castel Sant'Angelo, run along the Via della Conciliazione for just under 1 km (0.6 miles). This wide avenue will lead you straight to the Vatican, the world's smallest country.

48

Rome's River Run

ROME, ITALY

Following the flow of the River Tiber, this peaceful jog weaves through the Italian capital, taking in historic sights big and small along the way.

The River Tiber has been at the heart of Rome since its founding, almost 3,000 years ago. Starting at the edge of the ancient centre, this laid-back route traces a section of this sinuous river, following the flat, traffic-free path that runs along its leafy western bank.

On the way, runners will glimpse traces of the city's long history, including the ancient Temple of Hercules, one of the oldest buildings in Rome, and the 2,000-year-old Ponte Cestio, which crosses over to Tiber Island. They'll also be treated to a slice of tranquility; here, the sounds of the busy city are muted and the sun glitters off the calm surface of the river. All too soon, the 19th-century Ponte Vittorio Emanuele II comes into view, its beautifully carved form signalling that the run is nearing its end. One last sight awaits, however: the mighty Castel Sant'Angelo, a towering fortress built in 135 CE, which rises above joggers as they take their final steps.

SET OFF: *With most of this run following the quiet riverside path, it's a great run to do at any time of day.*

⊖ 2.5 KM (1.5 MILES)

◯ 17 M (56 FT)

⊖ PAVED

ELEVATION PROFILE

50 m (164 ft)

0

0   2.5 km (1.5 miles)

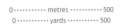

The **PORTA SANTA MARIA**, an arched gateway in the northern side of the walls, features a marble statue of the Virgin Mary.

Porta Santa Maria

Porta San Donato

LUCCA

Porta Elisa

Venture out onto the arrow-shaped **BALUARDO SAN DONATO**, the largest of several bastions along the walls.

Baluardo San Donato

Orto Botanico di Lucca

Start / Finish

49
Walls of Lucca

LUCCA, ITALY

Enjoy elevated views over historic Lucca on this circuitous jog, which runs along the town's wonderfully preserved Renaissance ramparts.

Peer into the **ORTO BOTANICO DI LUCCA**, an arboretum and botanical gardens that features a variety of Tuscan flora.

4.2 KM (2.6 MILES) 4 M (13 FT) PAVED

The rust-red walls surrounding the Tuscan town of Lucca are an impressive sight. Built during the 16th century to protect against attack from Florence, these 12-m- (39-ft-) high walls were later turned into a tree-lined walkway – one that, today, local joggers love. Starting at the leafy Piazzale Vittorio Emanuele, the town slowly reveals itself as you make your way around the top of the fortification. Views across the terracotta rooftops come thick and fast, as do glimpses into secret courtyards and onto splendid basilicas and old palaces. There's so much to see that you could easily spend an hour completing the 4.2-km (2.6-mile) loop – or you might even choose to take another turn around the ramparts.

SET OFF: *The walls are open 24 hours, but if you want some company, join the Mura di Lucca parkrun on Saturday at 9am.*

Running along the tree-lined Walls of Lucca on an autumn day

ELEVATION PROFILE

50 m
(164 ft)

0

0   4.2 km (2.6 miles)

50
Tour of Monaco

VIEILLE VILLE, MONACO

Looping through glam Monaco, this run takes you from the rainbow-hued old town to the glitz of Monte-Carlo and beyond.

7.5 KM (4.6 MILES)

236 M (774 FT)

PAVED

Nestled on the sun-drenched Côte d'Azur, Monaco is the world's second smallest country. Its diminutive size makes it a great place for a runseeing tour, with most of its highlights a mere stone's throw away from each other.

Starting in the pastel-hued Vieille Ville (old town), your feet will lead you past the fortress-like Place du Palais (Prince's Palace), the seat of the ruling Grimaldi family for eight centuries. From here, the sights come thick and fast: glistening Port Hercule and its planetary sized super yachts; the country's iconic Formula 1 track; and lavish Monte Carlo Casino, often surrounded by Ferraris and Aston Martins – there's no doubting that this is the playground of the rich and famous. At the halfway point lies Plage Larvotto, backed by the high-end Avenue Princesse Grace; its white sands are the perfect place for a quick break before looping back.

SET OFF: *Run early in the morning, before the crowds of tourists descend and the streets get busy.*

104

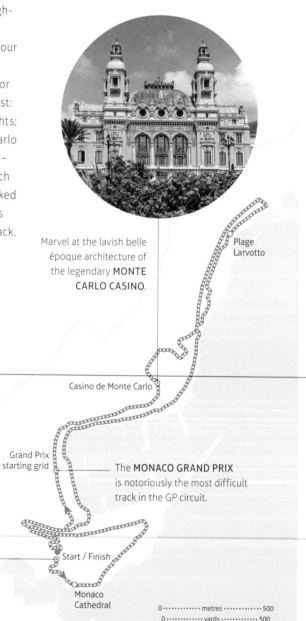

REFUEL
Head to Market

For a post-run snack, head to the Condamine Market on Place d'Armes, which has been operating since 1880. The stalls here are bursting with local specialities, including *socca* (a crispy chickpea pancake) and *barbagiuans* (a pastry filled with things like cheese and spinach).

Marvel at the lavish belle époque architecture of the legendary **MONTE CARLO CASINO**.

Plage Larvotto

Casino de Monte Carlo

ELEVATION PROFILE

100 m
(328 ft)

0

0   7.5 km (4.6 miles)

FRANCE

MONACO

Grand Prix starting grid

The **MONACO GRAND PRIX** is notoriously the most difficult track in the GP circuit.

Located on a high, rocky promontory overlooking the ocean, the **VIEILLE VILLE** is utterly striking.

Start / Finish

Monaco Cathedral

0 ············ metres ············ 500
0 ············ yards ············ 500

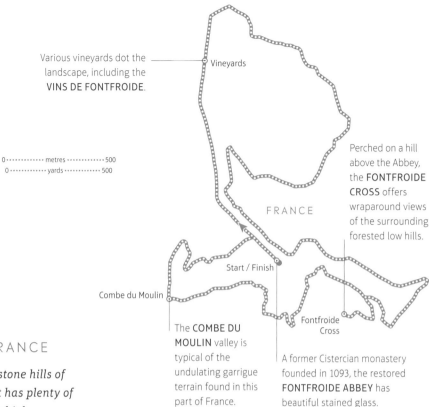

Various vineyards dot the landscape, including the **VINS DE FONTFROIDE.**

Vineyards

0 ·········· metres ·········· 500
0 ·········· yards ·········· 500

F R A N C E

Perched on a hill above the Abbey, the **FONTFROIDE CROSS** offers wraparound views of the surrounding forested low hills.

Start / Finish

Combe du Moulin

Fontfroide Cross

The **COMBE DU MOULIN** valley is typical of the undulating garrigue terrain found in this part of France.

A former Cistercian monastery founded in 1093, the restored **FONTFROIDE ABBEY** has beautiful stained glass.

51

La Ronde des Cistes

FONTFROIDE ABBEY, FRANCE

Running through the wooded limestone hills of southern France, this scenic circuit has plenty of ascent to keep the challenge-factor high.

9 KM (5.6 MILES) · 305 M (1,001 FT) · TRAIL

If the south of France conjures up images of mind-bogglingly expensive beach hotels, the La Ronde des Cistes is part of another world entirely. Set in the Occitanie country-side, this run winds through a dramatic limestone terrain of rugged hills, covered in shrubby vegetation known as garrigue.

The run is the shortest of the four organized events – often referred to col-lectively as the Trail de Fontfroide – that are held over the same weekend in March, with 15-km (9.3-mile), 34-km (21.1-mile) and 55-km (34.1-mile) versions also taking place. It begins, as the others do, at the 11th-century Fontfroide Abbey, before snaking across wooded slopes to complete

a deeply enjoyable circuit – although a taxing one. Runners will find their legs burning, thanks to the hilly terrain, which sees them tackle 300 m (984 ft) of ascent. Thankfully the views offer plenty of reason to pause for breath.

SIGN-UP: *Register in advance online at www.traildefontfroide.com.*

ELEVATION PROFILE

300 m (984 ft)

0

0   9 km (5.6 miles)

View over Fontfroide Abbey from next to the Fontfroide Cross

52

Le Marathon International du Beaujolais

FLEURIE TO VILLEFRANCHE-SUR-SAÔNE, FRANCE

Savour the party atmosphere on France's friendliest wine marathon, which winds among the golden stone villages, cornrow vineyards and crumbling châteaux of Beaujolais.

Top Tip
Alcohol dehydrates, so it's especially important to hydrate well during this run.

42.2 KM (26.2 MILES)   324 M (1,063 FT)   PAVED/TRAIL

For most of the year, the tiny wine-making region of Beaujolais, found just south of Burgundy, is a peaceful spot. On the third weekend of November, however, the rural quiet is turned on its head when around 15,000 runners take to the region's roads to run Le Marathon International du Beaujolais. The scene is carnivalesque. Gym kit is the exception rather than the rule, and you'll blend in better dressed as a bunch of grapes than clad in lycra.

The run starts in Fleurie, a terracotta-roofed village, passing through bucolic landscapes and wine estates as it makes its way to the town of Villefranche-sur-Saône. It's a sumptuous feast for the eyes – and for the tastebuds. Runners are actively encouraged to stop and sample the region's Beaujolais Nouveau at the 18 wine tasting stations en route, and there's chance to soak up the alcohol at a further 15 pitstops

for cheese and other local delicacies. (Thankfully for tipsy runners, the route descends more than it climbs.)

The party vibe is enhanced by brass bands and drumming groups, as well as live music performances and DJ sets in the chateaux the route passes; it's not unknown for runners to stop for a dance. Suffice to say that you won't be getting any PBs here – this marathon is one to savour.

SIGN-UP: *Reserve a place from June via* www.marathondubeaujolais.org.

ELEVATION PROFILE

300 m (984 ft)

0

0   42.2 km (26.2 miles)

Costumed runners making their way to the finish line in Villefranche-sur-Saône

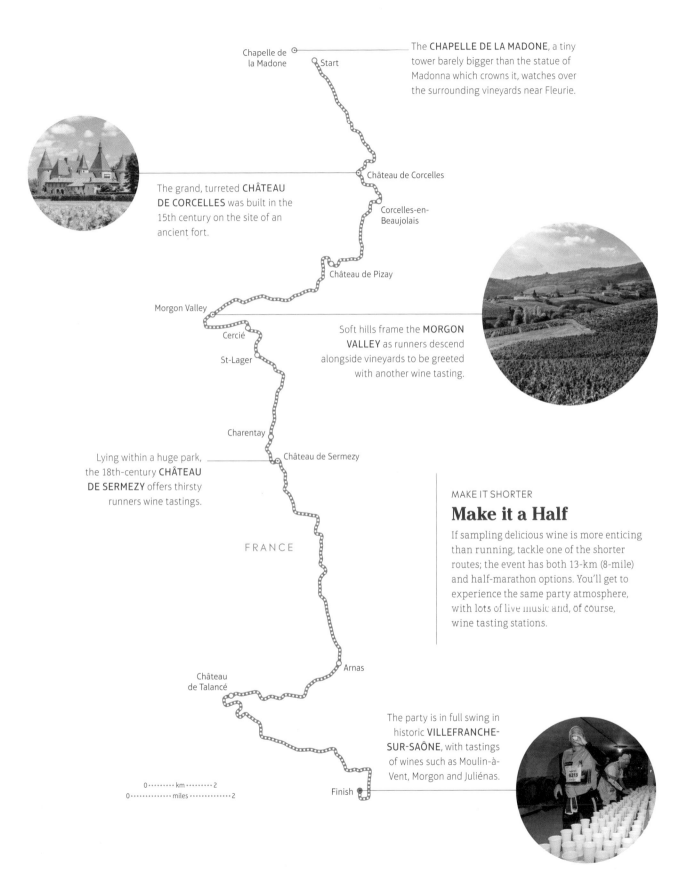

Chapelle de la Madone ○

Start ○

The **CHAPELLE DE LA MADONE**, a tiny tower barely bigger than the statue of Madonna which crowns it, watches over the surrounding vineyards near Fleurie.

Château de Corcelles

The grand, turreted **CHÂTEAU DE CORCELLES** was built in the 15th century on the site of an ancient fort.

Corcelles-en-Beaujolais

Château de Pizay

Morgon Valley

Cercié

St-Lager

Soft hills frame the **MORGON VALLEY** as runners descend alongside vineyards to be greeted with another wine tasting.

Charentay

Château de Sermezy

Lying within a huge park, the 18th-century **CHÂTEAU DE SERMEZY** offers thirsty runners wine tastings.

FRANCE

107

MAKE IT SHORTER

Make it a Half

If sampling delicious wine is more enticing than running, tackle one of the shorter routes; the event has both 13-km (8-mile) and half-marathon options. You'll get to experience the same party atmosphere, with lots of live music and, of course, wine tasting stations.

Arnas

Château de Talancé

The party is in full swing in historic **VILLEFRANCHE-SUR-SAÔNE**, with tastings of wines such as Moulin-à-Vent, Morgon and Juliénas.

0 ········ km ····· 2
0 ········ miles ········ 2

Finish ○

EUROPE

Runners tackling a rocky and ridged part of the trail near to Courmayeur

53

Ultra-Trail du Mont-Blanc

CHAMONIX, FRANCE

This is not a run for the faint-hearted – or for those without a head for heights. Circling soaring Mont Blanc, this gruelling race rises and falls through three countries and some truly spectacular mountain scenery.

171 KM (106 MILES)

10,050 M (32,972 FT)

TRAIL

Few long-distance trails cause as much of a stir as the Ultra-Trail du Mont-Blanc (more commonly known as the UTMB), a 171-km (106-mile) race that loops around Mont Blanc, the highest mountain in the Alps. Passing through France, Italy and Switzerland, this prestigious event is widely regarded as the crown jewel of trail running thanks to its unparalleled combination of challenging terrain, thigh-aching elevation gain and stunning alpine scenery. Simply put: it's possibly the most difficult and most spectacular race on earth.

Taking place around the end of the summer, the race is part of a week-long series of events that sees trail runners ▶

ELEVATION PROFILE

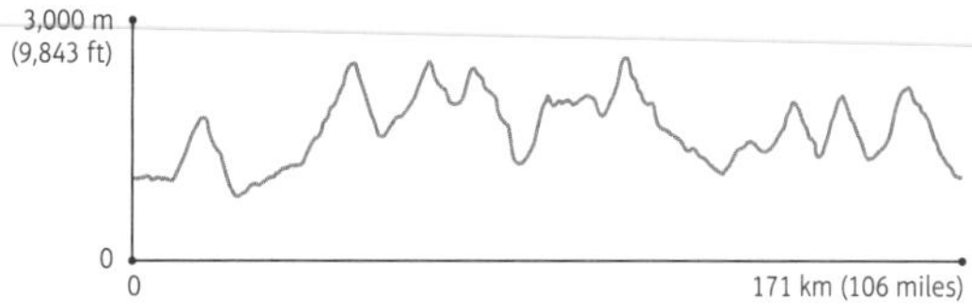

Top tip

Live tracking is on offer, helping supporters to keep track of a participant's movements.

REFUEL

Aid Stations

The main aid stations along the trail are stocked with sports drinks, water and all kinds of energy-packed snacks, including dried meat and cheese. A few of the larger stations even supply pasta dishes. Hot drinks are available at the stations during the night, along with a place to rest.

from across the globe – and their many supporters – descend on Chamonix in the French Alps. Among the other events on offer is the Courmayeur-Champex Lac-Chamonix (CCC), a 98-km (61-mile) route that follows the famous Tour du Mont Blanc hiking trail, and the Petite Trotte à Léon (PTL), a 300-km (186-mile) race where small teams navigate their way through alpine terrain. All the other races provide a mixture of challenge and beauty in spades – but the grand finale to them all is the UTMB.

The course itself is, simply put, a beast. To complete it, participants have to deal with extreme elevation, including long, steep descents and ascents, with around 10,000 m (32,800 ft) of climbing in total – that's more than it takes to reach the top of Everest. There's also highly technical terrain to tackle, which can range from hard-packed paths and steep, slippery grassy slopes, to rocky trails littered with stones and narrow, windswept ridges. At some of the most exposed points, runners will have to use ropes attached to the rock face to pull themselves onwards.

If this wasn't challenge enough, the region's ever-changeable weather can also pose problems, whizzing through all four seasons in one afternoon. Runners often have to deal with blistering, dehydrating heat during the day and freezing cold temperatures at night. Added to this is the chance of rainstorms that turn sections of the trail into thigh-splattering mud and snow and sleet showers that can make the path ahead vanish. To top it all off, participants also have to complete the course in under 48 hours. For most contenders, this will mean running for more than a day with few breaks – suffice to say, sleep deprivation can be a real issue.

With such energy-sapping difficulties to contend with, it's no wonder that this race is undertaken by only the very hardiest and most experienced of trail runners – and even then, they'll need to muster all their strength and willpower to make it through. Several places are reserved for elite athletes, many of whom manage to complete the course in around 20 hours. ▶

Runners setting off from Chamonix at the start of the UTMB

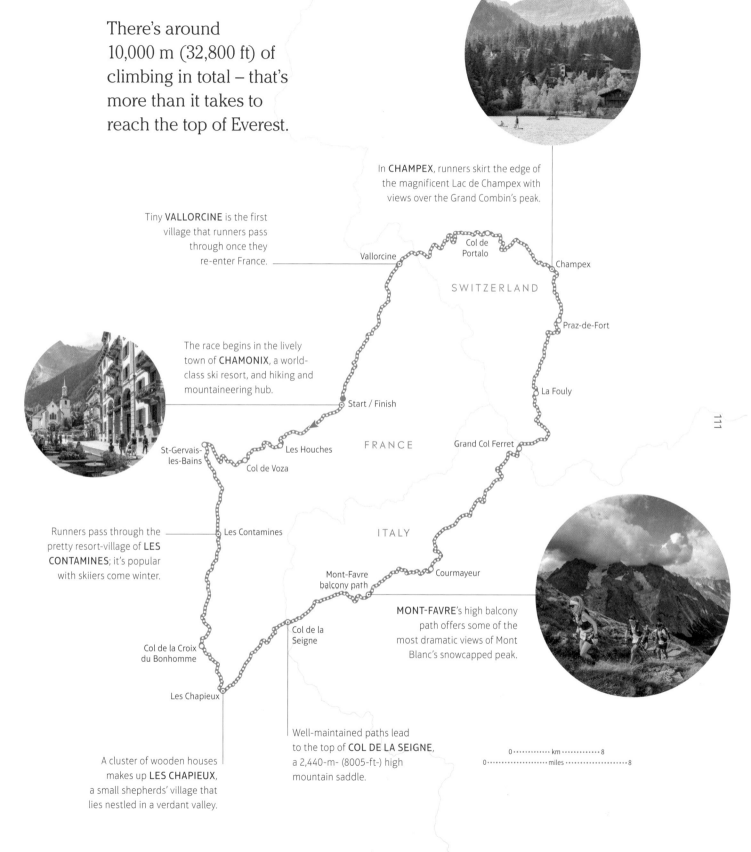

There's around 10,000 m (32,800 ft) of climbing in total – that's more than it takes to reach the top of Everest.

In **CHAMPEX**, runners skirt the edge of the magnificent Lac de Champex with views over the Grand Combin's peak.

Tiny **VALLORCINE** is the first village that runners pass through once they re-enter France.

The race begins in the lively town of **CHAMONIX**, a world-class ski resort, and hiking and mountaineering hub.

Runners pass through the pretty resort-village of **LES CONTAMINES**; it's popular with skiers come winter.

MONT-FAVRE's high balcony path offers some of the most dramatic views of Mont Blanc's snowcapped peak.

A cluster of wooden houses makes up **LES CHAPIEUX**, a small shepherds' village that lies nestled in a verdant valley.

Well-maintained paths lead to the top of **COL DE LA SEIGNE**, a 2,440-m- (8005-ft-) high mountain saddle.

Col de Portalo

Champex

Vallorcine

SWITZERLAND

Praz-de-Fort

La Fouly

Start / Finish

Les Houches

FRANCE

Grand Col Ferret

St-Gervais-les-Bains

Col de Voza

Les Contamines

ITALY

Mont-Favre balcony path

Courmayeur

Col de la Seigne

Col de la Croix du Bonhomme

Les Chapieux

0 ·········· km ·········· 8
0 ·········· miles ·········· 8

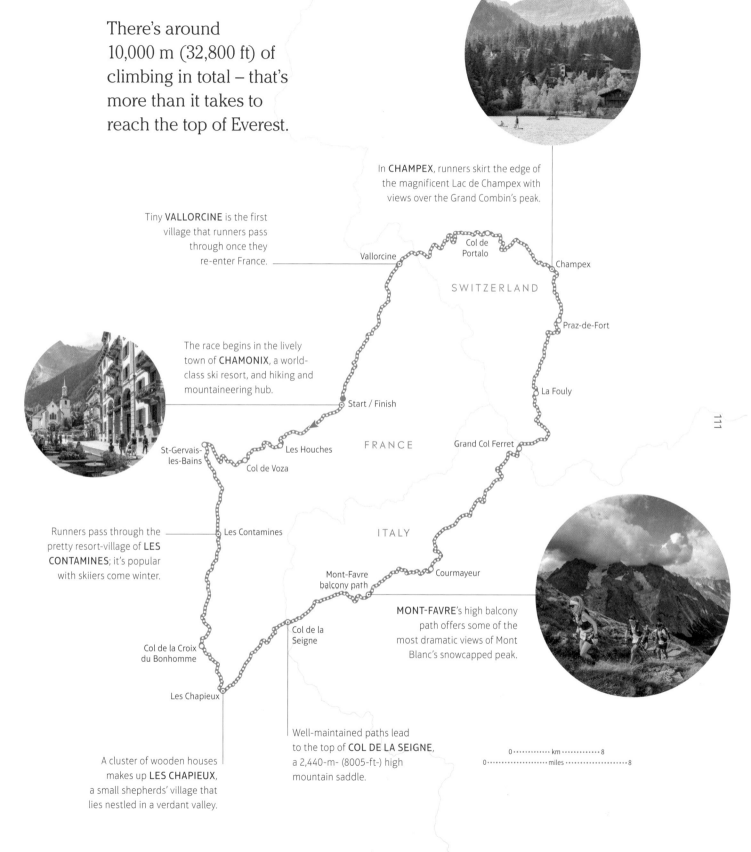

Frenchman François D'Haene holds the current record for the men's race, having finished the route in a staggering 19 hours, 1 minute and 32 seconds. The women's title, meanwhile, is held by American Courtney Dauwalter, who ran the UTMB in an impressive 22 hours, 30 minutes and 54 seconds. One of the most popular winners has got to be Italian Marco Olmo. Called a "metronome" by his fellow competitors, Olmo proved that age is just a number when he won the UTMB in 2006 at 58 years old. He won it the following year, too.

The rest of the places for the UTMB are filled via lottery – this doesn't mean that just anyone can enter. Runners must complete several other ultramarathons and hit specific qualifying times to even be considered for entry. Plus, even if they make the cut (there are only 2,300 places available, adding a further element of exclusivity to the UTMB) there's no guarantee that they'll finish the race. In fact, around 40 per cent of participants in the UTMB don't complete the full circuit.

IN FOCUS
A Running Legend

Hailing from Italy's Piemont region, ultra-running icon Marco Olmo didn't start jogging until his late 20s. In his 40s, he competed in some of Africa's most infamous ultramarathons, including Morocco's Marathon des Sables *(p142)* and Libya's Desert Marathon, winning the latter in 1998. From there he went from strength to strength: he's since won multiple ultras, including the UTMB twice and France's Gran Raid du Cro-Magnon an incredible six times.

Runners have to be at the top of their game to take this race on. So what's in it for them? For one thing, the pure satisfaction of having completed possibly the toughest trail-running race in the world. For another? The kudos it'll earn them among their running peers for having done so. Then there's the not-so-small matter of the location of the UTMB. Winding through the Alps, the route offers runners spellbinding scenery in spades: lush valleys cut through by silver streams; high alpine meadows sprinkled with wildflowers; glittering alpine lakes bordered by deep-green forests; and soaring granite peaks cloaked in ice-blue glaciers and iron-coloured clouds. Along the way, participants might catch sight of some of the wildlife that calls this landscape home, including ibex, chamois and golden eagles. To top it off runners will have near-constant views of the hulking mass of Mont Blanc, whose snow-capped peak towers over the landscape at 4,807 m (15,771 ft).

Ascending along a gravel road during the UTMB

France's François D'Haene crossing the UTMB finish line first in 2021

Despite the encouragement that such stunning scenery can bring, there's no denying that, at the end of the day, this race is a truly epic challenge. Those that manage to make it back to Chamonix are greeted by the roar of thousands upon thousands of supporters, who line the streets, often several people deep, all the way to the end. As runners cross the finish line, by now utterly spent and exhausted, they can bask in the knowledge that they've completed the most difficult trail race in the world.

SIGN-UP: *The race takes place at the end of August or start of September. Entry criteria can be found on the website at www.utmbmontblanc.com/en.*

MAKE IT SHORTER

The ETC

If you want to sample a flavour of the UTMB, then why not try the shortest event on offer, the Experience Trail Courmayeur (ETC)? This 15-km (9.3-mile) race winds through spruce and larch forests, crosses green mountain pastures and serves up epic views of Mont Blanc. There's still a fair amount of ascent to tackle (1,300 m/4,265 ft), but it's much more accessible than the UTMB thanks to the shorter distance.

ANOTHER WAY

Walk It

If you're more passionate about beer than running, there's always the option to walk the marathon. That way, you can stop at each brewery and have a cold beer before continuing on. There's also a shorter 25-km (15.5-mile) route that you can run or walk.

After the **FINISH LINE**, runners pose with giant cardboard beer bottles, toast fellow finishers and enjoy the great music and celebratory atmosphere.

Supporters happily sip foam-topped glasses of Tripel Karmeliet, a strong golden beer, at the **BOSTEELS BREWERY**.

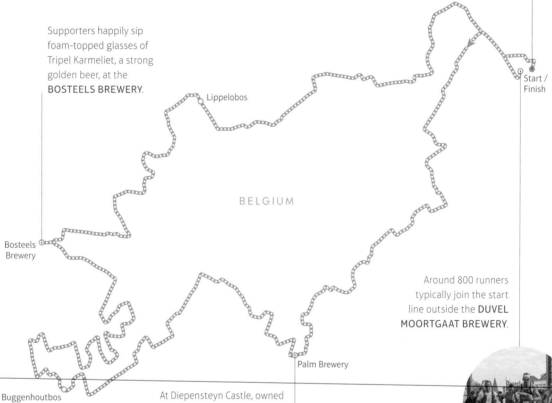

Lippelobos

BELGIUM

Start / Finish

Bosteels Brewery

Around 800 runners typically join the start line outside the **DUVEL MOORTGAAT BREWERY**.

Palm Brewery

Buggenhoutbos

At Diepensteyn Castle, owned by **PALM BREWERY**, a knight in armour patrols the grounds and offers high fives to runners.

0 ········ km ········ 1
0 ·········· miles ·········· 1

Great Breweries Marathon

DUVEL MOORTGAAT BREWERY, BREENDONK, BELGIUM

The ultimate run for beer lovers. This flat and pleasant route through the Belgian countryside goes via three breweries, with plenty of chances to sample their brews once you've crossed the finish line.

42.2 KM (26.2 MILES) 51 M (167 FT) PAVED/TRAIL

Belgium's beer is world-famous, and no wonder – the country has been brewing the stuff for over 1,000 years. Today, it's home to hundreds of breweries making thousands of different beers, including refreshing witbiers, strong golden ales, sweet-and-sour cherry beers and rich raisin-like quadrupels.

With such a reputation, it'll come as no surprise that Belgium is the location of this beer-focused marathon, which takes runners through three breweries. While participants don't sample any of the goods en route (they want to make it round the course, after all), the promise of a glass keeps them going until they cross the finish line.

There are plenty of reminders of the rewards in store along the way. At Palm, the first brewery on the route, colourful crates of beer create a chicane for runners through the packaging area, before leading them past a busy outdoor bar in a charming cobbled courtyard. A little further on, near the 230-year-old Bosteels Brewery, locals clap and wave, giving the competitors a boost as they pass the halfway mark. A small loop of this brewery's handsome red-brick yard takes in old beer delivery vans and drinkers relaxing in deck chairs while sipping bright amber beers.

Between the breweries, the route heads through the flat Belgian countryside, along tree-lined lanes, through quaint villages and past thriving hop gardens. Here, peace descends, with traffic free running on closed roads and a few short sections on light trails. Eventually, though, Duvel Moortgat appears on the horizon, its huge silver tanks the guiding beacons to the finish line. Here, runners collect their medal – which features a bottle opener, of course – and prepare to quench their marathon-size thirst with three well-deserved complementary beers.

SIGN-UP: *Registration opens around February, but it's often possible to get a space close to the race date; sign up at* www.greatbreweriesmarathon.be.

ELEVATION PROFILE

50 m (164 ft)

0

0   42.2 km (26.2 miles)

Tibidabo

Runners might catch glimpses of **TIBIDABO**, a hill crowned by the Sagrat Cor church.

Observatori Fabra

A short detour off the path, the **OBSERVATORI FABRA** is one of the oldest observatories in the world.

Finish

BARCELONA

| 0 ·········· metres ·········· 500 |
| 0 ··········· yards ··········· 500 |

End your run at the **FUNICULAR DEL TIBIDABO**, which has been taking visitors to the park since 1901.

Start

55

Carretera de les Aigües

BAR PEU DEL FUNICULAR TO FUNICULAR DEL TIBIDABO, BARCELONA, CATALONIA, SPAIN

Escape Barcelona's busy beaches and follow the locals into the hills of Collserola to admire the cityscape and Mediterranean from up high.

4.6 KM (2.9 MILES) 185 M (607 FT) TRAIL

Barcelona's Collserola Natural Park feels like something of a secret. Yet this protected area of forested hills is found just a stone's throw from the city centre. Come summer, locals head here to escape the heat – and the tourists – on the park's shady paths.

One of the best routes for joggers is the Carretera de les Aigües, a dirt trail that snakes along a ridge and offers stunning

views of the city. While the full route is 9 km (6 miles), the section from Peu de Funicular to Tibidabo Funicular offers up the same amazing vistas in half the distance. From this high, the city's sights – including the iconic Sagrada Família – look like miniature models, and the sea shimmers beyond in the distance. Even better, the pine trees that line the trail serve up lots of cooling shade. It's a tempting place to linger – handily, there are plenty of paths branching off from the route, providing lots of opportunities to extend your run.

SET OFF: *Reach the start by taking a ferrocarril (city train) to Peu del Funicular.*

ELEVATION PROFILE

300 m
(984 ft)

0

0   4.6 km (2.9 miles)

Runner climbing up a grassy slope during the SKY Baqueira Beret

SKY Baqueira Beret

BERET, CATALONIA, SPAIN

Take in emerald hills and snow-capped mountains on this up-and-down alpine route through the Pyrenees.

⊖ ⊗ ⊙

14 KM (8.7 MILES) 752 M (2,467 FT) TRAIL

Every July, trail runners flock to the verdant Val d'Aran for a series of epic events organized by the UTMB® World Series. While expert athletes take on the 55-km (34-mile), 105-km (65-mile) or 161-km (100-mile) options, those after their first taste of alpine running go for the SKY Baqueira Beret.

This route may only be 14 km (8.7 miles) long but it doesn't skimp on either challenge or views. Ascending past cow-munched meadows, the first 8 km (5 miles) are almost entirely uphill, causing your calves to ache and your lungs to gasp for the fresh alpine air. The peak is reached at Cap de Clòsos, where thankfully the tough part's over. Now all that's left is to follow the ridge back down, drinking in views of forested valleys and snow-dusted mountains all the way.

SIGN-UP: *Registration opens in October for the following July; book a place at* www.aranbyutmb.com.

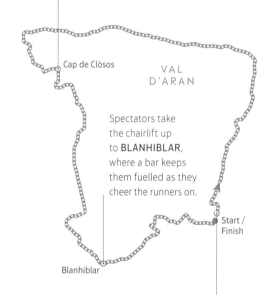

At 2,418 m (7,933 ft), **CAP DE CLÒSOS** is the highest point of the SKY Baqueira Beret.

Cap de Clòsos

VAL D'ARAN

Spectators take the chairlift up to **BLANHIBLAR**, where a bar keeps them fuelled as they cheer the runners on.

Start / Finish

Blanhiblar

Archaeological remains found in the ancient town of **BERET** date back as far as the Bronze Age.

0 ········· km ······· 1
0 ············· miles ············· 1

ELEVATION PROFILE

3,000 m (9,843 ft)

2,000 m (6,560 ft)

0   14 km (8.7 miles)

IN FOCUS

Aranese

In the Val d'Aran, you might hear Spanish, Catalan, French and Basque spoken. However, the valley actually has its own language, Aranese, a dialect of the Pyrenean language of Gascon. It was declared the third official language of Catalonia in 2010.

57

Transvulcania

FUENCALIENTE TO LOS LLANOS DE
ARIDANE, LA PALMA, SPAIN

*This super-tough ultra takes in unforgiving terrain and lots of
ascent and descent as it snakes across the otherworldly volcanic
beauty of the island of La Palma.*

75 KM (46.5 MILES) 4,423 M (14,511 FT) TRAIL

Found off the coast of Africa, the Canary
Islands' La Palma is known as La Isla Bonita,
or the Beautiful Island – something this
race proves with every step. Starting in
the soft dawn light, runners follow a trail
that winds up from the rocky shoreline at
Fuencaliente into what feels like another
world. It's a staggering landscape of bright-
green pine forests, their leaves contrasting
starkly with the dark volcanic earth, and
lunar-like hills and rocky ridges that tumble
down towards the azure ocean. On a good
day, the panoramic vistas can stretch across
the sun-soaked sea, sometimes even giving
glimpses of neighbouring Tenerife.

The views may be idyllic, but the event
itself most certainly is not – this ultra is
considered one of the most challenging
high-altitude races on the planet. Runners
must endure over 4,400 m (14,400 ft) of
ascent, including scaling craggy Roque de
los Muchachos, La Palma's highest peak at

2,426 m (7,959 ft). The terrain is tough and
technical, too, including soft black sand
littered with sharp rocks, rocky sections
and rugged, mountainous dirt trails.

The start of the trail is particularly
draining, involving a 16-km (10-mile) climb
on narrow trails that are wide enough for
just one person; those looking to overtake
need to come off the path onto even more
technical terrain. And that's not to mention
the monumental Caldera de Taburiente, a
huge volcanic crater that comes later in
the race. At points here, the path drops

ELEVATION PROFILE

3,000 m
(9,843 ft)

0

0   75 km (46.5 miles)

Competitors making their way down a
rocky path towards Playa de Tazacorte

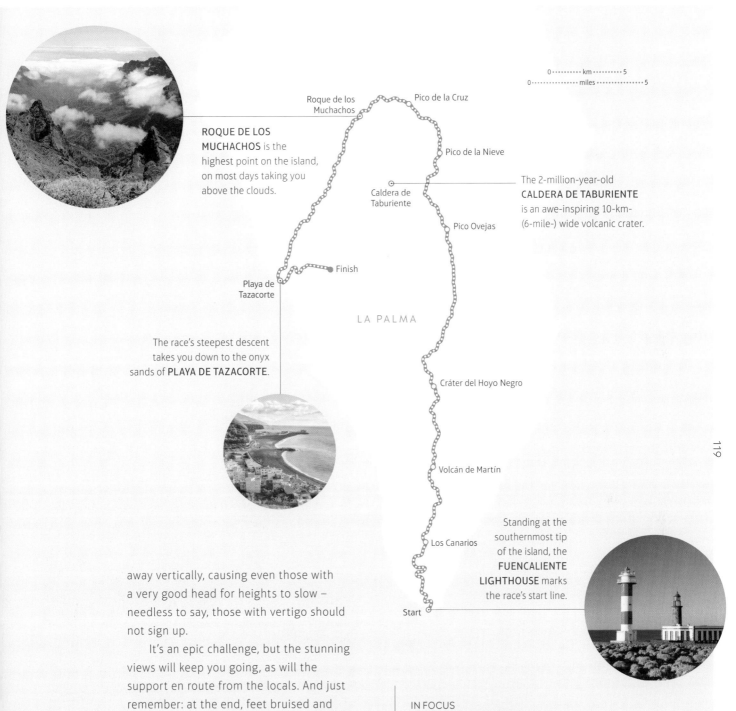

Roque de los Muchachos   Pico de la Cruz

ROQUE DE LOS MUCHACHOS is the highest point on the island, on most days taking you above the clouds.

Pico de la Nieve

Caldera de Taburiente

The 2-million-year-old **CALDERA DE TABURIENTE** is an awe-inspiring 10-km- (6-mile-) wide volcanic crater.

Pico Ovejas

Finish

Playa de Tazacorte

The race's steepest descent takes you down to the onyx sands of **PLAYA DE TAZACORTE**.

LA PALMA

Cráter del Hoyo Negro

Volcán de Martín

Standing at the southernmost tip of the island, the **FUENCALIENTE LIGHTHOUSE** marks the race's start line.

Los Canarios

Start

away vertically, causing even those with a very good head for heights to slow – needless to say, those with vertigo should not sign up.

It's an epic challenge, but the stunning views will keep you going, as will the support en route from the locals. And just remember: at the end, feet bruised and legs aching, you can bask in the knowledge that you've completed one of the toughest races in the world.

SIGN-UP: *Entry is by lottery and runners must prove they have run at least a marathon before. Register on* https://transvulcania.utmb.world *by 1 October.*

IN FOCUS
Cumbre Vieja

The island's Cumbre Vieja Volcano last erupted on 19 September 2021. The resulting lava flows destroyed 2,000 buildings, led to the evacuation of over 6,000 people and meant that that year's Transvulcanica could not take place.

The dramatic sight of the UNESCO World Heritage-listed **MOSTEIRO DOS JERÓNIMOS** greets you at the finish line.

LISBON

Terreiro do Paço

Cais do Sodre

Alcântara

Baixa de Algés

Finish

Admire the landmark **BELEM TOWER** as you run through the district of the same name.

Belem Tower

Start

Join thousands of runners streaming across the historic **PONTE DE 25 ABRIL** at the start of the race.

58

Lisbon Half Marathon

PONTE DE 25 ABRIL TO MOSTEIRO DOS JERÓNIMOS, LISBON, PORTUGAL

Run through Portugal's finest city on a river-hugging half marathon that doubles up as a spectacular sight-seeing tour.

With a riverfront route, historic surroundings and guaranteed good weather, it should come as no surprise that this half marathon is Portugal's most popular running event. It's a fast-paced course – the world record was broken here in 2021 by Jacob Kiplimo – but you won't want to PB this route. Passing by many of the city's most impressive sights, this is an event to savour. A highlight is the start point on the deck of the Ponte 25 de Abril – Europe's longest suspension bridge – which offers eye-catching views across the River Tagus to the red-roofs of the historic water-front. Keeping close to the turquoise-tinged Tagus, the route serves up more iconic sights, from the leafy Jardim Vasco da Gama to the medieval Belem Tower, before ending at one of the city's most famous spots: the grand Mosteiro dos Jerónimos.

Runners passing over the Ponte de 25 Abril, the start point of the Lisbon Half Marathon

⊖ 21.1 KM (13.1 MILES)

◇ 55 M (180 FT)

⊖ PAVED

ELEVATION PROFILE

100 m (328 ft)

0

0   21.1 km (13.1 miles)

SIGN-UP: *The race is held in May. Register in advance at* www. maratonaclubedeportugal.com.

59

Velika Paklenica Gorge

STARIGRAD PAKLENICA, CROATIA

Following a narrow gorge, this moderately challenging trail takes in soaring cliffs, gushing rivers and tumbling waterfalls.

15.8 KM (9.8 MILES) 658 M (2,159 FT) PAVED/TRAIL

Cleaving through the limestone rock of Croatia's expansive Velebit Mountains are two deep ravines: Velika Paklenica (Great Paklenica) and Mala Paklenica (Small Paklenica). This route heads straight up the former, crisscrossing the coursing river via boardwalks and heading past rocky waterfalls as it snakes up the canyon. The first half of the run might be uphill, but the soaring cliffs – which stand over 400 m (1,300 ft) high – provide regular shade. The halfway point at the leafy Paklenica mountain hut, hidden in lush forest next to a small pool, makes for a perfect pitstop. Lose the running shoes, dip your feet in the icy water and rehydrate for the downhill return.

SET OFF: *Head out early to beat the daytrippers visiting the caves, who tend to arrive later in the day.*

MAKE IT LONGER

Begin Beachside

Add an additional kilometre to each leg of the run by starting right at Starigrad's sweeping pebble beach, lined with bustling bars and restaurants. This way, you can also enjoy a refreshing dip in the cool Adriatic at the end of your run.

PAKLENICA MOUNTAIN HUT, concealed in the cool forest, is the turn-around point and a good place to refill your water bottle.

ELEVATION PROFILE

1,000 m (3,280 ft)

0

0   15.8 km (9.8 miles)

COTTAGE LUGARNICA is a simple, family-run hiking hut serving hot and cold drinks, cakes, grilled sausages and bean stews.

VELIKA PAKLENICA NATIONAL PARK

Paklenica Hut

Cottage Lugarnica

Manita Peć Cave

Return to visit **MANITA PEĆ CAVE**, part of the cave system that runs beneath the gorge. It has great views of the steepest cliffs.

0 ···· km ···· 1
0 ···· miles ···· 1

Start / Finish

EUROPE

0 ·········· km ········ 10
0 ················· miles ················ 10

ANCIENT CORINTH is a highlight of the race. Here, participants pass by crumbling Roman ruins, including the pillared Archaic Temple of Apollo.

Corinth Canal

Ancient Corinth

Archaea Nemea

GREECE

Lyrkia

Sangas Pass

A third of the way through the race, runners cross the famous yellow **PASSENGER BRIDGE**, which spans the Corinth canal.

REFUEL
Ancient Greek Treats

Multiple checkpoints line the route, each one offering a variety of international and locally inspired items of nutrition. If you wish to run like an ancient Greek then feast on the olives, dates and honey rather than energy gels and Coca Cola – but make sure your stomach is used to this sort of food in advance.

Tegea

Tackled in the dead of night, rugged **SANGAS PASS** is one of the most difficult parts of the route.

After crossing the finish line in Sparta, it's tradition for runners – now crowned with laurel wreaths – to kiss the foot of the **KING LEONIDAS STATUE**.

Finish

After Athens, the route runs beside the sparkling turquoise sea, with a particularly stunning stretch around **VARDARIS BEACH**.

Megara

Vardaris Beach

The race begins at the foot of the **ACROPOLIS** in Athens. Perched atop a rocky outcrop, this ancient citadel was developed over hundreds of years.

Start

Top Tip
Try to eat a little at each checkpoint; it will help keep you fuelled throughout the race.

60

Spartathlon

ATHENS TO SPARTA, GREECE

One of the world's toughest ultramarathons, this demanding run is based on the original marathon route between Athens and Sparta.

245 KM (152 MILES)

2,995 M (9,826 FT)

PAVED/TRAIL

The story of the Spartathlon begins over 2,500 years ago. According to an account by the famed historian Herodotus, in 490 BCE an Athenian messenger called Pheidippides was sent to Sparta to seek help against the Persians before the Battle of Marathon. He ran day and night to reach his destination, arrving in Sparta just a day after he'd left Athens. Thousands of years later, British RAF Wing Commander John Foden was so inspired by this legendary tale he decided to see whether the 245-km (152-mile) distance was actually runnable in this time. In 1982, he and four other RAF officers traveled to Greece to run the route; amazingly, three of the runners were successful in completing the distance, with John Scholtens the quickest in an impressive 34 hours and 30 minutes.

From there word spread and an official event blossomed, with more runners determined to follow in the footsteps of Pheidippides. Today, the race welcomes over 400 hardy souls from over 48 different countries, who come to tackle the gruelling route.

To say this ultramarathon is a challenge is something of an understatement: this is a race that breaks even the toughest, most experienced athletes, with only a third of ▶

ELEVATION PROFILE

1,500 m (4,920 ft)

0

0

245 km (152 miles)

Runners setting off from Athens, the start of the epic Spartathlon

those on the start line actually making it to the end. The length of the route plays an important role, of course, but it's not the only thing. The terrain is also unforgiving, with runners forced to navigate rough paths that kick up throat-burning dust when it's dry and turn to calf-sticking mud when wet. There's lots of climbing up steep, rugged hillsides, too, with almost 3,000 m (9,843 ft) of ascent in total. Then there's the weather, which can range from blisteringly hot to wild and rainy – often within the same race.

An added agony is the 75 checkpoints scattered along the route, each with a strict and demanding cut-off time. The 80 kms (50 miles) from Athens to Corinth must be completed in just 9 hours and 30 minutes – in

> An added agony is the 75 checkpoints scattered along the route, each with a strict and demanding cut-off time.

most other races, at least 13 hours would be allocated. If a participant comes in after the time limit, they're made to hand in their number. This time pressure often forces runners to push too hard too soon, leaving them struggling for energy later on.

They're going to need energy, too, especially for Sangas Pass, one of the

Heading along a flatter stretch of the course

Right Running along
the final stretch of the
route in Sparta

Bottom right
A competitor enjoying
a drink in front of the
statue of King Leonidas
near the finish line

toughest parts of the race. Found around
two thirds in, this 960-m (3,150-ft) pass
must be climbed in the dead of night;
headtorches on, participants push up to
the rocky summit, which is often blasted
by cold winds. At this point the challenge
is as much about mental stamina as it is
physical, with exhausted runners fighting
to keep going. The lack of sleep doesn't
help: in fact, athletes have been known
to start hallucinating in the final stages
following the climb.

How to survive it? Advance training is
crucial. In the preceding months, many runners complete 160-km (99-mile) training
weeks, adding in long downhills to prepare
their quad muscles for steep descents. For
the heat, they run indoors in winter gear and
spend time in saunas to acclimatize. Nutrition
is also key, both during training and on race
day; eating and drinking is often the last
thing runners want to think about during
the ultra, but it's crucial to maintain the
body's stores of things like carbohydrates,
sugars and electrolytes.

For those runners who do manage to
finish, the sense of triumph is immense.
On the final stretches, the streets of Sparta
are lined with crowds who roar their respect
as hardy participants cross the finish line.
Against all the odds, they've completed one
of the world's toughest ultramarathons.

SIGN-UP: *Registration opens for a month
at the end of January. Qualification criteria
is strict; see* www.spartathlon.gr/en.

IN FOCUS

A Modern-Day Pheidippides

In 2013, Mimi Anderson, a world-renowned ultra
runner, finished the Spartathlon within the 36-hour
cut off – then turned around and ran the same distance back to Athens. In doing so, she recreated what
many believe to be the return effort of Pheidippides,
who, after delivering the call for help to the Spartans,
ran back to Athens to relay their response.

61
Voskopojë

VOSKOPOJË, ALBANIA

Passing through dense evergreen forests and pastoral landscapes, this winding trail gives you a taste of rural Albanian life.

19.2 KM (11.9 MILES)

786 M (2,579 FT)

PAVED/TRAIL

Nestled in the southern highlands of Albania, 20 km (12.4 miles) west of the city of Korçë, is the little village of Voskopojë. The green hills surrounding it are laced with dozens of trails, allowing runners to immerse themselves in the bucolic landscape.

Leaving the village from the south, this trail climbs into the mountains, providing a good workout for both legs and lungs as it winds through a fertile landscape that's forested and pastoral by turns. You'll pass by emerald fields, grazing pastures and soaring silver firs, the paths occasionally lined by wild plums and apples.

At points you'll see Albanian shepherds, hard at work in their hay or corn fields, or tending to cows, sheep and goats. Settlements are few and far between, with diminutive Shipskë the only other village along the trail. Here, you'll likely be invited home for coffee or raki (a homemade plum spirit) by one of the welcoming locals.

SET OFF: *The most economical and eco-friendly way to reach Voskopojë is via bus from Korçë.*

Aerial view over the village of Voskopojë, surrounded by green mountains

126

ELEVATION PROFILE

2,000 m
(6,560 ft)

0

0   19.2 km (11.9 miles)

SHIPSKË is home to three 17th-century Orthodox churches; St George's has well-preserved frescos.

Shipskë

ALBANIA

Start / Finish

After your run, wander around VOSKOPOJË and admire its six Orthodox churches.

Detour to **PASHË TEPE** for views over the forests to the west and Voskopojë to the north.

Pashë Tepe

0 ·········· km ·········· 1
0 ·········· miles ·········· 1

The race starts in the small
village of **RAJCZA**, not far from
the church of Saint Lawrence,
a patron saint of the parish.

Start

Finish

Danielka

On the way, participants pass
through **DANIELKA**, a tiny
settlement surrounded by forest.

Muńcoł

ŻYWIEC
LANDSCAPE
PARK

Młada Hora

62

Mała Rycerzowa

RAJCZA TO UJSOŁY, POLAND

*This taxing mountain race snakes up to the top of Mała
Rycerzowa, offering views of the spruce-covered slopes
of the Żywiec Beskids on the way.*

Mała Rycerzowa

Every August, the beautiful Żywiec
Beskids, a forested range in the Polish
Beskid Mountains, plays host to the Chudy
Wawrzyniec, a weekend-long trail running
event. People from across Poland and
beyond come to tackle one of its four
routes, among them a tiring, calf-zinging
52 km (32.3 miles) and an exhausting,
leg-trembling 102 km (63.3 miles).

⊖ 20.7 KM (12.9 MILES)

⊘ 984 M (3,228 FT)

⊖ PAVED/TRAIL

At just over 20 km (12 miles), this option
may be the shortest of the four routes on
offer, but it still packs a punch. For one
thing, the race climbs several peaks along
the way, including the 1,207-m (3,960-ft)
high summit of Mała Rycerzowa; in fact,
the overall ascent comes to more
than 1,000 m (3,280 ft). Runners
also have to deal with steep
and rough terrain – especially
tricky for tired legs during the
downhill stretches on the way
to the finish. But the views
make it all worth it: from the
summit of Mała Rycerzowa, a
panorama of forested peaks,
punctuated here and there by golden
grassland, extends into the distance.

SIGN-UP: *Registration usually opens
in December of the preceding year.*

Musicians play Polish
folk songs near the peak
of **MAŁA RYCERZOWA**,
giving runners a much-
needed boost.

ELEVATION PROFILE

1,500 m
(4,921 ft)

0

0   20.7 km (12.9 miles)

EUROPE

Mountains enclose
the lake on either side,
providing a snow-
capped backdrop.

63

Lake Bohinj Loop

RIBČEV LAZ, SLOVENIA

Soak up the mountain views as you complete a lap of this lovely lake in the middle of Mount Triglav National Park.

11 KM (6.8 MILES)　80 M (262 FT)　PAVED/TRAIL

128

Lake Bled might be Slovenia's aquatic poster child, but Bohinj, just half an hour's drive further along the road, is easily its equal. This is the country's largest permanent body of water, and the beautiful setting – tucked into the foothills of the Julian Alps, in the heart of Triglav National Park – means Bohinj attracts plenty of visitors in summer. It's not difficult to lose them, though, as you take off on this run that circuits the entire perimeter of the lake.

The laid-back loop is fairly level, with only a few slight ascents and descents – so you could complete the run in a decent time if you set a punchy pace. But you'll thank yourself for leaving the stopwatch at home for this one; focusing on your feet is easier said than done when the scenery is this

exquisite. Mountains enclose the lake on either side, providing a snow-capped backdrop that's mirrored in the still waters throughout your run. There are onion-domed churches and wooden bridges along the way, as well as a highly picturesque half-way point: the Savica River, a tumbling ribbon of turquoise that glides over rocks and into the lake's western end.

Crossing over the pretty stone bridge in Ribčev Laz, with views of Lake Bohinj

ELEVATION PROFILE

600 m (1,969 ft)

500 m (1,640 ft)

0   11 km (6.8 miles)

Pause on the wooden bridge that crosses the **SAVICA RIVER** at the western end of the lake – the water is an incredible aquamarine.

If the going's hot, you can break your run at a tiny sliver of **BEACH** on the lake's northern shore, a beautiful spot for a swim.

The shimmering blue waters of **LAKE BOHINJ** are a near-constant presence throughout your run.

TRIGLAV
NATIONAL PARK

Beach

Lake Bohinj

Savica River

Ukanc

0 ········· metres ········· 800
0 ········· yards ·········· 800

Church of The
Holy Spirit

Start /
Finish

The exterior of the 18th-century **CHURCH OF THE HOLY SPIRIT** is covered with a large fresco of St Christopher, the patron saint of travellers.

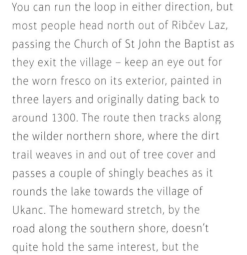

You can run the loop in either direction, but most people head north out of Ribčev Laz, passing the Church of St John the Baptist as they exit the village – keep an eye out for the worn fresco on its exterior, painted in three layers and originally dating back to around 1300. The route then tracks along the wilder northern shore, where the dirt trail weaves in and out of tree cover and passes a couple of shingly beaches as it rounds the lake towards the village of Ukanc. The homeward stretch, by the road along the southern shore, doesn't quite hold the same interest, but the scenery is no less special: sloping mountains across the water and another dinky church on the run-in to Ribčev Laz.

SET OFF: *The trail is accessible from dawn to dusk.*

IN FOCUS
Hidden Treasure

At the head of Lake Bohinj stands a statue of a goat: the Zlatorog, or Goldhorn, a fabled chamois whose golden horns were the key to treasures hidden high up in the Julian Alps. Legend has it that Zlatorog, injured by a hunter looking for the gold, took his revenge on the landscape, gorging the meadows into the rocky mountains you can see today.

Before your run, pop into the **CHURCH OF ST JOHN THE BAPTIST** in Ribčev Laz, home to some of the oldest frescos in Slovenia.

64

Transylvania 100

BRAN, TRANSYLVANIA, ROMANIA

This incredibly demanding ultrarun through a section of the Bucegi Mountains will push your limits – but it'll also offer the chance to explore a wildly beautiful, little-visited part of Transylvania.

100 KM (62 MILES) 6,444 M (21,142 FT) TRAIL

Forming part of the Transylvanian Alps, the snowy mountains and forested valleys of the Bucegi range feel very much off-the-beaten-track. Although the area is criss-crossed with trails, visitors are few and far between – you're more likely to meet a local farmer than a fellow explorer. Such a wild, rural idyll makes the perfect setting for the Transylvania 100, an epic ultra that will test your strength and stamina.

Set up in 2014, the race is a collaboration between Andy Heading, an expert British trail runner who has tackled ultras around the world, and local father-and-son team Marius and Vlad Cornea (both keen hikers and runners), who have unparalleled knowledge of the Bucegi Mountains' trail network. The event has quickly gained in popularity: more casual trail runners use the course to find out if technical mountain racing is for them, while hardcore

Running through the spectacular Bucegi Mountains on the Transylvania 100

veterans compete as a way to test their fitness ahead of other longer, even more intensive events. No matter the motivation, all are attracted by the epic challenge and the region's untamed natural beauty.

The weekend-long event has five different categories of distance, including a beginner's route of 20 km (12.4 miles) and a more challenging distance of 80 km (50 miles). The 100-km (62.1-mile) race is the best of them all, however: forming a grand, single-lap traverse of the Bucegi ▶

ELEVATION PROFILE

3,000 m
(9,843 ft)

0

0   100 km (62 miles)

The race starts and finishes at **BRAN CASTLE**. Perched atop a cliff, this imposing stronghold is Transylvania's most famous sight.

Dracula's Castle

Bran Castle is widely regarded as the home of Dracula, the title character in Bram Stoker's famous novel, yet there is little evidence that the author knew about it. However, it's the only castle in Transylvania that matches Stoker's description of the vampire's lair, so it remains Dracula's Castle to most.

Around 16 km (9.9 miles) in, runners slog their way up **HORNUL MARE**, the hardest climb of the whole route.

The **SPHINX OF BUȘTENI** is a 12-m-(40-ft-) tall rock formation that resembles the Egyptian icon.

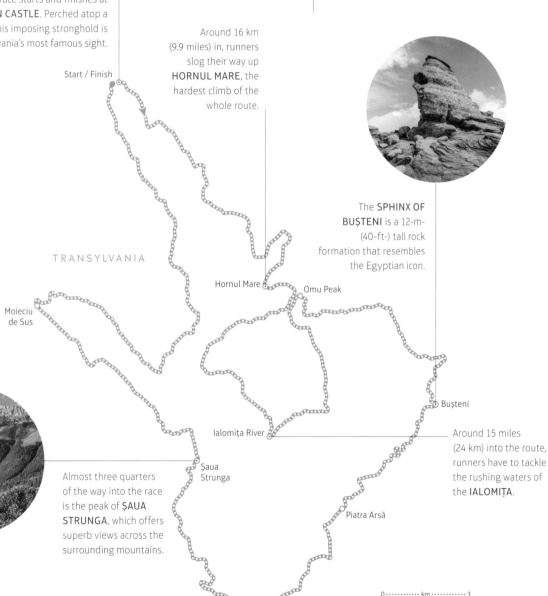

Start / Finish

TRANSYLVANIA

Moieciu de Sus

Hornul Mare

Omu Peak

Bușteni

Ialomița River

Șaua Strunga

Piatra Arsă

Almost three quarters of the way into the race is the peak of **ȘAUA STRUNGA**, which offers superb views across the surrounding mountains.

Around 15 miles (24 km) into the route, runners have to tackle the rushing waters of the **IALOMIȚA**.

| 0 ·········· km ··········· 3 |
| 0 ·········· miles ··········· 3 |

Participants heading off
from the starting line
beneath Bran Castle

6,400 m (21,000 ft) of elevation gain – and it's no wonder that this race is regarded as one of the toughest in Europe.

The most demanding of the climbs is the Hornul Mare. Known simply as "The Chimney", this sweeping pass takes runners up to the top of Omu Peak, whose rocky summit soars high at 2,500 m (8,202 ft). With over 500 competitors, there is often a long snake of participants grinding their way up to the top, following each other's footsteps in snow that can be a leg-trembling 0.6–0.9 m (2-3 ft) deep.

Yet there is positive payback for all the pain – runners will, after all, be immersed in the wild beauty of the Bucegi Mountains. The route flows through tree-blanketed valleys carved out by gushing rivers; along rocky ridges that offer up panoramas of deep-green valleys and snow-capped mountains; and up through barren ravines surrounded by hulking mounds of iron-grey rock. Wildlife makes an appearance, too. Participants will likely spot red deer grazing on the grassy slopes and birds of prey circling in the air high above. While

range, the route forces runners to tackle ancient forest trails and twisting single-tracks across mountain plateaus and ridges. The running is highly technical: the trail is often very narrow, and can be sprinkled with loose rocks, crossed with tree trunks or cut through by rushing rivers. At other points – including in icy gullies and on snow-dusted peaks – it disappears entirely, with only the occasional marker to guide you; suffice to say, participants need to be adept at backcountry navigation. Add to this extremes of temperature, which range from around 20° C (68° F) in the valleys to freezing temperatures at the highest peaks, and a series of endless climbs – there's over

The route forces runners to tackle ancient forest trails and twisting singletracks across mountain plateaus and ridges.

it's unlikely that wolves and bears will make an appearance, it's always a good idea to keep your wits about you. The lurking presence of these wild animals is another reminder that you've undertaken a truly epic journey into the remote heart of rural Transylvania.

SIGN-UP: *Registration opens in October at www.transylvania100k.com; to qualify, you'll need to have run a 60-km (37-mile) trail on similar terrain.*

MAKE IT SHORTER
First Timers

For runners looking to sample technical mountain trail running, the event also offers shorter 20 km (12.4 miles) and 30 km (18.6 mile) routes. These routes still take in a fair bit of ascent – 1,230 m (4,035 ft) for the former and 2,365 m (7,759 ft) for the latter – and pass through similar spectacular scenery. Check the race organizer's website for qualification information for both routes.

Trail runners making their way up a snow-covered slope during the Transylvania 100

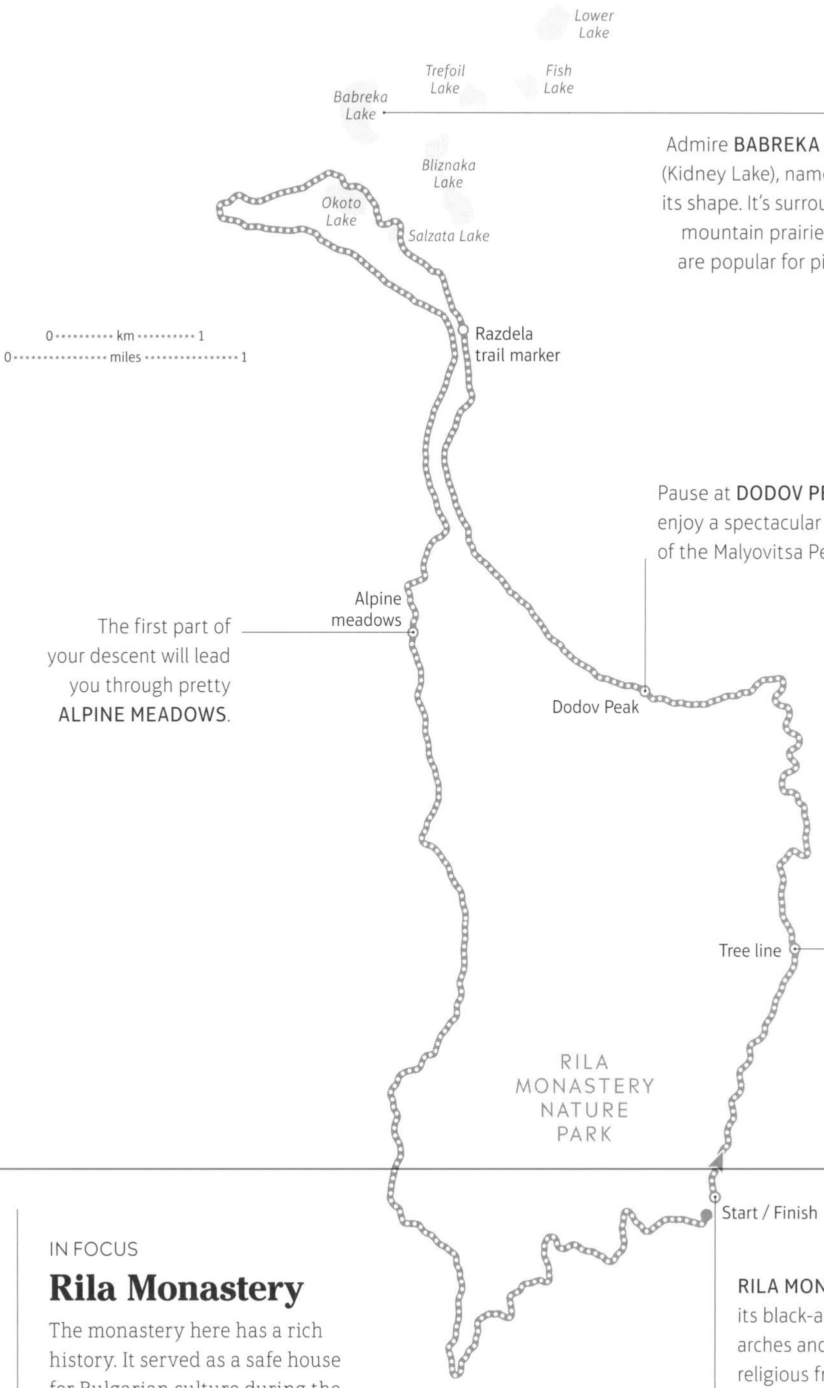

Lower Lake

Trefoil Lake

Fish Lake

Babreka Lake

Admire **BABREKA LAKE** (Kidney Lake), named for its shape. It's surrounded mountain prairies that are popular for picnics.

Bliznaka Lake

Okoto Lake

Salzata Lake

0 ·········· km ·········· 1
0 ·········· miles ·········· 1

Razdela trail marker

Pause at **DODOV PEAK** to enjoy a spectacular full view of the Malyovitsa Peak to the east.

Alpine meadows

The first part of your descent will lead you through pretty **ALPINE MEADOWS**.

Dodov Peak

Near the treeline, keep a look out for a glimpse of an **EURASIAN CAPERCAILLIE**.

Tree line

RILA MONASTERY NATURE PARK

Start / Finish

IN FOCUS

Rila Monastery

The monastery here has a rich history. It served as a safe house for Bulgarian culture during the Ottoman Empire, protecting important archives and artworks; then, under Communism, it was given protected status. Today, it is one of the most revered sites in Bulgaria for religious pilgrims and architecture enthusiasts.

RILA MONASTERY is famed for its black-and-white striped arches and intricate Orthodox religious frescos.

65

Rila Monastery and Seven Lakes Loop

RILA MONASTERY, BULGARIA

Departing from Bulgaria's most iconic monastery, this leg-burning run weaves through some of the country's oldest forests before emerging into a lake-dotted alpine wonderland.

27 KM (16.7 MILES)

1,954 M (6,411 FT)

PAVED/TRAIL

Nestled amid protected old-growth forest, the 1,000-year-old Rila Monastery makes an impressive starting point for this challenging loop. Setting off, the chants of Bulgarian Orthodox Monks rise through the air as you head up a steep trail that darts beneath Macadonian pine and beech. As you climb higher, the landscape transforms from dense forest to starkly beautiful mountain peaks. The path will throw up rocks and roots, and the ascent will cause your legs to burn and chest to heave – it's good training ground for trail runners. Respite awaits at the top of the Dodov Peak, however, where the climb becomes much gentler. The windswept ridge between its summit and nearby Damga (2,677 m/8,783 ft) offers you a first glimpse

of the Seven Lakes, a group of glacial pools that dot the rugged terrain, each named for their physical characteristics. The path traces down to the water's edge of Salzata Lake (Tear Lake), which is exceptionally clear, before winding past the blue waters of Okoto Lake (Eye Lake). A little further on, a viewpoint offers a stunning panorama over all of the lakes, including the Twins, an hourglass-shaped body of water that becomes two separate pools in the warmer months.

From here, an unmarked trail leads back towards the monastery, passing through cow- and goat-dotted alpine pastures and plunging into shady forest, home to the endemic Rila oak, a species only found in this river valley. Soon, the chants of the monks will rise through the air once again – a sign that you've reached journey's end.

SET OFF: *Start your run fresh by reserving a bed at the monastery; book in advance via the contact number found on* www. rilskimanastir.org.

ELEVATION PROFILE

3,000 m (9,843 ft)

0

0   27 km (16.7 miles)

66

Salomon Cappadocia Short Trail

ÜRGÜP, CAPPADOCIA, TURKEY

Weaving through a surreal landscape of fluted hills and towering "fairy chimneys", this trail takes runners through thousands upon thousands of years of geological and human history.

38.6 KM (23.9 MILES) 1,120 M (3,675 FT) PAVED/TRAIL

Rising from the windswept and austere Anatolian plains, Cappadocia feels like it's been plucked straight out of a fairytale. This landscape of otherworldly rock formations is made up of soaring "fairy chimneys" (narrow towers of rock reaching as high as 40 m/130 ft) and folded stone hills. These unusual forms were created 60 million years ago when tuff (soft volcanic rock) was first covered by a layer of basalt and then slowly eroded by wind and rain. But it's not just nature that's worked magic here. The Byzantines carved entire villages into and under the rock, forming a honeycomb network of caves that included everything from churches to living quarters and stables – many of which remain in use to this day. It is a humbling story of humanity etched in stone over hundreds of years.

Plotting a course through this lunar-like landscape is the Salomon Cappadocia

Trail, the most popular trail race in Turkey. While the hardcore runners take on the 119-km (73.9-mile) or 63-km (39.1-mile) routes, first-time or more laid-back long-distance runners head off on the shorter option, a 38-km (23.6-mile) loop that winds past some of the region's best sights. ▶

A group of runners jogging through the stunning scenery of Cappadocia

ELEVATION PROFILE

1,500 m
(4,921 ft)

500 m
(1,640 ft)

0   38.6 km (23.9 miles)

Cave churches and monasteries like the **DIREKLI KILISE** (Column Church) date to the Byzantine period. There are Orthodox-style frescos painted on the walls and ceilings.

As you run, you might catch a glimpse of hot-air balloons; they take off next to **SUNSET POINT**.

Direkli Kilise

Rose Valley

RED AND ROSE VALLEYS are named after the colours the sun splashes across the sandstone rocks at sunset.

Meskendir Cave Church

Göreme

Just off the route, the **GÖREME OPEN AIR MUSEUM** preserves the vestiges of a monastery that dates back to the 4th century.

Sunset Point

Göreme Open Air Museum

GÖREME HISTORICAL NATIONAL PARK

Start / Finish

Ortahisar

The caves in **ORTAHISAR** are known for being used to store fruit. Temperatures here hover around 10° C (50° F) all year long.

Ibrahimpaşa

REFUEL

Homemade Treats

Head to Tık Tık Kadın Emeği (İstiklal Caddesi 13) after your run. At this women's cooperative, friendly staff serve up lots of delicious local grub, including *mantı* (a Turkish version of ravioli) and *bulamac* (a dessert made with grape syrup and walnuts).

0 ·········· km ·········· 1
0 ·············· miles ·············· 1

Above left Runners passing through İbrahimpaşa, almost 10 km (6.2 miles) into the route

There's 1,120 m (3,674 ft) of rolling ascent to tackle, and the paths in the valleys have frequent twists and turns, but the route isn't technically demanding. The terrain is mostly soft rock or dried red dirt, so there's little risk of catching your foot on a root – leaving you free to look up and take in the views.

And what incredible sights you'll see. Near the start of the race, the route passes through the village of Ortahisar, where you'll run in the shadow of a 90-m- (295-ft-) high castle, known as Sivrikaya, that's been hewn directly from the rock. Further on,

just past the tiny village of İbrahimpaşa, lies Pigeon Valley. A collection of pigeon roosts were carved into the soft rock here by the local people, who used these birds to send messages and collected their droppings for fertilizer. Alongside pigeons, you might also spy olive tree warblers and goldfinches or, if you're lucky, Golden-faced Egyptian vultures.

The trail leads onwards, past sun-bleached grassy fields, lush vineyards and valleys of pale corrugated rock to reach Göreme, the busiest village of the region. This settlement, cut into the honey-coloured rock, is utterly enchanting and it can be a struggle to keep to the path here. The village's narrow alleyways and carved churches beckon you to explore, as do examples of cone-shape "fairy chimneys", their pointed heads reaching up to the sky.

> This settlement, cut into the honey coloured rock, is utterly enchanting.

Shortly after Göreme, the route weaves through Meskendir, a valley of pale stone where the rocks resemble meringues. Meskendir Cave Church, once part of a larger monastic complex, is found here; its rounded ceilings are well-preserved considering it dates from around 1000 C.E. A little further on, the path passes through the Red and Rose valleys, whose furrowed hills glow different shades of pink through-out the day. The best view is from Sunset Point en route: take a breather here and enjoy sweeping views of the ridged sand-stone rocks, noticing how the light seems to dance in the twists and crags of the formations. It's a sight you'll never forget.

SIGN-UP: *Register for entry by the end of September at* www.cappadocia ultratrail.com.

MAKE IT LONGER

Explore Further

The two other routes on offer provide the opportunity to explore the region further. The 63-km (39.1-mile) Medium Trail includes a stop in the village of Uçhisar, while the 119-km (73.1-miles) Ultra Trail explores every corner of the region, including little-visted villages like Karlik, Cemil and Mustafapaşa.

Above centre The spectacular town of Göreme, built directly into the rock

Above right A runner with walking poles tackling a slope during the race

140

MOROCCO

67

WESTERN SAHARA

MAURITANIA

SENEGAL

GAMBIA

GUINEA-BISSAU

GUINEA

73

SIERRA LEONE

CÔTE D'IVOIRE

LIBERIA

AFRICA AND THE MIDDLE EAST

TUNISIA

SYRIA

LEBANON

IRAQ

IRAN

PALESTINE

JORDAN

68 ⊙ ISRAEL ⊙ **69**

ALGERIA

KUWAIT

LIBYA

EGYPT

SAUDI
ARABIA

QATAR

UAE

OMAN

MALI

NIGER

SUDAN

ERITREA

YEMEN

CHAD

DJIBOUTI

URKINA
FASO

BENIN

NIGERIA

SOMALIA

70 ⊙

GHANA

TOGO

CENTRAL
AFRICAN REPUBLIC

SOUTH
SUDAN

ETHIOPIA

CAMEROON

EQUATORIAL
GUINEA

REPUBLIC
OF THE
CONGO

UGANDA

KENYA

GABON

⊙ **71**

DEMOCRATIC
REPUBLIC
OF THE CONGO

RWANDA

BURUNDI

TANZANIA

ANGOLA

MALAWI

ZAMBIA

⊙ **74**

MOZAMBIQUE

ZIMBABWE

MADAGASCAR

⊙ **72**

NAMIBIA

MAURITIUS

⊙ **75**

BOTSWANA

ESWATINI

LESOTHO

SOUTH
AFRICA

⊙ **76**

Runners making
their way across the
Moroccan desert

67

Marathon des Sables

VARIES, MOROCCO

Looking for the ultimate running challenge? Try taking on half a dozen marathons, one after the other, in less than a week – all in scorching heat across the Sahara.

233 KM (145 MILES) 6,097 M (20,003 FT) TRAIL/DESERT

142

It takes a certain kind of character to run six back-to-back marathons. Even more so when they take place across the searing sands of the Sahara Desert – with competitors required to carry everything they need to survive for six days on their back. But that's exactly why the Marathon des Sables, the "Marathon of the Sands", is regarded as the toughest footrace on earth.

The race was set up by French explorer, Patrick Bauer, who, in 1984, had walked for 350 km (217 miles) across the Sahara – on his own. Captivated by the desert, and aware that others would be similarly inspired by the challenge, he founded the Marathon des Sables just two years later. ▶

ELEVATION PROFILE

1,000 m
(3,280 ft)

500 m
(1,640 ft)

0   233 km (145 miles)

Top Tip

The mandatory kit list for the race includes a head torch, lighter and anti-venom pump.

REFUEL
Self-sufficiency

Runners have to carry their food supplies with them. Exactly what they pack will depend on their own nutritional needs and the amount of weight they want to carry, but they must have at least 14,000 k/calories' worth of food. Runners need 6–7 litres (1.5–2 gallons) of water per day; this can be topped up at each camp.

The day before the race runners arrive at **TIMGALINE**, where they'll sleep in Berber tents before setting off the next day.

Start

The towering dunes of the mighty **ERG CHEBBI**, a vast "sand sea" buffering up against the border with Algeria, are the highlight of Stage 6.

Finish · Stage 6 start
Erg Chebbi

Mfis

144

STAGE 2 sees competitors climb the legendary Jebel el Oftal; the summit is reached via a 25-degree slope, requiring the use of ropes in some sections.

Stage 2 start

MOROCCO

Jebel el Oftal
Stage 3 start

Stage 5 start

Stage 4 start

STAGE 4 is the longest section of the race; competitors run well into the night to cover the 85 km (53 miles) or so.

Near the end of Stage 5, runners head past **MFIS**. Once a mining settlement, this town was abandoned in the mid-20th century.

0 ········ km ········· 10
0 ············· miles ················ 10

The night before the race starts is all nervous energy and last-minute kit checks

The course is different every year, with the exact route kept secret from the competitors until the day before the race. But the route is always torturously long (around 260 km (160 miles), the terrain harsh and the heat intense. Runners can expect a mix of stony plains, rocky mountains, huge dunes (known as *ergs*), sandy wadis and dried-up riverbeds – ideal habitats for venomous beasties like scorpions, puff adders and horned vipers. Sandstorms are a common occurrence, too, reducing visibility to a few metres and whipping sand against any skin that's been left exposed to the elements. Temperatures, meanwhile, regularly top 45° C (113 ° F), dropping rapidly at night, when you'll wish you hadn't tried to save a few kilos by opting for a thinner sleeping bag. With all this to contend with, it's little surprise that a few won't make it – around 30 or so runners drop out along the way each year. In fact, in 2021, when the temperatures were particularly extreme, almost half of those who started the race never reached the end.

The night before the race starts is all nervous energy and last-minute kit checks

– after all, you have to carry everything you need with you, including a sleeping bag, clothes, and food and water. Many runners bring shoes that are two sizes too big for them – feet swell in the heat, and few people can complete the Marathon des Sables without having to tape up their feet at some point during the race. Most also wear gaiters, essential for keeping out the sand (veterans stitch theirs to their shoes, as glue just melts in the heat), and a legionnaire hat with a flap at the back to protect their necks from the sun. Some also carry walking poles to help tackle the ups and downs of wave after wave of sand dunes. As you'll be navigating your way across the desert, other necessities include a map (which you'll be given) and a compass (which you need to bring with you).

By 6am on the first race day, the tents have been pulled down (each day a team of Berbers drives ahead to the next bivouac to erect them all again) and the runners are ready. Stage 1 is a taster of what's to ▶

Participants navigating rocky dunes during the Marathon des Sables

come over the next six days. Dune fields, rocky ascents, stony scrub and parched wadis all make an appearance as the runners navigate the 30.3 km (20 miles) that lie between Timgaline and that night's bivouac at West Aguenoun N'oumerhiout.

Every stage is different and every one presents a fresh challenge to body and mind. Stage 2, for instance, sees competitors tackle the brooding hulk of Jebel el Otfal. Hauling yourself up this 250-m (820-ft) vertical ascent of sandy mountain – whose final section is so steep that ropes have been pegged into the rocks to help you – is a gruelling business. The downhill isn't much better, with a super-steep 20 per cent gradient to tackle on soft sand littered with boulders.

Colours shift throughout the day, from rich honey to flat yellow to flaming orange, as the scorching Moroccan sun flares then fades. As night falls, the runners retreat to their Berber tents, which protect them against the wind, and the cold of night and heat of early morning. Eight people sleep side by side in a tent, on bed rolls they've carried with them through the day, using the shelter to eat, recover, sleep, share stories and make life-long friends.

They'll need the support for Stage 4. This is the Long One, the "Big Scary", the day many runners dread. Always the toughest, this stage is over twice as long as the next longest, in some years knocking on 90 km (55 miles) in distance covered. Stage 5, meanwhile, sees runners plough through even more rocky, sandy desert, pushing their battered bodies towards the finish line. While the competitive element is present at the end of this stage – with winners declared and medals awarded – so is a sense of camaraderie. Those who've already completed the course gather to cheer their fellow participants across the finish line.

All that's left to do after this is Stage 6, a blissfully short 7.7-km (4.6-mile) celebratory trot towards Merzouga. Done in aid of UNICEF, this section doesn't count towards the rankings, so runners can take their time, savouring one last stretch of desert together as they bask in the knowledge that they've just completed the toughest footrace on earth.

SIGN-UP: *The route described here is the 2022 course; the exact route changes each year. Reserve a place well in advance at* www.marathondessables.com/en.

Top Passing through golden sand dunes surrounded by camels

Bottom left A competitor climbing to the summit of Jebel El Oftal using ropes

Bottom right Keeping cool during the Marathon des Sables

IN FOCUS
Survival Skills

In 1994, Italian Mauro Prosperi, a former Olympic pentathlete, spent nine days lost in the desert during the race after getting caught in a sandstorm. He survived by eating lizards and snakes and by drinking bats' blood, and was eventually found in Algeria, nearly 300 km (185 miles) off track. Since then, he has run the race six times – successfully completing each one.

AFRICA AND THE MIDDLE EAST

68

Pyramids Half Marathon

GIZA, CAIRO, EGYPT

Race through 5,000 years of history on this majestic half marathon, which runs past the iconic Pyramids of Giza – the last remaining Wonder of the Ancient World.

21.1 KM (13.1 MILES)

256 M (840 FT)

PAVED

148

Top Tip
For useful information on the half marathon, visit the Race Expo on Arkan Plaza before race day.

On the edge of bustling Cairo lies one of the most famous burial sites on earth: the vast Giza Necropolis, home to the iconic Pyramids of Giza. Rising high above the arid desert landscape, these imposing limestone-and-granite tombs were built around 2550 to 2490 BCE to house the remains of the country's deceased pharaohs.

The area is normally packed with archeologists and camera-toting tourists, but for one day each year it becomes the realm of runners for the Pyramids Half Marathon. This relatively flat race whisks runners around the complex, taking in all three of the pyramids along the way. Participants run past Menkaure, the youngest of the tombs, first, before heading on towards Khafre, which is remarkably still topped by some of its original limestone cladding. At last they reach Khufu: the largest and oldest of all the pyramids, it was built out of over

Runners jogging past the world-famous Pyramids of Giza

2 million stone blocks as a tomb for the fourth-dynasty pharaoh Khufu.

These aren't the only sights that runners will see as they head across the golden sands, the early morning sun beating down on them. Equally striking structures also dot the route, including smaller pyramids, built for the pharaohs' families, and the grand Tomb of Queen Khentkaus I, who ruled Egypt independently at the end of the fourth dynasty. Then, around halfway into the route, another of Egypt's iconic sights appears:

ELEVATION PROFILE

200 m (656 ft)

0

0   21.1 km (13.1 miles)

It's a Date

Aid stations are dotted along the route, serving up water and energy-boosting sports drinks. Sweet dates, which the Ancient Egyptians once used to make syrupy wine, are also on offer to help give flagging participants a boost.

0 ·········· metres ·········· 750
0 ·········· yards ·········· 750

A highlight of the route is the soaring **GREAT PYRAMID OF KHUFU**, built in the 26th-century BCE.

○ Great Pyramid of Khufu

Pyramid of Khafre ○

Great Sphinx ○
of Giza

Pyramid of ○
Menkaure

Pass by the **PYRAMID OF KHAFRE**; it's the second tallest and second largest of the tombs found here.

Start ○
Finish ●

GIZA

The **GREAT SPHINX OF GIZA** was buried up to its shoulders in sand for thousands of years, before it was eventually excavated in the early 19th century.

the Sphinx, a reclining human-headed lion with the wings of a falcon. The sight of this monumental mythical creature will spur runners on towards the finish line – with more views of the lofty pyramids along the way.

SIGN-UP: *The race takes place in December. Register in advance at* www.thetrifactory.com/pyramids halfmarathon.

69
Dead Sea Marathon

EIN BOKEK, ISRAEL

The world's lowest marathon traces the edge of the Dead Sea, before leading runners into the very heart of these briny waters.

Straddling the border between Israel and Jordan, the pale blue waters of the Dead Sea lie nestled amid a rocky desert landscape. This salty, landlocked body of water sits at an incredible 400 m (1,300 ft) below sea level – making it the lowest point on earth. It's a stunning setting for this speedy marathon.

Following largely flat paths, the course traces a line around the sea's southern shores, before heading out onto a breakwater that stretches into the centre of the sea itself. This embankment, which marks the border between Israel and Jordan, is usually inaccessible to visitors – it's only opened once a year for race day. As you run across this thin strip of earth, take in the sublime views: roughly hewn, tawny hued hills stretch down towards the mirror-flat sea, fringed with piles of salt crystals that look like sparkling mounds of snow.

SIGN-UP: *The race is held each February. Register at* www.deadsea.run/en.

⊖ 42.2KM (26.2 MILES)

⊗ 177 M (581 FT)

⊖ PAVED/TRAIL

ELEVATION PROFILE

-300 m (-984 ft)

-400 m (-1,312 ft)

0   42.2 km (26.2 miles)

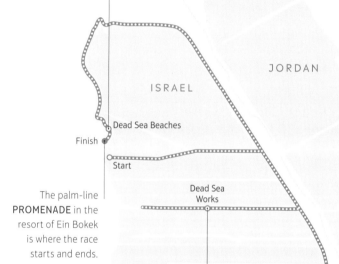

0 ···· km ···· 2
0 ···· miles ···· 2

Ein Bokek is home to two **SANDY BEACHES** – the perfect place to recuperate post-race.

JORDAN

ISRAEL

Dead Sea Beaches

Finish

Start

Dead Sea Works

The palm-line **PROMENADE** in the resort of Ein Bokek is where the race starts and ends.

The embankment dyke, known as the **DEAD SEA WORKS**, is opened by Israel's security forces specifically for the race.

150

During the route, runners pass by **ADDIS ABABA PARK**, a shady sliver of tree-dotted green.

ADDIS ABABA

Normally filled with city traffic, the busy **RAS MEKONNEN AVENUE** is closed during the race.

Addis Ababa Park

Ras Mekonnen Avenue

Start / Finish

St. Urael Square

Mexico Square

Expansive **MESKEL SQUARE** in the heart of Addis Ababa marks the start of the race.

0 ······· km ······· 1
0 ·········· miles ·········· 1

70

Great Ethiopian Run International

MESKEL SQUARE, ADDIS ABABA, ETHIOPIA

Sweeping through central Addis Ababa, this popular running event is essentially one giant street party, with participants dancing and singing their way towards the finish line.

10 KM (6.2 MILES)   147 M (482 FT)   PAVED

Back in 2001, Olympic gold medalist Haile Gebrselassie set up this race through the centre of the Ethiopian capital – it was the first time an athletic event of this scale had occurred in the country. All 10,000 spaces sold out in the blink of an eye, thanks to Gebrselassie's popularity as a sporting icon and locals' love for their national sport. Today, the event is Africa's biggest road race, with 45,000 participants taking part.

A handful of elite runners come here to compete, but for most people this event is simply a joyful celebration of life. Some participants spontaneously break into song as they jog along; others enjoy impromptu dance breaks, fuelled by music from the roadside; and yet others pause to meditate or quench their thirst with a beer or two. Suffice to say, few PBs are achieved – but who cares when the party vibe is this good?

SIGN-UP: *The race takes place in November. Register via* www.ethiopianrun.org/race.

ELEVATION PROFILE

2,500 m (8,202 ft)

2,300 m (7,546 ft)

0   10 km (6.2 miles)

Runners lining up in Meskel Square at the start of the race

71

Lewa Safari Marathon

LEWA WILDLIFE CONSERVANCY, KENYA

This challenging run makes a double loop through a treasure trove of biodiversity, rewarding participants with sightings of some of the continent's most renowned wildlife.

42.2 KM (26.2 MILES) 438 M (1,437 FT) TRAIL

152

Even the most seasoned runners are unlikely to have shared a track with a hyena or a giraffe. But those who tackle this race through northern Kenya's Lewa Wildlife Conservancy are some of the few people on earth that can claim such an honour.

Lying largely on the Laikipia Plateau, this vast reserve is a safe refuge for many of Africa's most important and iconic species. This marathon goes right through the area, making two laps of the half marathon route – all the better to glimpse the incredible wildlife. Jogging across Lewa's golden, grassy plains, runners might see herds of curious elephants drinking from watering holes or hungry giraffes chomping on acacia trees. There's the chance to see lions and leopards, too, but from a distance only – park rangers on the ground and in the air ensure these animals keep their distance.

This marathon is all about the wildlife, and not just because it can be seen along the route. The race is organized by the Tusk Trust to raise money to protect Lewa's rich biodiversity. Over the last 22 years, the event has supported numerous wildlife conservation projects across the country, plus social initiatives. The funds raised have supported the critically endangered Grevy's zebra and have helped bring Kenya's black rhino back from the brink of extinction.

The wildlife sightings will help give you a boost as you run – and you'll need it. This race is a challenge (though perhaps not for Kenya's elite long-distance runners,

ELEVATION PROFILE

1,800 m (5,905 ft)

1,500 m (4,920 ft)

0   42.2 km (26.2 miles)

Zebras crossing the path, with runners jogging ahead in the distance

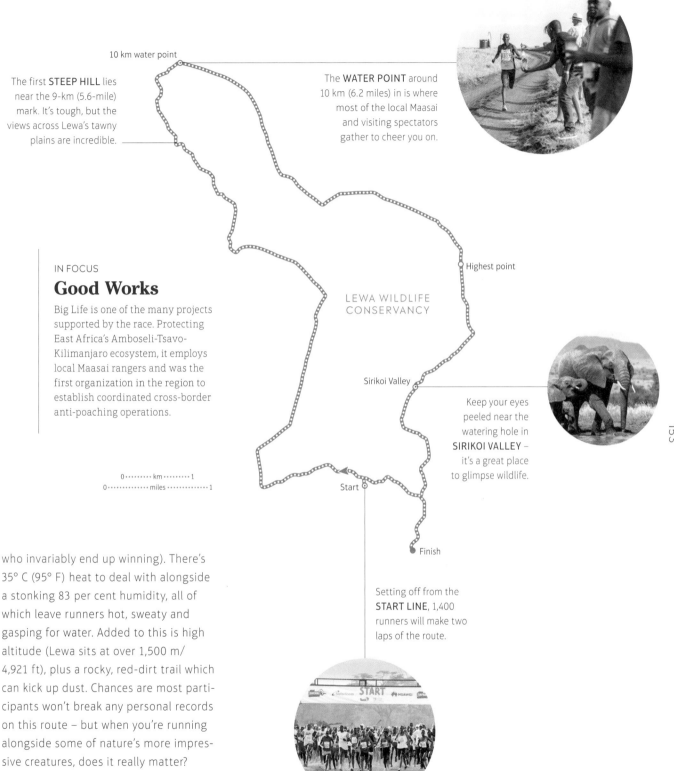

10 km water point

The first **STEEP HILL** lies near the 9-km (5.6-mile) mark. It's tough, but the views across Lewa's tawny plains are incredible.

The **WATER POINT** around 10 km (6.2 miles) in is where most of the local Maasai and visiting spectators gather to cheer you on.

Highest point

LEWA WILDLIFE CONSERVANCY

IN FOCUS
Good Works

Big Life is one of the many projects supported by the race. Protecting East Africa's Amboseli-Tsavo-Kilimanjaro ecosystem, it employs local Maasai rangers and was the first organization in the region to establish coordinated cross-border anti-poaching operations.

0 ·········· km ·········· 1
0 ·········· miles ·········· 1

Sirikoi Valley

Keep your eyes peeled near the watering hole in **SIRIKOI VALLEY** – it's a great place to glimpse wildlife.

Start

Finish

who invariably end up winning). There's 35° C (95° F) heat to deal with alongside a stonking 83 per cent humidity, all of which leave runners hot, sweaty and gasping for water. Added to this is high altitude (Lewa sits at over 1,500 m/ 4,921 ft), plus a rocky, red-dirt trail which can kick up dust. Chances are most participants won't break any personal records on this route – but when you're running alongside some of nature's more impressive creatures, does it really matter?

SIGN-UP: *Register at* www.lewasafari marathon.com; *there's a minimum fundraising requirement of £1,750 per person.*

Setting off from the **START LINE**, 1,400 runners will make two laps of the route.

153

0 ········· km ········· 2
0 ········· miles ········· 2

Maconde Viewpoint

Baie du Cap

St Martin

With white sugary sand lapped by turquoise waves, **ST. FELIX BEACH** is one of the most beautiful spots on the island.

Surrounded by sugarcane fields, the village of **BEL OMBRE** is home to a series of luxury resorts and golf courses.

Bel Ombre

MAURITIUS

Beau Champ

Start / Finish

Near the turnaround point is the famous **MACONDE VIEWPOINT**; visit it post-race for views across Baie du Cap village and the southern coast.

154

72

Mauritius Half Marathon

ST. FELIX BEACH, MAURITIUS

Explore the stunning tropical scenery of Mauritius on this coastal half marathon, which winds its way past sandy shores and rustling palms.

21.1 KM (13.1 MILES)
124 M (407 FT)
PAVED

Lying off the southeast coast of Africa, the idyllic island nation of Mauritius rises up out of the azure Indian Ocean. With its foliage-clad hills, powdery beaches and tranquil lagoons, this tiny isle feels like paradise. Lucky runners get to explore it during the Mauritius Half Marathon, which tracks a route along the island's beautiful south coast.

Starting from St. Felix, one of Mauritius's most gorgeous beaches, the relatively flat route sticks close to the waterside, following a smooth road to the Baie du Cap fishing village and back again. The island shows its best side along the way: rocky bays lined by casuarina trees and palm fronds; peaceful beaches made of fine golden sand; and lush green fields of sugarcane. At Baie du Cap, the halfway point, runners can soak in the views over the sparkling ocean before running the scenic route in reverse.

SIGN-UP: *The half marathon takes place every July. Register at www.mauritiusmarathon.com.*

> The idyllic island nation of Mauritius rises out of the azure Indian Ocean.

ELEVATION PROFILE

100 m
(328 ft)

0

0   21.1 km (13.1 miles)

73

Sierra Leone Marathon

MAKENI, SIERRA LEONE

Explore the jungles and villages of Central Sierra Leone on this strenuous marathon, which helps to support local children.

42.2 KM (26.2 MILES) | 344 M (1,129 FT) | PAVED/TRAIL

This marathon is a test of endurance. Runners contend with 35° C (95° F) heat and staggering 95 per cent humidity as they navigate the red-clay paths that weave through dense green jungle and past tiny corrugated-iron-roofed villages. It's a sweaty, sticky challenge that will have participants gasping for water – but it's all for a good cause.

Participants are asked to raise over £2,000 each for the race's organizer, Street Child, a UK-based charity that helps to support local children through education. Visits to some of the villages aided by the charity take place before the marathon, so runners can see first hand some of the good work that their fundraising will do. It's this knowledge that will keep them going for mile upon hot-and-humid mile.

SIGN-UP: *The race takes place in June. Register at* www.street-child.org.

The red clay roads are temporarily replaced by the **KAMAKWIE-MAKENI BRIDGE** as you cross the Mabole River.

Tambianu

Kamakwie-Makeni Bridge

Kunshu

0 ·······km······· 2
0 ·······miles············ 2

Manke

SIERRA LEONE

The route crosses an iconic **DISUSED RAILWAY** line that once carved its way through the jungle.

Disused railway crossing

Panlap

Start / Finish

Makeni's **WUSUM SPORTS STADIUM** marks both the start and the end of the race. Crowds pour into the stadium at the finish line.

Runners crossing the finish line, found next to the Wusum Sports Stadium

ELEVATION PROFILE

200 m
(656 ft)

0

0   42.2 km (26.2 miles)

74

Victoria Falls Half Marathon

VICTORIA FALLS TOWN, ZIMBABWE

Natural wonders abound on this half marathon, which takes runners past the majestic Victoria Falls.

21.1 KM (13.1 MILES)

149 M (489 FT)

PAVED/TRAIL

156

Known as Mosi-oa-Tunya ("the smoke that thunders") by Zimbabwe's Lozi people, Victoria Falls is one of the seven natural wonders of the world. At 1,708 m (5,604 ft) wide and 108 m (354 ft) high, this is the largest sheet of falling water on earth. It's an awe-inspiring sight – and just one of many on this race in western Zimbabwe.

Leaving from Victoria Falls town, the route crosses the bridge next to this thundering cascade, close enough to feel the spray of the water. From there, it jumps briefly across the border into Zambia, before looping back into Zimbabwe. Participants then run through a forest of baobab trees, home to the colossal Big Tree, whose trunk is a vast 22.4 m (73.5 ft) wide, and loop through a section of Zambezi National Park. Its teak woodlands and savannah are home to countless animals, including impala, baboon and lions – so don't be surprised if a flighty gazelle bounds across the path as you jog on towards the finish.

SIGN-UP: *Register in advance at* www.vicfallsmarathon.com.

ELEVATION PROFILE

1,000 m (3,280 ft)

800 m (2,625 ft)

0

21.1 km (13.1 miles)

Zambezi River

Zambezi National Park

Zambezi Nature Sanctuary

Finish

At approximately 2,000 years old, the **BIG TREE** is thought to be the oldest tree in Zimbabwe and one of the oldest in the world.

ZAMBIA

You might see wildlife such as warthogs, elephants and leopards in **ZAMBEZI NATIONAL PARK**. Field rangers help to ensure runners' safety here.

Big Tree

A UNESCO World Heritage Site, **VICTORIA FALLS** is around twice as wide and twice as high as Niagara Falls.

Victoria Falls

Start

Victoria Falls Bridge

ZIMBABWE

0 ····· km ····· 1
0 ······· miles ··········· 1

Aerial view
across ocean-side
Swakopmund, fronted
by a sandy beach

75

Swakopmund parkrun

SWAKOPMUND, NAMIBIA

Enjoy a beachside jog alongside the Atlantic Ocean on this laid-back parkun, one of Africa's first.

When this parkrun began in Swakopmund in April 2017, it became the continent's only town outside of South Africa to stage the popular running event. Today, there's a tight-knit community of weekly parkrunners, including kids from Mondesa Youth Opportunities – a non-profit trust for underprivileged children.

It's fair to say that "parkrun" is a bit of a misnomer for this particular route. True, the flat, ocean-facing course begins (and ends) on the grass at the bottom of Strand Street, but it very quickly gives way to a wide expanse of open beach, the apt setting for most of the run – this is Namibia, after all, home to four deserts, including the mighty Namib. As runners amble, jog or sprint along, the route offers up beautiful views of this golden sandy stretch and of the deep-blue Atlantic beyond.

SIGN-UP: *As with all parkruns, register (once) on the website to get a barcode, then simply bring it to the event.*

The race marshal near the **PLATZ AM MEER** shopping centre marks the half-way point; turn around here for the homeward leg.

Platz am Meer

5 KM (3.1 MILES) 16 M (52 FT) PAVED

Head out into the sands on a **PATHWAY** that cuts right across the beach.

Beach path

SWAKOPMUND

Sea wall

Start / Finish

Enjoy the sea breeze from the Atlantic as you join the **COASTAL PATH** near the start of the race.

0 ········ metres ········ 500
0 ········ yards ········ 500

ELEVATION PROFILE

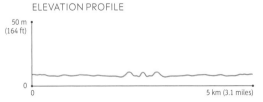

50 m
(164 ft)

0

0   5 km (3.1 miles)

AFRICA AND THE MIDDLE EAST

76

Two Oceans Marathon

NEWLANDS TO RONDEBOSCH,
CAPE TOWN, SOUTH AFRICA

This achievable ultramarathon takes you on a breathtaking coast-to-coast course around Cape Town's Table Mountain.

56 KM (35 MILES) ⊖ 624 M (2,047 FT) ⊗ PAVED/TRAIL ⊗

Regarded as one of the most beautiful races in the world, this ultra showcases the Cape Peninsula's stunning scenery in spades: soaring cliffs, wave-lashed bays, and the blue waters of the Atlantic and Indian Oceans (hence the name of the course). At just 14 km (9 miles) longer than a standard marathon, it's also the perfect option for those looking to cut their teeth on their first ultra.

Starting in the shadow of Table Mountain, the first section winds through some of Cape Town's southern suburbs and along the edge of the Indian Ocean. It's pretty flat and easygoing, but you don't get views as spectacular as this without a bit of effort – there are two tough ascents to come, the first being Chapman's Peak. Tarmac turns to trail as runners climb the 165-m (541-ft) mountain on cramping legs; thankfully, the panoramic vistas at the top offer the perfect excuse to ease off. To the north, green cliffs stretch down to placid Hout Bay, while to the south the white sands of Long Beach are

Runners passing along a stunning section of the Cape Peninsula's coastline

lapped by Atlantic waves. Plenty of runners have lost a minute or two to these views.

Descending to the coast once again, the course follows a road that wraps itself around high cliffs all the way to the powdered sands of Hout Bay Beach. From here there's one more big climb to scale: the infamous Constantina Nek, a pass in the Table Mountain range and the highest point on the route at 212 m (695 ft). Legs will be aching by this point, but after cresting the summit, runners are spurred on by the sight of Table Mountain – and by the knowledge that the climbs are done and dusted.

SIGN-UP: *Register at* www.twooceans marathon.org.za. *Entry is by ballot.*

ELEVATION PROFILE

300 m (985 ft)

0

0   56 km (35 miles)

158

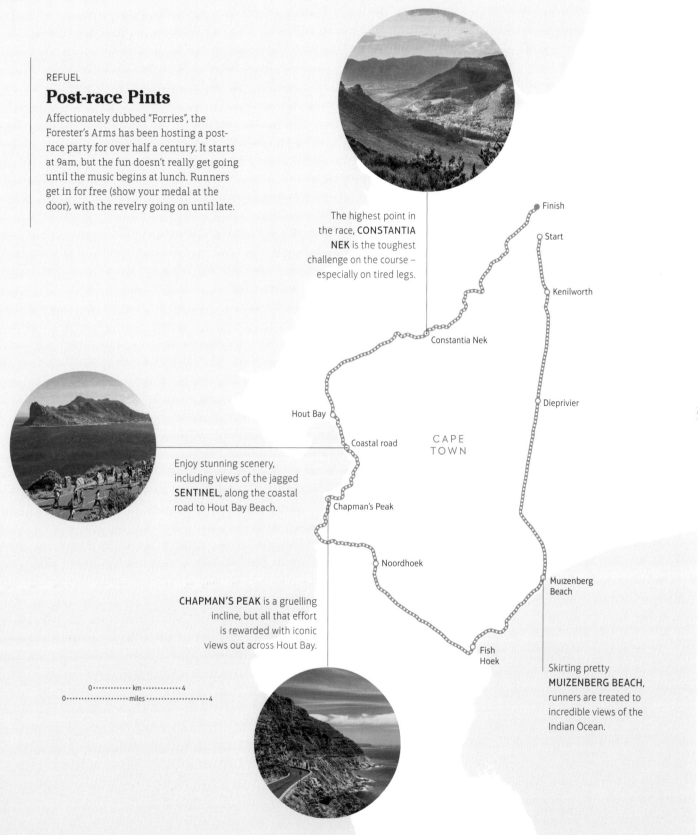

REFUEL

REFUEL

Post-race Pints

Affectionately dubbed "Forries", the Forester's Arms has been hosting a post-race party for over half a century. It starts at 9am, but the fun doesn't really get going until the music begins at lunch. Runners get in for free (show your medal at the door), with the revelry going on until late.

The highest point in the race, **CONSTANTIA NEK** is the toughest challenge on the course – especially on tired legs.

Enjoy stunning scenery, including views of the jagged **SENTINEL**, along the coastal road to Hout Bay Beach.

CHAPMAN'S PEAK is a gruelling incline, but all that effort is rewarded with iconic views out across Hout Bay.

Skirting pretty **MUIZENBERG BEACH**, runners are treated to incredible views of the Indian Ocean.

Finish
Start
Kenilworth
Constantia Nek
Dieprivier
Hout Bay
Coastal road
CAPE TOWN
Chapman's Peak
Noordhoek
Muizenberg Beach
Fish Hoek

0 ·········· km ·········· 4
0 ················ miles ················ 4

RUSSIA

90 ⊙

KAZAKHSTAN

MONGOLIA

UZBEKISTAN   KYRGYZSTAN   86 ⊙   NORTH
                                                                                    KOREA
             77 ⊙
TURKMENISTAN   TAJIKISTAN
                                                                              84 ⊙
                                                                                    SOUTH
AFGHANISTAN   CHINA   KOREA 88 ⊙

PAKISTAN   80 ⊙   NEPAL
                      78 ⊙   BHUTAN

                   BANGLADESH

                                                                    TAIWAN
INDIA   ⊙ 85
                              MYANMAR   ⊙ 83
                                    LAOS

       ⊙ 79

                              THAILAND

                         82 ⊙   VIETNAM
                              CAMBODIA
                                                            PHILIPPINES

             SRI
             LANKA   81 ⊙

                                              ⊙ 89
                                        BRUNEI

                              MALAYSIA
                         SINGAPORE

                                        INDONESIA

                                                    TIMOR-
                                                    LESTE

ASIA

77

Samarkand Half Marathon

REGISTAN, SAMARKAND, UZBEKISTAN

Winding through the UNESCO World Heritage Site of Samarkand, this historical half marathon takes you past some of the city's most beautiful and storied architecture.

21.1 KM (13.1 MILES) 198 M (650 FT) PAVED

Top Tip

Travel from Tashkent, the Uzbek capital, to Samarkand on the super-fast Afrosiyob bullet train.

With more than 3,000 years of history flowing through its streets, Samarkand is one of the oldest continually inhabited cities in Central Asia. Its location along the Silk Road – an ancient trading route between China and the Mediterranean – made it both a crossroad of cultures and an important strategic location, with the likes of Alexander the Great and Genghis Khan attempting to conquer and control the city. Samarkand's heyday was in the 14th century, when it became the capital of the empire of Amir Timur (also known as Tamerlane); this ferocious leader – who was said to make pyramids from the skulls of those who resisted him – created an empire that stretched all the way from Ankara in Turkey to Delhi in India. During this time, the city became a key economic hub and an important centre for Islamic scholarly study.

Running past the Registan during the Samarkand Half Marathon

A unique way to explore its history is by running the Samarkand Half Marathon. The race twists and turns its way through the heart of the historic centre, an area that contains some of Central Asia's most stunning architecture, including buildings that date from the time of the Timurid Empire. It's pretty easygoing, being flat and along smooth tarmac, making it easy for runners to dedicate most of their attention to the bejewelled mosques, *madrassas* and mausolea that they'll pass on the way. ▶

ELEVATION PROFILE

800 m (2,625 ft)

600 m (1,969 ft)

0   21.1 km (13.1 miles)

A grassy plateau to the north, **AFROSIAB** contains archaeological remains of the city's first incarnation, which was destroyed during the 13th-century Mongol invasion.

S A M A R K A N D

Ulugbek
Observatory

Afrosiab

IN FOCUS

Inclusivity in Sport

The half marathon is organized by Uzbekistan's Art and Culture Development Foundation (ACDF), which aims to promote inclusivity in sport and culture. Runners of all abilities are encouraged to take part in the race and proceeds from entry fees are donated to charities, in particular those helping disabled people to find work in the cultural sector.

The vast **BIBI KHANYM MOSQUE** was built by Timur; it can hold around 10,000 worshipers.

Bibi Khanym
Mosque

Shah-i Zinda
Necropolis

Start / Finish

The race both begins and ends in the **REGISTAN**, a sublime square enclosed on three sides by mosaic-covered *madrassas* (educational institutions).

Central Park

The 14th-century **RUKHOBOD** is the mausoleum of Sheikh Burhanuddin Sagarji, the spiritual mentor of Timur.

Rukhobod

Gur-i Amir

The glittering **GUR-I AMIR** is the burial place of Timur. Its design provided inspiration for Humayun's Tomb in Delhi.

ASIA

The beauty of the buildings that you'll pass is matched by the richness of their histories.

Bounding along the route, with one of the city's mosques in the background

The beauty of the buildings that you'll pass is matched by the richness of their histories. Near the start of the route lies the Shah-i Zinda, a beautiful tomb complex richly decorated with tiles. Translating as "The Living King", its name is a reference to the grave of Qutham ibn Abbas; a cousin of the Prophet Muhammad, ibn Abbas is credited with bringing Islam to Uzbekistan. Legend has it that he was decapitated, but by some miracle didn't die, and now lives forever beneath the foundations of the city, acting as its protector. Further on lies the Gur-i Amir, the tomb of Timur himself. Its magnificent tile work, coloured in shades of turquoise and lapis lazuli blue, is stunning, but it's the tomb's recent history that will

give runners pause for thought. When Soviet archaeologists exhumed Timur here in June 1941, they found an inscription inside the grave reading "Whomsoever opens my tomb shall unleash an invader more terrible than I." A day later, Nazi Germany invaded the Soviet Union in Operation Barbarossa – allegedly, Soviet leader Stalin was so disturbed by the possible link between the two events that he demanded Timur be reburied straight away, with full Islamic burial rites.

With so much beauty and history surrounding you, it can be easy to forget you're running a half marathon (despite aching legs), but keep going, as the most impressive section is undoubtedly the final stretch from Ulugbek's Observatory to the finish line at the Registan. Every few minutes of effort brings another UNESCO masterpiece, all of their exteriors decorated with exquisite mosaic and majolica tilework in intricate patterns. There's the astronomical observatory of the great medieval scientist Ulugbek, who produced his important catalogue of 1,018 stars here; the mighty Bibi Khanym Mosque with its stunning turquoise dome, which is dedicated to Timur's wife and is one of the largest of the largest religious structures in Central Asia; and, last of all, the Registan, a vast square surrounded by three of the most stunning *madrassas* (educational institutions) in the Islamic world, each of them covered by incredibly complex mosaics.

The best thing? Once you've crossed the finish line and recouped your energy, Samarkand will still be there, waiting for you to explore it a little further and – thankfully for your legs – at a much more leisurely pace this time.

SIGN-UP: *The race takes place in November. Register online at* www.samarkandhalfmarathon.uz *anytime before the event.*

Platefuls of Plov

Uzbekistan's national dish is *plov*: a high-carb rice dish flavoured with lamb or beef, yellow carrots, onions and cumin. Chefs in Samarkand claim that their recipe, which features hard boiled quails' eggs and dozens of garlic cloves, is the best in the country, so refuel with a plateful at the end of your run for a tastebud-tingling culinary experience.

Some of the exquisite tile work found at the Shah-i-Zinda Mausoleum

Ascending a rocky path in the Himalayan foothills during the Impact Half Marathon Nepal

78

Impact Half Marathon Nepal

KAKANI, NEPAL

Immerse yourself in Nepal's welcoming culture and stunning mountain scenery on this demanding run. It's an unforgettable adventure – and one that gives back to the local community along the way.

21.1 KM (13.1 MILES)   1,104 M (3,622 FT)   PAVED/TRAIL

Blanketing a large swathe of the mighty Himalayas, Nepal has long been regarded as a haven for trekkers and trail runners. Each year, countless adventurers come to walk, hike and run the paths that snake through its incredible mountain scenery.

You don't have to make for the big peaks for good trail running, though. A few hours' bumpy drive from Nepal's capital, Kathmandu, lies Kakani, a tiny hillside village in the Himalayan foothills, surrounded by swathes of terraced farmland. Every year this unassuming little spot plays host to one of the country's best trail-running events: the Impact Nepal Half Marathon. ▶

ELEVATION PROFILE

2,500 m
(8,202 ft)

1,500 m
(4,920 ft)

0   21.1 km (13.1 miles)

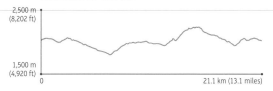

Top Tip
Spend some time exploring Nepal's cultural capital, Kathmandu, post-race.

166

Push on up **HELL HILL**. It's the steepest part of the race, but you'll be treated to spectacular views from the top.

Hell Hill

Stupa

Start / Finish

Shivapuri National Park

Pause to admire the views one last time before crossing the finish line back in **KAKANI**.

Sitting atop infamous Hell Hill, the village's beautiful **BUDDHIST STUPA** isn't far from the end of the race.

Passing through the gates into **SHIVAPURI NATIONAL PARK**, you'll enter a forested wonderland home to a wide range of wildlife.

This isn't your standard half marathon – and not just because it takes place at high altitudes, on rocky trails and with views of some of the world's most spellbinding mountains. No, what makes this race truly special is its focus on the local community.

The event is set up by Impact Marathon, an organization that uses running as a way to empower underprivileged communities around the world. Participants arrive in Kakani four days before the half marathon is due to take place; during this time, they immerse themselves deeply in local life, helping out with community projects such as reinforcing the road into the village, which is frequently eroded by the heavy monsoon rains. Participants also get to see first hand how their dedicated fundraising efforts support Childreach Nepal, a charity that sets up educational projects to help prevent child trafficking.

The days in Kakani before the race also give runners a chance to prepare for the half marathon itself. Participants set up camp at the colourful pop-up athlete's village by the Scout Centre. Here, each morning, they unzip their tents to reveal a 180-degree view of snow-capped Himalayan peaks in the distance. An acclimatization run follows, helping runners to get used to the high altitude – Kakani sits at a staggering 2,030 m (6,660 ft) above sea level – before breakfast is served, accompanied by steaming mugs of chai.

Regular yoga sessions are on offer, too, as are nightly dinners and drinks. Here, as the glowing sun sets over the

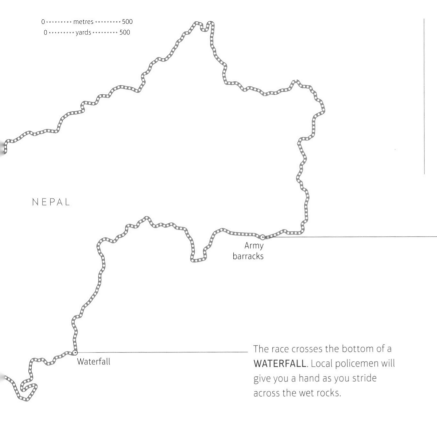

0 ···· metres ···· 500
0 ···· yards ···· 500

NEPAL

Army
barracks

Waterfall

ANOTHER WAY

Make an Impact

Race organizers Impact Marathon also run five other events around the world. If you're after a desert challenge, tackle the marathon in Jordan, which passes through Martian-like Wadi Rum. Fancy something a little greener? Try the hill-running route on Scotland's Isle of Mull.

The **ARMY BARRACKS** is where Nepalese running sensation Mira Rai got her big break. After outrunning local soldiers, she was invited back to train with them.

The race crosses the bottom of a **WATERFALL**. Local policemen will give you a hand as you stride across the wet rocks.

Competitors making
their way through
Shivapuri National Park

surrounding 7,000-m- (23,000-ft-) high peaks, participants get to know one another over plates piled high with dal bhat; this filling combo of steamed rice, lentils and various spiced vegetables is perfect for pre-race carb loading.

Eventually race day arrives. Beginning at the start line in Kakani village, where multicoloured prayer flags wave in the wind, the route briefly heads along tarmacked roads before entering forested Shivapuri National Park. Here, it cuts a path through pockets of chir pine, ring-cupped oak and wild Himalayan cherry trees; the forest is home to countless species of birds, as well as pangolins, wild boars and Himalayan black bears. ▶

170

Above left Runners undertaking the first section of the half marathon through Kakani village

Every so often there's a break in the trees, the foliage parting to reveal panoramas of rolling green foothills stretching away towards the Himalayas' soaring peaks, their jagged forms dusted with decent helpings of snow.

The scenery is beautiful, but the going can be tough. Runners will need to watch their footing on a mixture of dusty gravel tracks and rocky singletrack trails. Then there's the amount of ascent. Hardy locals maintain that the course runs along "Nepali flat" trails – essentially ones that are just

This calf-cramping climb marks the highest point of the race at 2,233 m (7,326 ft).

"a little bit up, a little bit down", as they end up at the same altitude. Well, not quite: there's in fact 1,104 m (3,622 ft) of ascent, including more than one relentlessly steep climb.

One of the toughest is "Savage Summit": found two-thirds of the way in, this calf-cramping climb marks the highest point of the race at 2,233 m (7,326 ft). Another ascent, the ominously named "Hell Hill", lies cruelly near the end of the route. It's only half a mile long, but with a sharp 150 m (490 ft) in altitude gain, it can be brutal, forcing runners to push their by now aching legs up the steep slope towards the gold-and-white stupa that marks the summit. From here, runners are rewarded with some of the best views of the race: to the west lie the famous peaks of the Annapurna range, while to the north sit the lofty summits of the Langtang region.

At the finish line, both members of the local community and those participants who have already finished gather to cheer on the remaining runners. The finish line ticker tape is raised for everybody, giving them all the chance to fully appreciate that arms-out-wide, head-tilted-back adrenaline rush as they cross the line. There's a party vibe, with runners clapping each other on the back and hugging, comparing blisters and bruises as well as tales of their time on the trail. The jubilation of completing the course – and the knowledge that you've supported the community of Kakani – all makes you wish you could go back to that first morning, with it all still to come.

SIGN-UP: *Register at* www.impact marathon.com. *In future, the race location will move to Batase, another village in the Himalayan foothills.*

MAKE IT LONGER

Makc a Second Loop

If you fancy an even bigger challenge, why not tackle the full marathon. It undertakes a second loop of the same course, adding on an even bigger section of Hell Hill. It will test even the most experienced of trail runners.

Above centre Looking out over the village of Kakani in the Himalayan foothills

Above right Jogging past the stupa at the top of "Hell Hill", found near the end of the race

ASIA

A riot of colourful
wildflowers and shrubs,
some of them very rare,
spill across the scenic
KAAS PLATEAU.

Kaas
Plateau

79

Satara Hill Half Marathon

SATARA, INDIA

*One of India's most popular half marathon routes takes runners
on a challenging journey up a mighty hill, rewarding them with
sights both cultural and natural along the way.*

21.1 KM (13.1 MILES)   420 M (1,378 FT)   PAVED

Don't expect a quick time on this majestic half marathon, which winds from the storied city of Satara to the top of its eponymous hill. For one thing, there's the long, steady, thigh-burning ascent to reach the 1,058-m (3,471-ft) summit. For another, there's the heat and humidity to contend with. But mainly, it's because you'll be distracted by wonders along the way.

To begin with, the course passes historic buildings epic in their scale and grandeur, starting with the Ajinkyatara Fort, a mighty 18th-century castle. There are also sanctuaries of quiet reflection on the route, such as Dholya Ganpati Mandir, a Hindu temple devoted to the worship of the elephant-headed god Ganesh.

Leaving the city, the ascent begins, with nature replacing culture as the

Colourfully dressed runners making
their way up Satara Hill

ELEVATION PROFILE

1,500 m
(4,920 ft)

500 m
(1,640 ft)

0   21.1 km (13.1 miles)

172

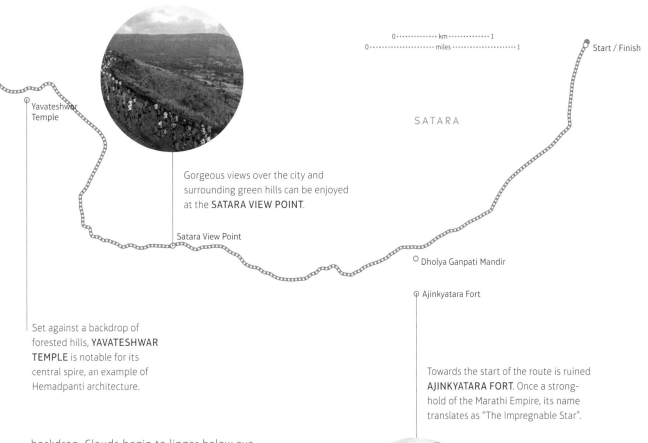

Yavateshwar
Temple

0 ·········· km ·········· 1
0 ·········· miles ·········· 1

Start / Finish

Gorgeous views over the city and
surrounding green hills can be enjoyed
at the **SATARA VIEW POINT**.

Satara View Point

Dholya Ganpati Mandir

Ajinkyatara Fort

Set against a backdrop of
forested hills, **YAVATESHWAR
TEMPLE** is notable for its
central spire, an example of
Hemadpanti architecture.

Towards the start of the route is ruined
AJINKYATARA FORT. Once a stronghold of the Marathi Empire, its name
translates as "The Impregnable Star".

173

backdrop. Clouds begin to linger below eye
level and verdant green mountainsides,
peppered with colourful shrubs and flowers,
line the road. Ultimately, the route skirts
the fringes of the famed Kaas Plateau,
ascribed a UNESCO World Heritage Site for
its abundance of gorgeous wildflowers.
Among the strange and beautiful flora
here are white toothbrush orchids, named
for their bristly flowers, and carnivorous
plants like the insect-guzzling *drosera indica*.

By the top of Satara Hill, the views are
at their best: the flower-strewn expanse of
the Kaas Plateau sits on one side, ancient
Satara on the other, making the effort all
seem worthwhile. Now there's just the
small matter of getting back down again.

SIGN-UP: *It's essential to book a place in
advance at* www.runsatara.com. *Registration opens in May for four days only.*

REFUEL
Pav Bhaji

Satara is famous for its Marathi cuisine:
rich, spicy and restorative. Head to the
Black Pearl *(Uttekar nagar, Sadar Bazar)*
in the centre of town to feast on *pav
bhaji*, a beloved local delicacy that sees
robust vegetable curries paired with
soft bread rolls.

Jantar
Mantar

The **JANTAR MANTAR**, Delhi's open-air astronomical observatory, brims with instruments for measuring the stars.

Rajpath

India
Gate

Sitting in the middle of a huge roundabout, the **INDIA GATE** is dedicated to Indian and British soldiers who died in World War I.

DELHI

0 ·········· km ·········· 1
0 ·········· miles ·········· 1

Start / Finish

Once the main venue for the 2010 Commonwealth Games, the **JAWAHARLAL NEHRU STADIUM** is where the race starts and ends.

80

Delhi Half Marathon

JAWAHARLAL NEHRU STADIUM,
DELHI, INDIA

This community-focused race sees runners take over Delhi's frenetic streets, raising money for charity along the way.

21.1 KM (13.1 MILES)   60 M (197 FT)   PAVED

It's rare to see Delhi's bustling streets come to a standstill – but that's exactly what happens during this half marathon. Tracing a path through the heart of New Delhi, the route takes in some of the city's most iconic sights. Look out for the India Gate, an imposing World War I war memorial built by the British, and the Jantar Mantar, an 18th-century observatory built by Sawai Jai Singh II, a ruler of Jaipur.

There may not be the roar of traffic on the streets, but you'll definitely hear the roar of the crowd, with spectators lining the course in their thousands. There's a huge community feel to this race, and not just because everyone is encouraged to take part, with the event including both a Wheelchair Race and a Senior Citizens' Run. It's also because this is one of the largest charity events in the country, with some £8 million raised since the half marathon launched in 2006. It's a reminder that running a race can be about far more than simply putting one foot in front of the other.

SIGN-UP: *The race takes place in November. Register in advance at:* https://delhihalfmarathon.procam.in.

ELEVATION PROFILE

250 m
(820 ft)

200 m
(656 ft)

0

21.1 km (13.1 miles)

81

Laguna Phuket Marathon

LAGUNA PHUKET, PHUKET, THAILAND

Twisting through Phuket's popular northeast, this bewitching marathon takes runners on a journey from luxurious resorts all the way to a little-visited beach – and back again.

◯ 42.2 KM (26.2 MILES) ◯ 176 M (577 FT) ◯ PAVED

Possibly Thailand's most famous island, Phuket is known for being the perfect place for a sun, sand and sea getaway. The island is dotted with countless resorts – including the expansive Laguna Phuket, an upmarket area home to lots of impressive five-star hotels. This tropical half-marathon begins here, plotting a course along a stunning white-sand seafront that's deservedly popular with beachgoers.

Yet this marathon doesn't keep to the tourist trail. Instead, it heads further north, weaving along quiet roads lined by dense rainforest and passing by tranquil, rainbow-coloured temples – it's an area that could well be dubbed Phuket's last wild frontier. In particular, the section alongside Nai Yang Beach is as pristine as the island could be. To one side is a swathe of tropical foliage, hiding rubber and pineapple plantations, as well as an abundance of wildlife that ranges from buzzing kingfishers to squealing macaques. To the other, is a sandy shore lined by the aquamarine Andaman Sea. Here, the only sounds you'll hear will be the rhythmic woosh-woosh of the waves, a smattering of birdsong and the steady plod of your own feet.

SIGN-UP: *The race takes place in June. Register at:* www.phuketmarathon.com.

Running past a temple during the Laguna Phuket Marathon

NAI YANG BEACH is a joy to run alongside, with its palms, golden sands and sparkling blue water.

Nai Yang Beach

0 ······ km ······ 2
0 ······ miles ······ 2

PHUKET

Wat Phra Thong temple

Start / Finish

LAGUNA PHUKET is a purpose-built tourism hotspot, complete with five-star hotels, golf courses and restaurants.

The **WAT PHRA THONG** temple is home to a gigantic, half-hidden golden Buddha statue.

ELEVATION PROFILE

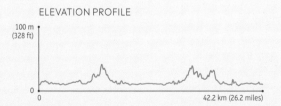

100 m (328 ft)

0

0   42.2 km (26.2 miles)

0 ········· km ········· 1
0 ········· miles ········· 1

Home to vine- and root-tangled walls and doors, **TA PROHM** is famous for its role in the first Tomb Raider film.

Jog right through **ANGKOR THOM**, a huge temple complex; it's home to the striking Bayon, a temple covered in carved faces.

○ Ta Keo

○ Angkor Thom

○ Ta Prohm

Banteay Kdei ○

The end is in sight at the restored **SOUTH GATE**, an impressive structure whose central tower is adorned with three faces.

○ South Gate

ANGKOR

Prasat Kravan ○

176

Angkor Wat ○

Start / Finish

REFUEL
Good-Cause Grub

Sister Srey *(Pokambor Avenue)* is all about delicious food with a community focus. Come here to devour organic grub, including poached eggs on toast and dragonfruit smoothie bowls. This sister-run café donates a percentage of its profits to a landmine clearance charity, as well as helping out with other community projects.

Runners get a stunning view of **ANGKOR WAT** at both the start and end of the race.

82

Angkor Wat International Half Marathon

ANGKOR WAT, ANGKOR ARCHAEOLOGICAL PARK, CAMBODIA

Cambodia's number one distance race, this half marathon delves into the heart of Angkor Archaeological Park, snaking through a jungle teeming with tree-tangled ruins.

Jogging through the beautifully carved South Gate of Angkor Thom

Angkor is surreally spellbinding. Built from the 9th to the 15th century, it was the capital city and religious heart of the Khmer Empire, which, at its peak, covered much of modern-day Cambodia, Laos, Thailand and southern Vietnam. The area is home to countless magnificent temples, including the world-famous Angkor Wat, the largest religious complex in the world. Today, many of these now-crumbling places of worship lie half-shrouded amid the dense, humid jungle.

⊖ 21.1 KM (13.1 MILES)

⊗ 27 M (89 FT)

⊖ PAVED/TRAIL

ELEVATION PROFILE

50 m
(164 ft)

0

0   21.1 km (13.1 miles)

Most visitors come here on a whirlwind trip, shuttling between the main temples by tour coach or auto rickshaw – but those in the know travel on foot.

Set up in 1996, the Angkor Wat Half Marathon captured the imagination of road racers right away. Of course, the setting was undeniably hard to beat, as was the course itself, which loops past some of the park's most impressive sights – but so was its raison d'être. The race was launched to raise funds and relief for victims of landmines. Unexploded ordnance remains a hangover from the days of the Khmer Rouge, the Pol Pot-led regime which terrorised huge swathes of the country from the mid to late 1970s. In the past two decades, however, this government-backed marathon has raised millions for landmine charities and NGOs, helping support a ban on the manufacture and use of anti-personnel mines. ▶

ASIA

Top Tip

Book your transport to Angkor Wat (usually a taxi or auto rickshaw) in advance.

178

A tuk-tuk travelling past some of the ruins of Angkor Archaeological Park

To avoid the energy-sapping Southeast Asian heat, the race begins at 5:30am, when the dawn sunlight colours the stone temples in hues of blushed crimson, soft pink and burnished orange. And what a start it is: the first kilometre (0.6 miles) winds past the mighty Angkor Wat itself. Built in the 12th century, this intricately carved temple complex is an iconic symbol of Cambodia – its image is found everywhere, from the country's national flag and its bank notes, to souvenir t-shirts and beer bottles.

As runners jog onwards, a series of ruined temples peek out of the lush jungle: the moated Prasat Kravan, a 10th-century

Hindu monument; Bat Chum, made up of a trio of now-crumbling towers; and peaceful Banteay Kdei, known for its carvings of dancers. At 12 km (7.5 miles) in, the route reveals one of Angkor's most famous relics: Ta Prohm. This 12th-century temple has been half swallowed by the jungle, with the tangled roots of fig, banyan and kapok trees wrapping their tendrils around its walls. Wildlife makes an appearance as the route continues on: wag-tails and rock thrushes announce their arrival with cries from the canopy, while macaques follow participants' progress as they clamber over remains of the ruined temples like ghostly spirits.

From here, the route winds beneath the soaring victory gate, one of five gates that mark the entrance to Angkor Thom, a vast complex housing temples and the homes of priests and palace officials. Here, runners will catch a glimpse of the Terrace of the Elephants, an impressive stone wall

> As runners jog onwards, a series of ruined temples peek out of the lush jungle

decorated with carvings of these impressive creatures, before heading to the Bayon – for many the highlight of Angkor. This dreamlike temple is adorned with over 200 faces, which smile down serenely on runners as they make the final push under the South Gate. All too soon, participants fling themselves across the finish line, ending up back where they began – in front of the otherworldly Angkor Wat.

SIGN-UP: *Register in advance via the World's Marathons website:* www.worlds marathons.com/marathon/angkor-wat-international-half-marathon.

MAKE IT LONGER

Beyond Angkor Wat

If you fancy discovering more of the area around Angkor Wat, then why not tackle the Khmer Empire Full Marathon? Half of this adventurous race covers similar ground to the half marathon, including starting and ending in the shadow of majestic Angkor Wat. However, it also takes runners further afield, giving them the chance to discover lush green rice fields and far-flung Angkor-era temples along the way.

Below Running through Angkor Archaeological Park

Below left The stunning Terrace of the Elephants

The 17th-century **TÂY HỒ TEMPLE** is dedicated to Liễu Hạnh, a sacred mother saint and one of Four Immortals in Vietnamese folk religion.

At over 1,000 years old, the wood-carved **VAN NIEN PAGODA** is a highlight of the tree-lined western edge of the lake.

Van Nien Pagoda

HANOI

Kim Liên Temple

Tây Hồ Temple

Võng Thị Temple

West Lake

Start / Finish

Trấn Quốc Pagoda

0 ·········· km ·········· 1
0 ·········· miles ·········· 1

Jog past the soaring red **TRẤN QUỐC PAGODA**, its form reflected in the lake.

83
West Lake Loop

HANOI, VIETNAM

Offering a slice of serenity in bustling Hanoi, this lakeside route beautifully blends old and new as it passes by ancient temples and scenes of modern life.

Best known for its bustling Old Quarter – with narrow streets and a ceaseless flow of scooter traffic – Hanoi can seem frenetic. Yet just north of the historic centre, casual joggers can find some calm and a cool breeze on this runseeing tour around Hồ Tây (West Lake).

As the flat, paved route passes by centuries-old pagodas and temples, the fragrant aroma of incense fills the air. Look out for the historic Trấn Quốc Pagoda; built over 1,500 years ago on a small island within West Lake, this eye-catching red shrine is Hanoi's oldest Buddhist monument. Modern life is just as present, too. As the route weaves along shady tree-lined embankments, you'll pass by couples strolling hand-in-hand and old friends playing board games over a cup of Vietnamese coffee; you might even spot a few fishermen looking to catch their lunch. It all feels wonderfully peaceful.

SET OFF: *Many temples have strict dress codes, so come back post-run to explore them further.*

⊖ 14.8 KM (9.2 MILES)

⊗ 12 M (39 FT)

⊖ PAVED

Casual joggers can find some calm and a cool breeze on this runseeing tour around Hồ Tây

ELEVATION PROFILE

50 m
(164 ft)

0

0   14.8 km (9.2 miles)

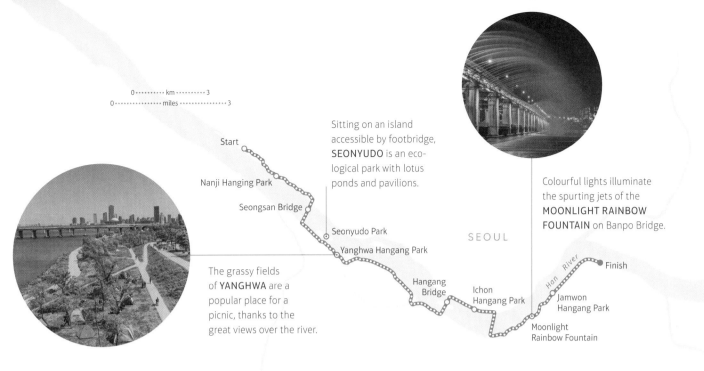

Start

Nanji Hanging Park

Seongsan Bridge

Sitting on an island accessible by footbridge, **SEONYUDO** is an ecological park with lotus ponds and pavilions.

Seonyudo Park

Yanghwa Hangang Park

The grassy fields of **YANGHWA** are a popular place for a picnic, thanks to the great views over the river.

Colourful lights illuminate the spurting jets of the **MOONLIGHT RAINBOW FOUNTAIN** on Banpo Bridge.

SEOUL

Han River Finish

Hangang Bridge

Ichon Hangang Park

Jamwon Hangang Park

Moonlight Rainbow Fountain

84

Hangang Riverside Park

SEOUL, SOUTH KOREA

All types of runners take to the pleasant trails of Hangang Riverside Park, which stretches for miles along Seoul's iconic Han River.

MAKE IT SHORTER

Take Public Transport

The park is surrounded by good public transport links, including a metro, making it easy to shorten your run. For an easier jog, run roughly 10-km (6.2-miles) from Banpo Hangang Park, near Banpo Bridge, to Yanghwa Hangang Park.

23 KM (14.3 MILES) | 178 M (584 FT) | PAVED

Hugging the edge of the Han River – a wide ribbon of water that winds through the South Korean capital – is Hangang Riverside Park, home to Seoul's most popular running route. Here, paved paths connect no fewer than 12 separate areas, from the ponds and pavilions of Mangwon to the glimmering fountains of Nanji. Runners of all inclinations descend on the park, ambling, jogging or sprinting along the mixture of smooth concrete paths and wooden boardwalks that link each green space to the next. At points fields of muhly grass appear, their fluffy pink seed heads looking like candy floss; at others, runners are treated to staggering views of Seoul's space-age skyline. As you go, you're just as likely to see seasoned athletes preparing for the Seoul Marathon, which passes through the park each spring, as you are to spot sociable amateur jogging clubs. It's a welcoming spot, so lace up your shoes and join in.

SET OFF: *The park's smooth paths make it a good spot for interval training.*

ELEVATION PROFILE

50 m (164 ft)

0

0 23 km (14.3 miles)

Hong Kong's highest peak at 957 m (3,140 ft), **TAI MO SHAN** is the final climb of the race.

Grassy Hill

Finish

Tai Mo Shan

Needle Hill

HONG KONG

As you can probably guess from the name, **NEEDLE HILL** is yet another sharp climb.

Lion Rock

Looking like a lion's head, the distinctive form of **LION ROCK** can be spotted from many points along the route.

85

HK 100

PAK TAM CHUNG TO TAI MO SHAN COUNTRY PARK, HONG KONG

One of the most challenging fixtures on Hong Kong's trail racing calendar, this brutal route offers a mix of thigh-burning elevation and awe-inspiring panoramas.

103 KM (64 MILES) 5,180 M (16,995 FT) PAVED/TRAIL

Hong Kong may be famous for its urban skyline, but the HK 100 shows runners a different side of the city. Largely following the MacLehose Trail, one of Hong Kong's four long-distance footpaths, the course winds across the New Territories, revealing the city's less familiar face: hidden beaches, forested parks and hills – lots of hills.

The mountainous terrain means that the trail serves up more than 5,100 m (16,700 ft) of elevation gain, with much of that heavily loaded into the latter half. It isn't an easy race – in fact, many seasoned marathon runners have struggled on these relentless ascents and descents.

Climbing up one of the verdant hills in Hong Kong's New Territories

It starts off deceptively, however. The first half, looping around Sai King East Country Park, is relatively easy, with few hills and some fast paved sections. It's tempting to push hard here, but don't: you'll need to

Hoi Ha

Kai Kung Shan

Ma On Shan

Start

Tai Long Wan

Take in the golden sands of **TAI LONG WAN**, with views over the turquoise sea and wooded coastline.

Sai Wan Shan

High Island Reservoir

Near the saddle-shaped **MA ON SHAN** (702 m/2,303 ft), there are great views of the surrounding tree-blanketed peaks and island-dotted ocean.

keep plenty of juice in the tank for the serious, steep climbs. Gentle ascents aren't really a thing here, as the city loves efficiency too much: after all, why build switchbacks when it's quicker to go straight up?

Thankfully, the challenging nature of the route is more than matched by its beauty. Quaint villages and hidden beaches dot the first half, while the second offers plenty of staggering panoramas – courtesy of those same leg-aching climbs. At first, densely forested hills spread out in all directions, the pale-blue sea shimmering in the distance; then around two-thirds in, the glittering high-rises of the Hong Kong skyline appear.

Nearing the end, runners face the final hurdle of Tai Mo Shan. It's definitely not one

ANOTHER WAY
Sample a Section

HK 100 sound too tough? Then just run a section of it. Handily, the route is accessible at several points by public transport, so doing point-to-point sections is easy to arrange. The first 25 km (15.5 miles), for example, won't gain too much elevation and offers the chance to run along the stunning bay of Tai Long Wan.

of Hong Kong's most beautiful mountains (there's a weather observation station on the summit) but it is the highest, with awe-inspiring vistas across the water to the outlying islands of Tsing Yi and leafy Lantau. Thankfully, it's all downhill from here – although the winding, tarmacked descent to the finish line provides one final dose of punishment for your now-aching quads. Just try to remember those beautiful views.

SIGN-UP: *The race takes place in February. Places can fill up fast, so sign-up quickly once registration opens in November or December:* www.hk100-ultra.com.

ELEVATION PROFILE

1,000 m
(3,280 ft)

0

0   103 km (64 miles)

REFUEL

Bowls of Stew

The cuisine of Hebei province is rich and hearty, perfect for refuelling after running all those gruelling miles. In the town of Gubeikou, close to the end point of the race, head to the many food stalls in the main square to try a bowl of buckwheat noodles with meat stew.

One of five mountain passes the Wall traverses, **HOUCHANKOU PASS** is the steepest part of the trail, so be careful on the steps.

0 ·········· km ·········· 1
0 ·········· miles ·········· 1

Start / Finish

CHINA

Longyukou Pass

Houchankou Pass

Big Jinshan Tower

184

Kylin Tower

The **BIG JINSHAN TOWER** has visible arrow slits in its walls; these enabled archers to defend against enemies.

General Tower

KYLIN TOWER is famous for an ornate screen wall carved with sculptures of Kylin, a mythical chimera with hooves, antlers and a dragon-like head.

With thick buttressed walls, the mighty **GENERAL TOWER** was the most important defensive fortification along this stretch of the Wall.

Once a year in May, this wonder of the world becomes a running track like no other

86

Jinshanling Great Wall Marathon

JINSHANLING, CHINA

Toughened runners flock to the Great Wall of China to tackle this taxing marathon, which runs along a section of the Wall itself and through the forested mountains surrounding it.

42.2 KM (26.2 MILES) 1,856 M (6,089 FT) PAVED/TRAIL

It's not every day you run a race atop the Great Wall of China. In fact, it's incredible that such a thing is possible at all. Yet once a year in May, this wonder of the world becomes a running track like no other thanks to the Jinshanling Great Wall Marathon.

Jinshanling refers to a stretch of the Wall running for 10.5-km (6.5-mile) through mountainous countryside in Hebei province, northeast of Beijing. Like the rest of the Wall, Jinshanling was built to defend ancient China from the attacks of outsiders, particularly nomadic tribes from the Eurasian Steppe. A defensive wall stood here from as early as the 5th century CE, but the structures seen today date from around the 16th century, during the reign of the Ming Dynasty. All of the Wall's iconic architectural hallmarks are present, with 70 beacons and towers connected by crenelated stepped walkways, winding across five mountain passes.

This mighty fortification makes up a third of the route, with the rest on rocky dirt trails that wind through the surrounding tree-shrouded mountains. The twisting course and steep ascents mean that this is one for hardcore experts. Only the very fit need apply – indeed, you'll be in the company of some of the world's finest runners. If your lungs and knees are up to it, though, the views over the green mountains, as the Great Wall snakes off into the horizon, are worth every step.

SIGN-UP: *It's essential to apply in advance at* www.greatwall-jingshanling.com.

ELEVATION PROFILE

1,000 m
(3,280 ft)

0

0   42.2 km (26.2 miles)

Marathon runners tackling a section of the Great Wall of China

185

87

Tokyo Marathon

SHINJUKU TO CHIYODA CITY, TOKYO, JAPAN

Both one of the world's most celebrated races and Asia's premier marathon, this route takes runners on a speedy tour of Tokyo, heading past modern marvels and historic sights along the way.

Set up in 2007, the Tokyo Marathon has quickly become one of the most popular races in the world. Why? The flat, fast course – perfect for breaking personal bests – has something to do with it, as does the sheer number of city sights that competitors pass along the way. The support from the public has played a big role, too, with around 1 million spectators lining the city's streets each year to cheer runners on.

Today, the Tokyo Marathon sees 38,000 competitors take part – putting it in a similar league in terms of size to the likes of the London and Chicago marathons. It's no wonder, then, that in 2012 the race was made a member of the World Marathon Majors, an elite club of six of the world's best marathons. It's the only one in Asia to have been afforded the honour.

The race begins in the world-famous neighbourhood of Shinjuku, famed for its space-age jungle of neon screens, boisterous karaoke bars and classy hotels. Here, runners set off across the starting line, with some of the stars of endurance running leading the way. The race attracts lots of elite athletes, including current marathon world-record holders Eliud Kipchoge and Brigid Kosgei, who both hail from Kenya. ▶

Top Tip

Enter as a charity runner to boost your chances of securing a place.

SHINJUKU, the starting point of the marathon, is classic Tokyo: looming modern towers decked in glaring neon.

Start

⊖ 42.2 KM (26.2 MILES)

⊗ 60 M (197 FT)

⊖ PAVED

ELEVATION PROFILE

100 m
(328 ft)

0

0   42.2 km (26.2 miles)

Jogging through the Ginza neighbourhood, known for its wealth of shops

Go Sumo

To sate your sumo-sized appetite, try *chankonabe*, a wrestler's signature broth of chicken, tofu, and vegetables like pak choi, served with plenty of rice and a beer. Try it at Chanko Ho (*www.ho-ginza.net*) in Ginza, not far from the finish line.

Claiming the crown of the world's tallest tower, the **TOKYO SKYTREE** dominates the view around Sumida.

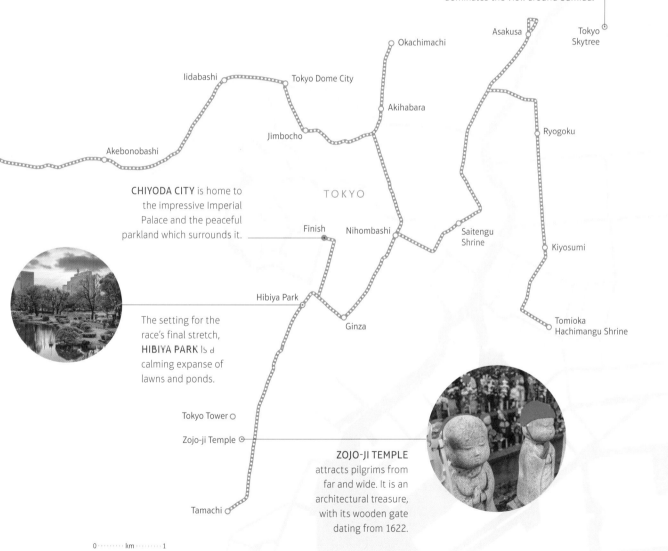

CHIYODA CITY is home to the impressive Imperial Palace and the peaceful parkland which surrounds it.

TOKYO

The setting for the race's final stretch, **HIBIYA PARK** is a calming expanse of lawns and ponds.

ZOJO-JI TEMPLE attracts pilgrims from far and wide. It is an architectural treasure, with its wooden gate dating from 1622.

Okachimachi
Asakusa
Tokyo Skytree
Iidabashi
Tokyo Dome City
Akihabara
Ryogoku
Jimbocho
Akebonobashi
Finish
Nihombashi
Saitengu Shrine
Kiyosumi
Hibiya Park
Ginza
Tomioka Hachimangu Shrine
Tokyo Tower
Zojo-ji Temple
Tamachi

0 ·········· km ·········· 1
0 ·········· miles ·········· 1

187

ASIA

Left Runners heading off from the start line in Shinjuku

Below A marathon participant running in fancy dress

The route flows alongside a cherry tree-lined canal that was once the moat of a mighty castle

Right A wheelchair racer competing in the Tokyo Marathon

One professional athlete who made history at the Tokyo Marathon is Yonas Kinda. Forced to flee Ethiopia in 2012, he became the first refugee to compete in the race as an elite runner in 2020. One of the most popular local runners, meanwhile, is Mariko Yugeta, who is still the only woman over 60 to have run a marathon in under 3 hours (on more than one occasion). Needless to say, during the 2022 Tokyo Marathon she powered past the competition to win the 60-plus category, being cheered across the finish line by jubilant crowds.

If such inspirational stories of triumph don't keep runners going, the profusion of city highlights along the route definitely will. At times participants might feel like they're on a highlights tour of Tokyo, such is the density of sights that line the route. As they pound the city streets, runners pass by the bustling Shinjuku railway station, the busiest in the world; the soaring Tokyo Skytree, the tallest tower on earth; and the lofty Tokyo Tower, a pleasingly bizarre edifice which resembles the Eiffel Tower dressed up as a traffic cone.

Snippets of an older Tokyo are also on display. Just after Shinjuku, the route flows alongside a cherry tree-lined canal that was once the moat of a mighty castle, while a little later, it passes through the Jinbōchō neighbourhood; named for a fearsome samurai of the 17th century, it's now filled with quaint bookshops and

cafés. Several shrines line the course, too, including Fukutoku with its vermilion *torii* (gate), and Tomioka Hachimangu, known as the birthplace of sumo wrestling. It may be prudent for runners to clap twice while passing them – this traditional Shinto custom is said to rouse the attention of the gods, in the hope of attracting good favour.

Then, near the end of the route, participants get a glimpse of one of the most majestic sights of all. Passing along the final stretch of the route. which winds past the elm trees and azaleas of Hibiya Park, the outline of the elegant Imperial Palace, residence of the Emperor of Japan for hundreds of years, emerges beyond the finish line. It's a fitting end for such a glorious race.

SIGN-UP: *Registration opens between July and September of the previous year – register in advance at* www.marathon. tokyo/en/. *Entry is by lottery.*

MAKE IT SHORTER

Hit the Highlights

If a marathon is too far, but you'd still like to run a race that takes in the best of Tokyo, sign up for the 10.7-km (6.6-mile) race. It runs from the neon-lights of Shinjuku, past the regal Imperial Palace, and finishes by Tokyo Station.

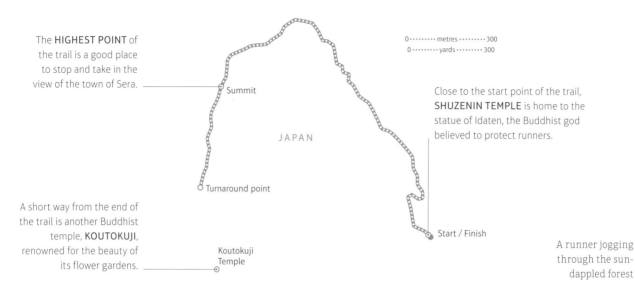

The **HIGHEST POINT** of the trail is a good place to stop and take in the view of the town of Sera. ———— Summit

0 ·········· metres ·········· 300
0 ·········· yards ·········· 300

JAPAN

Close to the start point of the trail, **SHUZENIN TEMPLE** is home to the statue of Idaten, the Buddhist god believed to protect runners.

○ Turnaround point

A short way from the end of the trail is another Buddhist temple, **KOUTOKUJI**, renowned for the beauty of its flower gardens. ————

Koutokuji Temple ◉

● Start / Finish

A runner jogging through the sun-dappled forest

190

88

Hiroshima God of Running Route

SERA, JAPAN

Ascending sharply through a verdant forest outside Hiroshima, this lovely mountain trail is watched over by a rare statue depicting a Buddhist god of running.

⊖ ⊘ ⊗ TRAIL

4.7 KM (2.9 MILES) 235 M (771 FT)

If you feel your running times could benefit from a little divine intervention, head for the hills outside the Japanese city of Hiroshima, to the town of Sera. Here, at the foot of a forested mountain trail, sits the only outdoor stone statue in Japan dedicated to Idaten: a Buddhist deity celebrated for his swiftness in chasing down demons, and worshipped as a god of running. There's a lovely community spirit about this place, with the path maintained by retired volunteers and used as a practice running trail by local students.

The route itself is challenging and you might find yourself pining for god-like stamina as you tackle the mountain path, which is steep in places and runs along the uneven forest floor. But the shade provided by the trees, and the scent of cedar that wreathes the forest, will boost your spirits – even if it won't boost your running time.

SET OFF: *To reach Sera, take the train from Hiroshima; the journey takes around 2 hours.*

ELEVATION PROFILE

500 m (1,640 ft)

200 m (656 ft)

0   4.7 km (2.9 miles)

89

Borneo International Marathon

KOTA KINABALU, MALAYSIA

Mountains, ocean and a modern metropolis are all within sight on this magnificent marathon on the island of Borneo.

42.2 KM (26.2 MILES) 60 M (197 FT) PAVED

The very name Borneo conjures images of vivid adventure, and this unforgettable marathon route certainly lives up to that promise. The route takes in the modern city of Kota Kinabalu, capital of the Malaysian state of Sabah, with the South China Sea glittering on one side and the mighty Mount Kinabalu looming imperiously on the other. Glitzy hotels, colourful street art and historic buildings provide eye-catching distraction from the marathon's biggest challenge: the tropical heat. And this factor also means that an early start is essential. You may find yourself questioning your life decisions when the 3am alarm goes off, but your reward – the sight of the sun rising behind the majestic Mount Kinabalu – makes it all more than worth it.

SIGN-UP: *Register in advance for the marathon at* www.borneomarathon.com.

ELEVATION PROFILE

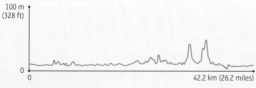

100 m (328 ft)

0

0   42.2 km (26.2 miles)

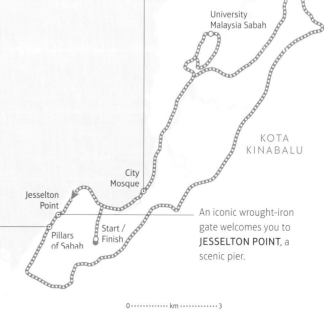

The **CITY MOSQUE** sits in a self-enclosed pool, which reflects its gorgeous pillars and dome in a beautiful symmetry.

University Malaysia Sabah

KOTA KINABALU

City Mosque

Jesselton Point

Start / Finish

Pillars of Sabah

An iconic wrought-iron gate welcomes you to **JESSELTON POINT**, a scenic pier.

The rotating **PILLARS OF SABAH** street art installation sees stone pillars painted with colourful murals by local artists.

0 .... km 3
0 .... miles 3

ASIA

At the **CHICHEE AID STATION**, runners can refuel with plenty of warm tea and hot soup.

Chichee Pass

Chichee aid station

CHICHEE PASS is the highest point of the marathon, offering some of the race's best views over the lake and the steppes.

Ongolog aid station

MONGOLIA

At **KHIRVESTEG PASS** (2150 m/ 7,053 ft), runners circle the sacred *oovo* (a cairn made of rocks and branches) three times clockwise; it's believed to ward off bad luck.

Khirvesteg Pass

0 ·········· km ·········· 2
0 ·········· miles ·········· 2

Runners wind through deep-green **FOREST** as they approach the end of the race.

Start / Finish

The race starts and ends at **CAMP TOILOGT**. Most runners spend a week here beforehand, relaxing ahead of the race.

MAKE IT LONGER
Try an Ultra

For those who want to push themselves further, there's a 100-km (62-mile) option. It follows the marathon route for the first section, then heads south along the lakeshore to Jankhai Pass (1,900 m/6,233 ft), before heading downhill to the finish line.

90

Mongolia Sunrise To Sunset

LAKE HOVSGOL NATIONAL PARK, MONGOLIA

Run one of the world's most isolated and beautiful trail races, which winds past vast Lake Hovsgol, across rugged mountains and through pristine forest.

Lake Hovsgol National Park is utterly remote. Found around 1,000 km (620 miles) from Ulaanbaatar, the Mongolian capital, this protected area is a mix of golden steppe grasslands, iron-grey peaks and deep-green taiga forest, with the huge freshwater Lake Hovsgol itself lying at its heart. It's an epic location for this race, which beautifully combines challenge with stunning scenery.

Following the misty lakeshore, the first section of the race is gentle and flat, providing the perfect warm-up. Before long, however, the trail turns inland to the west – and gains plenty of elevation as it heads for the 2,300-m (7,545-ft) Chichee Pass. This is the biggest climb of the route – one that causes legs to burn with effort. As you climb, the sun begins to illuminate the surrounding landscape: the inky water of the lake gradually turns a brilliant blue, the steppe is transformed into a golden carpet, and the hills change from grey to green. Thankfully, the race's cut-off times are generous – as the name suggests, you have from sunrise to

Running through Mongolia's beautiful Lake Hovsgol National Park

sunset – allowing runners plenty of chances to take a break and enjoy those views.

An exhilarating scramble down the mountain follows, the course fluctuating between fast-flowing single track, horse paths and untrodden fields. Then the next big climb appears – there may not be any horizon-reaching views here, but luckily this section weaves through a fairytale forest, so there's plenty to take your mind off burning quads: mosses dazzle with yellow luminescence and ancient fir trees glow green. Even better, once you reach the top of the climb, it's downhill all the way to the finish line.

SIGN-UP: *Registering in advance is essential – do so at www.ms2s.dk.*

ELEVATION PROFILE

AUSTRALIA

91 ⊚

AUSTRALASIA

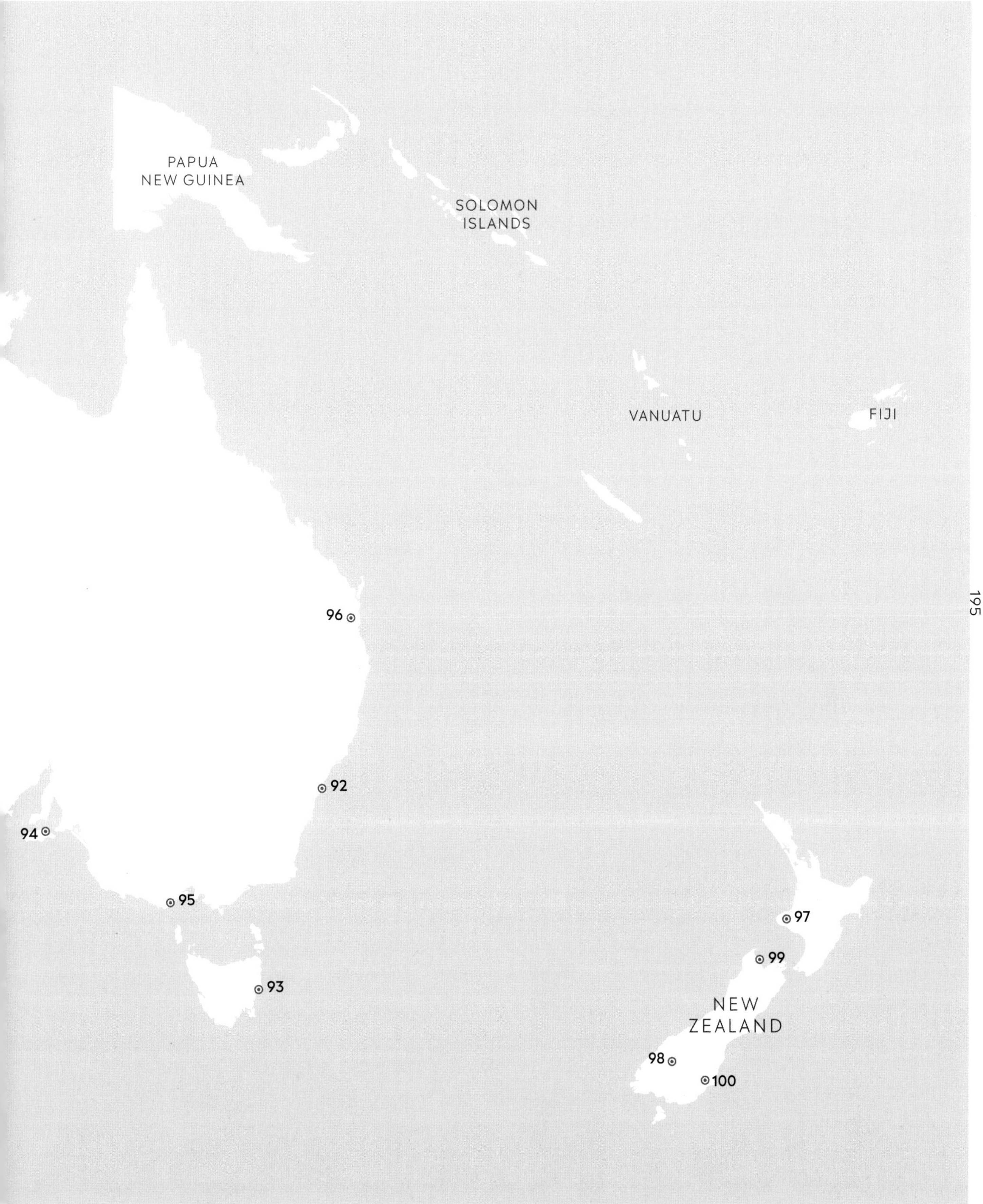

PAPUA
NEW GUINEA

SOLOMON
ISLANDS

VANUATU

FIJI

96 ◉

◉ 92

94 ◉

◉ 95

◉ 97

◉ 99

◉ 93

NEW
ZEALAND

98 ◉

◉ 100

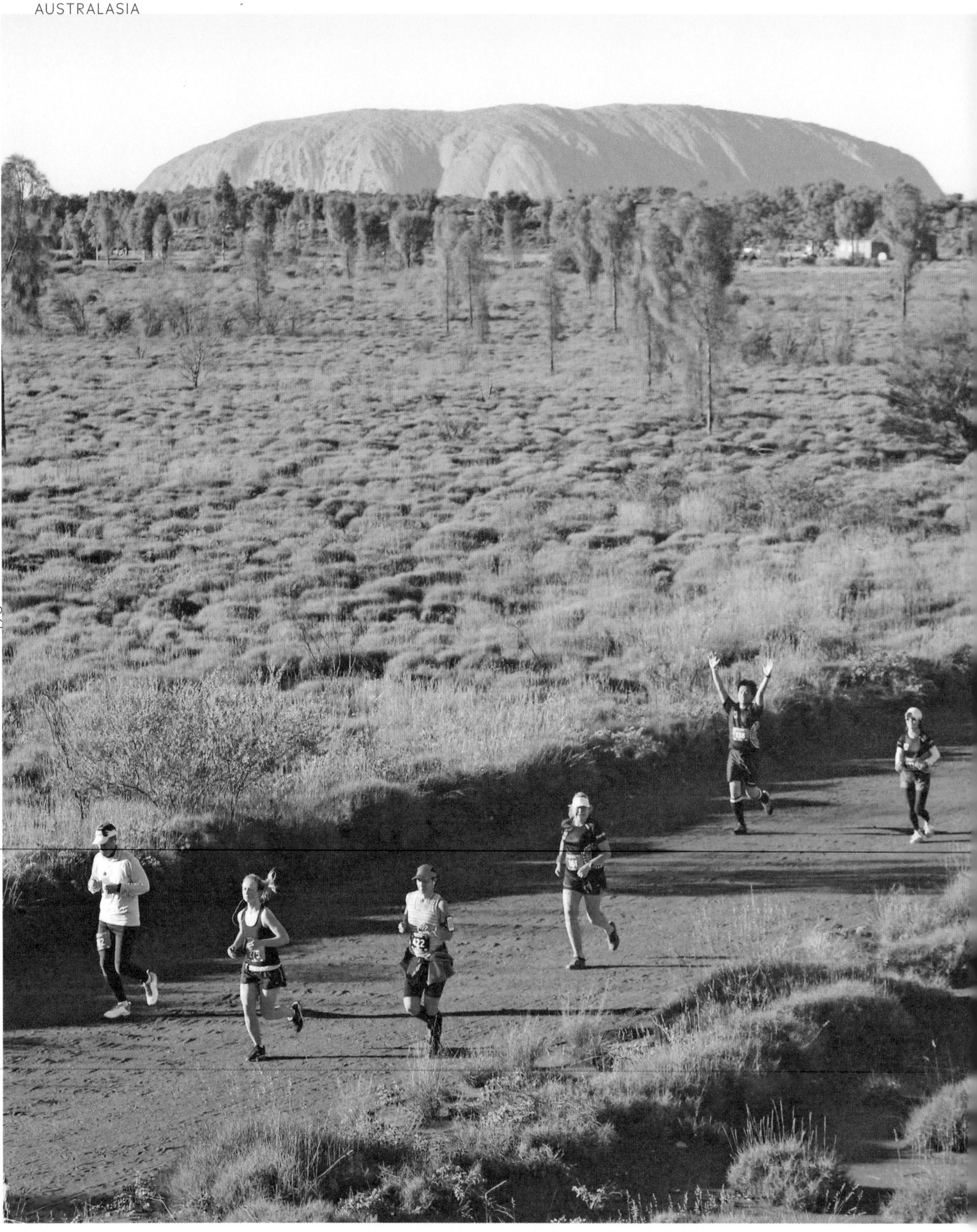

Running through
Australia's Red Centre,
with majestic Uluṟu
in the background

91

Australian Outback Marathon

NORTHERN TERRITORY, AUSTRALIA

This race winds into the heart of Australia's Red Centre, a place of deep spiritual significance to Aboriginal peoples.

42.2 KM (26.2 MILES) | 117 M (389 FT) | PAVED/TRAIL

Found at the centre of Australia's rugged and remote Outback, the Red Centre is an arid expanse of marmalade-hued desert plains, which stretch in a seemingly endless sea to the horizon. This is Australia's geographical heart – and its spiritual one, too.

The crimson-coloured land here is sacred to the country's Aboriginal peoples, especially the Aṉangu, who have called the area home for over 30,000 years. One of the world's oldest living cultures, the Aṉangu believe that this place was created during the Tjukurpa, a period of creation by ancestral beings, and that it remains a resting place for ancestral spirits. The area is home to two of their most important ▶

Top Tip
Take a tour of Uluṟu after the race with an Aṉangu guide. See *www.maruku.com.au* for more details.

ELEVATION PROFILE

550 m
(1,804 ft)

450 m
(1,476 ft)

0   42.2 km (26.2 miles)

197

AUSTRALASIA

At the **34-KM (21.1-MILE) MARK**, the course offers stunning views of Kata Tjuṯa to the right and Uluṟu to the left.

Approaching Connellan Airport, there are a few small **DUNES** to navigate. It's tiring, but spectacular views of Uluṟu await over almost every bump in the road.

Dunes

0 ·········· km ·········· 1
0 ·········· miles ·········· 1

Lasseter Highway

34 km mark

Around 21 km (13 miles) in, participants nip over the tarmacked **LASSETER HIGHWAY** before heading off into the bush once again.

Ayers Rock Campground

Yulara Village

NORTHERN TERRITORY

Runners skirt the edge of **YULARA VILLAGE**, home to a training academy that provides opportunities for Aboriginal peoples.

Start / Finish

Yulara Coach Campground

The race starts and ends next to the **FIELD OF LIGHT**, an art installation by Bruce Munroe made up of 50,000 solar stems that light up at night.

As runners make their way around the course, Uluṟu is a regular presence on the horizon.

Stay Hydrated

To ensure runners are well-hydrated throughout the race – particularly those who may not be used to the dry desert heat the Australian Outback is known for – drink stations are located every 3 km (1.8 miles). This means that you're always within easy reach of some much-needed hydration.

spiritual sights: Uluṟu and Kata Tjuṯa. These crimson-coloured rock formations stretch towards the sky, providing a striking contrast to the surrounding flat desert.

It's a privilege to be granted the chance to explore such a place – something runners are lucky enough to do during the Australian Outback Marathon. The event was set up in 2010 by keen runner Mari-Mar Walton and her husband Michael, who between them have run more than 50 marathons and ultramarathons. After taking part in the Alice Springs Marathon, the pair took a trip to Uluṟu and were so inspired by the beauty and significance of the place that they decided to set up a marathon right in the centre of the Australian Outback.

This isn't just a marathon, however. Participants arrive several days before the race to explore the area and learn about the history and heritage of its Aboriginal peoples. Depending on which "race package" is chosen, they spend three to six days in the Red Centre, taking time to visit Uluṟu and Kata Tjuṯa, and to speak to members of the Aṉangu. It's a powerful introduction to the legacy of this land and something that allows them to appreciate its importance before they step over the start line.

On marathon day itself, runners set off as the sun rises, watching as the landscape is bathed in hues of rose, cherry and

scarlet. Most of the course flows along trails made from the soft and sandy "red earth" that the area is so renowned for (although there are also sections along unsealed roads, rocky fire breaks, bush tracks and tarmac). Because of this, the previous month's weather will often determine how difficult the race will be: if it's rained in the weeks beforehand, the sandy trail will be more compacted, making running easier; if not, the soft surface underfoot may slow participants down. Thankfully, the course is relatively flat, with only a handful of inclines to tackle on the way, among them some sand dunes (they're not high, but as with any dunes expect aching calves).

As runners make their way around the course, Uluṟu is a regular presence on the horizon. Rising taller than the Eiffel Tower ▶

199

Passing along the "red earth" trails that make up most of the course

AUSTRALASIA

The rounded peaks of Kata Tjuṯa rising above the orange desert

at almost half a kilometer high, this monolithic mass of stone – whose name means "Great Pebble" – looms above the flat, arid landscape. As runners travel around the course, they'll see it change in colour from grey to pink to a blistering bright red as the sun moves position in the sky. The Aṉangu have many stories associated with Uluṟu. These are not written down, but are taught and remembered through *imma* (songs), ritual dances and rock art (indeed, the base of Uluṟu is decorated with paintings that date back over 5,000 years). One tale tells of Kuniya Tjukurpa, a battle that took place at Muṯitjulu, a waterhole next to Uluṟu; here, Kuniya (a python-woman) confronted her foe Liru (a venomous snake-man).

Other stories are more closely guarded, including those regarding Kata Tjuṯa; this cluster of large rock formations can also be spotted throughout the run. Access to cultural knowledge of this site is restricted to initiated men only – stories are not shared with visitors. Yet the weathered, domed peaks still make for an impressive sight as runners gaze to the southwest.

Participants might also glimpse some of the region's wildlife. Kangaroos bound across the flat plains, violet-hued *mirilyirilyii* (splendid fairy-wrens) forage among the shrubs and *ngiyari* (thorny devils) scuttle across the red earth. Other animals are especially important to the Aṉangu: stories tell that the *lungkaṯa* (blue-tongued lizard) once burned the land around Uluṟu and Kata Tjuṯa, while the tiny ruftons harewallaby is thought to embody the spirit of the Mala, the Aṉangu's ancient ancestors.

The race has tales of its own, too. Several years ago, Jo Penkins, a runner with multiple sclerosis, completed the race. She ran 1 km (0.6 miles) each day in the 41 days leading up to the event, before concluding the final stretch of almost 2 km (1.2 miles) on the day of the marathon. The race organizers now hand out two medals in her honour each year: one for perseverance, given to the runner who elects to enjoy the course the longest, and one to the person the organizers think deserve it the most. It was recently handed to an 89-year-old grandmother doing her first-ever organized event.

Violet-hued *mirilyirilyii* (splendid fairy-wrens) forage among the shrubs and *ngiyari* (thorny devils) scuttle across the red earth.

While finishing any marathon is an amazing achievement, there's no doubt that crossing the finish line of this one is a truly special and humbling experience. After all, runners have been given the opportunity to make their way through a sacred land – the memory of which will live on long after tired legs have stopped aching.

SIGN-UP: *Entries are only available as part of a package trip. Register at* www. australianoutbackmarathon.com.

ANOTHER WAY
Make It Snow

Looking for cooler climes? Trade desert for snow and give Australia's Big Foot Snow Marathon a try. Held in September, the race traverses through the high country of Victoria, which will likely be covered by a thick blanket of snow. Participants will need spiked running shoes and – potentially – snow shoes to complete the course.

Crossing the finish line at the end of the Australian Outback Marathon

The 1.5-km- (1-mile-) long crescent of sand that forms **BONDI BEACH** is arguably one of the best-known beaches in the world.

Start / Finish

0 ·········· metres ·········· 300
0 ·········· yards ·········· 300

Bondi Icebergs Swimming Club

Dating back to 1929, **BONDI ICEBERGS SWIMMING CLUB** is beloved for its surfside swimming baths nestled among the craggy shoreline.

SYDNEY

Mackenzies Point

Tamarama Beach

The more relaxed **BRONTE BEACH** is a popular spot for picnics and barbecues.

Bronte Beach

Keep your eyes peeled for the Aboriginal rock engravings carved into the flat seacliff at **MACKENZIES POINT**.

IN FOCUS
Bondi Lifeguards

The Bondi Surf Bathers' Life Saving Club dates back to 1907 when local swimmers gathered at Bondi's Royal Hotel to discuss forming a lifesaving organization. The now-iconic lifeguards deal with everything from swimmers and surfers in need of help to treating jellyfish stings. They also inspired the immensely popular Australian TV series *Bondi Rescue*.

92

Bondi to Bronte Beach

BONDI BEACH, NEW SOUTH WALES, AUSTRALIA

Showcasing laid-back Aussie beach culture at its finest, this run features three classic sandy shores and panoramic ocean views.

4.4 KM (2.7 MILES)

118 M (387 FT)

PAVED

Regularly touted as one of the world's greatest stretches of sand, Bondi Beach is the place where Sydneysiders come to see and be seen. It's also the starting point of this easygoing out-and-back jogging route.

Runners start by taking in the beach scene of the Bondi Promenade: chilled-out surfers cutting arcs across the waves, swimmers paddling about in the azure waters and lightly clad flocks of sunsoakers kicking back on the golden sands. From here, the trail gently climbs low cliffs as it heads south. It's an undulating route, but not a strenuous one, and the presence of a refreshing ocean breeze helps keep you cool – even when temperatures soar.

The ocean itself is a constant companion as you jog, and at the top of the bluff at Mackenzies Point, it stretches ahead in a sparkling expanse. From here, it's possible to spot humpback and southern right whales during their annual migration (May and November), as well as bottlenose dolphins (September to May). The point is also home to Aboriginal rock engravings, including one

Running along the rocky coastline between Bondi and Bronte Beach

depicting a large sea creature, possibly a whale, which could be up to 2,000 years old.

After this, the route is all about beautiful beaches. Dipping back down, the path leads to the small but perfectly formed Tamarama Beach, also known as "Glamarama" due to the trendy beachgoers who frequent its sands. Then it's just a hop, skip and a jump to Bronte; framed by sandstone cliffs. Pause to admire the views before wending your way back to Bondi, where golden sands and a refreshing dip await.

SET OFF: *This route follows a section of the popular Bondi to Coogee Coastal Walk and so can get very busy; run in the morning for a quieter path.*

ELEVATION PROFILE

50 m
(164 ft)

0

0   4.4 km (2.7 miles)

93
Wineglass Bay Loop

WINEGLASS BAY CAR PARK,
TASMANIA, AUSTRALIA

*Hit the fabulous Freycinet Peninsula for some of the most
amazing running in Australia, which takes in a menagerie
of Ozzie wildlife and one of the best beaches in the country.*

11 KM (6.8 MILES) 369 M (1,210 FT) TRAIL

Stretching into the aquamarine Tasman Sea, the Freycinet
Peninsula is a blush-pink crumple of granite peaks, fringed
with dazzling-white sand and blanketed in native bush.
It's a stunning natural wonderland – and one enjoyably
explored on this easy-to-follow running route.

First tracing the peninsula's western edge, the trail
runs past shady eucalyptus trees and rocky outcrops, with
views across boat-sprinkled Coles Bay. Keep your eyes
peeled here for local wildlife: Bennetts wallabies and spiny
echidnas lurk in the bush, while seals and dolphins frolic
offshore. After the long, wild expanse of Hazards Beach,
the route curves east towards the peninsula's marshy
interior, before emerging onto Wineglass Bay – an elegant
crescent of sand that ranks among Australia's best. Pause
to take in its pristine beauty before facing the route's main
challenge: a strenuous set of steps leading to the top of
the saddle between mounts Mayson and Amos. It's tough,
but worth it for views over Wineglass and the waves beyond.

SET OFF: *It's best to do the route anti-clockwise,
so that you leave the stunning views of Wineglass
Bay until (almost) last.*

ELEVATION PROFILE

200 m
(656 ft)

0

0   11 km (6.8 miles)

204

0 ···· km ···· 1
0 ···· miles ···· 1

WINEGLASS BAY doesn't get its name
from its shape but, more grimly, from the
19th-century whalers who flensed their
catches here, turning the water wine red.

Start / Finish

TASMANIA

Wineglass
Bay

Hazards Lagoon

Hazards Beach

At **HAZARDS
BEACH** are the rock
shelters of the area's
first inhabitants, the
Oyster Bay nation.

The peninsula's
narrowest point
is **HAZARDS
LAGOON,** where
a pair of pools
spread south of
the trail.

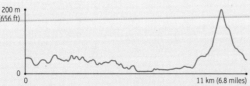

MAKE IT LONGER
Peninsula Track

For a more testing challenge, extend
this route to a 34.5-km (21.4-mile)
loop. Rather than turning east at
Hazards Beach, continue south,
following the Peninsula Track. This
route returns north past Mount
Freycinet, rejoining the shorter
trail at Wineglass Bay.

Top Tip

To reach Kangaroo Island, take the 45-minute ferry from Cape Jervis.

The run starts and ends at the **KINGSCOTE TIDAL POOL**. It's perfect for a plunge after a hard-and-hot run.

The run winds past the **KANGAROO ISLAND YACHT CLUB**, a local oceanfront landmark since 1961.

Start / Finish

Kangaroo Island Yacht Club

KANGAROO ISLAND

Brownlow Beach

The halfway point is found next to **BROWNLOW BEACH**, a pretty strip of white sand.

0 ········· metres ········· 750
0 ········· yards ········· 750

94

Kangaroo Island parkrun

KANGAROO ISLAND, SOUTH AUSTRALIA, AUSTRALIA

Winding along the edge of Kangaroo Island, this easygoing out-and-back jog offers some of the best coastal views and wildlife watching of any parkrun.

5 KM (3.1 MILES) · 13 M (43 FT) · PAVED

Since launching in 2017, the Kangaroo Island parkrun has become a laid-back Saturday morning ritual for local runners and walkers. Gathering on the edge of the small seaside town of Kingscote, loyal joggers set off along the coastline, drinking in the mirror-like waters, leafy green bush and white-sand beaches as they go. In the distance, the island's coastline curves around the bay, sitting like a ribbon of green on the horizon.

It's not just gorgeous views that make this run special – there's plenty of wildlife to be seen, too. It's unlikely that you'll spot the island's namesake kangaroos, as they live further inland, but frolicking seals will often make an appearance, as might ospreys and white-bellied sea eagles. If you're particularly lucky, you might even see whales breaching the ocean's surface – pretty good for a lazy morning run.

SIGN-UP: *The event takes place every Saturday at 8am; first-timers must register beforehand at www.parkrun.com.au.*

ELEVATION PROFILE

50 m (164 ft)

0

0   5 km (3.1 miles)

Jogging along the coast during the Kangaroo Island parkrun

Looking out over the
Twelve Apostles, one of
the highlights of the
Great Ocean Walk 100s

95

Great Ocean Walk 100s

APOLLO BAY TO TWELVE APOSTLES,
VICTORIA, AUSTRALIA

Following the path of the Great Ocean Walk, this challenging ultramarathon rewards runners with iconic Australian coastal scenery and snapshots of local wildlife.

100 KM (62.1 MILES)
2,950 M (9,678 FT)
TRAIL

Running from the golden sands of Apollo Bay to the imposing rocky forms of the Twelve Apostles, the Great Ocean Walk follows a stunning stretch of the southern Australian coastline. The 104-km (64.6-mile) walking trail mirrors a section of the Great Ocean Road, one of the world's most iconic driving routes thanks to its selection of soaring cliffs and eye-catching rock formations, sandy beaches and lush rainforest. In fact, the point-to-point walking route was created as a way for visitors to explore the area's coastal beauty more sustainably, without having to drive.

It's not just walkers who tread this trail, however. Every year, a group of hardy runners descend on the route to tackle the Great Ocean Walk 100, a truly epic ultramarathon. Set up in 2009 by Andy

Hewat, one of the most experienced ultra runners in Australia, the 100-km (62.1-mile) race is a challenging undertaking. There's the sheer length of the route, with runners completing more than two marathons in a single day. Then there's the terrain: most of the course follows singletrack paths, mercifully smooth at times, but liable to turn to slippery, leaf-strewn mud or cross sections of beach at others. The course is undulating for much of the way, too, perhaps not as extreme as other ultramarathons but with enough ascent and descent to keep the heart pounding.

Oh, and there's one more thing: the climate. The race usually takes place at a time of unpredictable weather. Runners could start with blisteringly hot and dry conditions in the morning, before coming up against torrential rain and gusty winds closer to evening. The winds are particularly infamous: howling across the ocean from Antarctica and causing the sea to thrash against the coastline, these gales have been responsible for many shipwrecks. In fact, around 700 ships have floundered ▶

ELEVATION PROFILE

50 m
(164 ft)

0

0   100 km (62 miles)

Top Tip

Venomous snakes are a potential hazard; see the official event website for useful safety guidance.

Heading across one of the sandy beaches
that dot the Great Ocean Walk 100s

here, helping to give this stretch of shore
the nickname the Shipwreck Coast.

Yet while these winds and waves have
caused destruction, they've also helped to
sculpt the limestone coastline here into a
series of eye-poppingly beautiful cliffs and
rock formations. It's this stunning coastal
scenery that will keep runners going; here,
clifftop paths offer views of rugged, bush-
clad hills tumbling towards the glittering
ocean. Meanwhile, those soft sandy beach
crossings provide glimpses of slate-blue
Fairy Penguins – the smallest penguins in
the world – and Australian fur seals, which
cluster in groups on the shore. It's not
uncommon to spot a rusty anchor or a
fallen mast here and there – direct evidence
of the coast's propensity for shipwrecks.

The route occasionally heads inland,
dipping in and out of the Great Otway

An iconic highlight
of the Great Ocean Road,
the **TWELVE APOSTLES**
are constantly being
shaped and reshaped by
erosion; today only eight
remain standing.

Finish

Princetown

MOONLIGHT HEAD
offers 180-degree views
of the stunning coastline;
there is a water stop for
the event here, too.

Wreck Beach

Johanna
Beach

Moonlight Head

It's this stunning coastal
scenery that will keep runners going; here, clifftop
paths offer views of rugged,
bush-clad hills tumbling
towards the glittering ocean.

On the infamous **WRECK BEACH**,
runners pass by the anchors of
the *Marie Gabrielle*, wrecked in
1869, and the *Fiji*, from 1891.

World War I
War Memorial

The Great Ocean Road was built between 1919 and 1932 by around 3,000 soldiers who had returned from World War I. It was constructed in memory of those killed during the war and is regarded as the world's biggest war memorial.

National Park. Here, participants find shade from the sun as they wind through a landscape of lush rainforest and native bush, the path lined by bushy giant ferns, graceful blackwood trees and giant eucalyptus trees. This is a great place for wildlife spotting: noisy rainbow parakeets and cockatoos zip above runner's heads, while koalas rest atop nearby eucalyptus branches and spiny

echidnas waddle across the path. Eventually, the route flattens out as runners wind across the wetlands of the Gellibrand River Estuary. It's home to a number of rare and threatened species, including the duck-billed platypus and white-spotted quoll.

From here, it's not far to the finish line, where the spires of the Twelve Apostles – one of the coast's most famous sights – rise up. The sight of these soaring limestone rock formations brings with them a sense of victory – made all the sweeter by the fact that you've reached them under your own steam, rather than from behind the wheel.

SIGN-UP: *Register at* www.gow100s.com. *Entries are capped at 100 runners and are offered on a first-come, first-qualified basis; previous ultramarathon experience needed.*

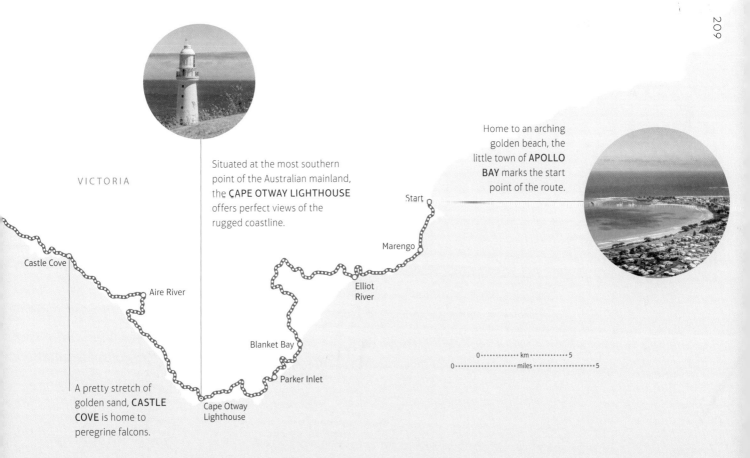

VICTORIA

Situated at the most southern point of the Australian mainland, the **CAPE OTWAY LIGHTHOUSE** offers perfect views of the rugged coastline.

Home to an arching golden beach, the little town of **APOLLO BAY** marks the start point of the route.

Start

Marengo

Castle Cove

Aire River

Elliot River

Blanket Bay

Parker Inlet

Cape Otway Lighthouse

A pretty stretch of golden sand, **CASTLE COVE** is home to peregrine falcons.

0 ·········· km ·········· 5
0 ·········· miles ·········· 5

96
Twin Falls Circuit

SPRINGBROOK NATIONAL PARK,
QUEENSLAND, AUSTRALIA

This short yet scenic run winds its way through swathes of ancient rainforest, taking in a series of cascading waterfalls as it goes.

An area of forested valleys and hills, emerald-green Springbrook National Park forms part of the Gondwana Rainforests of Australia World Heritage site – the most extensive area of subtropical rainforest in the world. Runners can explore a section of this vast forest on a short looping trail, which winds along the edge of, and then down into, a tree-covered canyon.

It's a relatively easy jog on forest paths, although legs might protest about the ups and downs. The path winds past Antarctic beech trees, their rough trunks covered in moss, and ancient Box Bush trees, known for their dome-like shape, leathery leaves and smooth, pink bark. The forest here is peppered with waterfalls, and the route takes in four of them; the trail goes by tumbling Tamarramai and Tallanbana falls, as well as sweeping behind the silvery curtain of Blackfellow Falls (be prepared to get wet). Best of all is the trail's namesake, Twin Falls, which tumbles over a fern-clad rock face into a pool below – it's an ideal spot for a quick dip.

SET OFF: *To see the falls at their very best, visit during the summer wet season.*

Twin Falls, nestled in the forest in Springbrook National Park

⊖ 4.1 KM (2.5 MILES)

⊘ 145 M (476 FT)

⊝ PAVED/TRAIL

ELEVATION PROFILE

800 m
(2,625 ft)

700 m
(2,297 ft)

0   4.1 km (2.5 miles)

SPRINGBROOK
NATONAL
PARK

TWIN FALLS is well worth the effort of the walk down – the waterfall makes an invigorating natural shower.

The **CANYON LOOKOUT** viewing platform offers jaw-dropping views that span the entire Gold Coast.

Canyon Lookout

Twin Falls

The route starts and ends at the **TALLANBANA PICNIC AREA**; pack a picnic to enjoy on one of the benches here post-run.

Start / Finish

0 ···········metres···········500
0 ···········yards···········500

210

97

Maketawa Hut Circuit

TE PAPAKURA O TARANAKI/EGMONT
NATIONAL PARK, NEW ZEALAND

*Tackle the legendary Taranaki Maunga on this moderate
route, which passes through changing volcanic landscapes.*

8.6 KM (5.3 MILES)

712 M (2,336 FT)

TRAIL

Soaring above a patchwork of flat fields, Taranaki Maunga
(Mount Taranaki) is a sight to behold. According to Māori
legend, this conical volcano is the quiet mountain on Te Ika-
a-Māui (the North Island), who tries to keep the peace
between the island's four other warring volcanic summits:
Tongariro, Ngauruhoe, Ruapehu and Pihanga. Interestingly,
it's the only one of these peaks that's still an active volcano.

    This looping run winds around an eastern section of
the volcano's slopes, taking in the "Goblin Forest" – an
emerald-hued kingdom of twisting kāmahi trees – before
climbing higher to a more open expanse of hardy native
shrubs. Here lie the Maketawa Hut and the Tahurangi
Lodge, both offering well-earned rest breaks and stunning
views of the sublimely symmetrical Mount Taranaki.

SET OFF: *Break up the run by spending the night at
Tahurangi Lodge. Book at:* www.taranakialpineclub.co.nz.

In the **GOBLIN FOREST**,
native kāmahi grow on old
tōtara and rata trees that
were destroyed by volcanic
eruptions long ago.

211

Start /
Finish

Goblin Forest

EGMONT
NATIONAL
PARK

Maketawa Hut

0 ······· metres ······· 500
0 ······· yards ······· 500

Tahurangi
Lodge

ELEVATION PROFILE

1,500 m
(4,921 ft)

500 m
(1,640 ft)

0

8.6 km (5.3 miles)

TARANAKI MAUNGA
can be glimpsed during
the run; it last erupted
around 400 years ago.

Taranaki
Maunga

Set among native bushland,
the **MAKETEWA HUT** is a
great rest stop with sweeping
views of the fertile plains
surrounding the mountain.

98

Moonlight Track

QUEENSTOWN TO ARTHUR'S POINT, NEW ZEALAND

*Winding through Queenstown's mountainous surrounds, this run
takes you on a tour of the area's gold-mining history.*

15.5 KM (9.6 MILES)

720 M (2,362 FT)

TRAIL

Offering up a range of adrenaline-packed activities, Queenstown is the undisputed adventure capital of New Zealand. Yet it was once famous for something else: gold. In 1860, the area became the site of one of the biggest gold rushes in the world after several discoveries of the metal were made. Prospectors flocked here in droves: veterans of gold mining descended from California and Australia, while newcomers came from as far afield as Europe and China, all looking to make their fortunes.

Glimpses of this once-golden history are revealed on this difficult route, which winds through mountainous scenery all the way to diminutive Arthur's Point. Starting in Queenstown, runners jump on the gondola for a pain-free ascent to Bob's Peak. (It's possible to run to the peak from the town, but this saves your legs for the mountain trails later on.) At the top, rocky paths lead upwards to the Ben Lomond Saddle, where views of deep-blue Lake Wakatipu and the ragged peaks of the Remarkables will steal what little breath you have left.

A pair of runners fording a stream
on the Moonlight Track

From here, a series of poles skirt the edge of the mountain, marking out the rugged path to the historical mining town of Sefferstown, which was home to around 3,000 people at its peak in 1863. Not much of the settlement is left today, other than stone foundations and trees used to mark traffic paths and doorways. Yet these ruins, nestled amid alpine tussock and shrub, are enough to evoke the memory of those who previously trod this way in their search for gold. A little further along a grassy path are more remnants of the gold-mining era, including the remains of the Moke Creek school, where prospectors' children were educated, and terraces on the hillside where miners sluiced for gold.

ELEVATION PROFILE

1,500 m
(4,921 ft)

0

0   15.5 km (9.6 miles)

IN FOCUS

George Fairweather Moonlight

The Moonlight Track was named after George Fairweather Moonlight, a Scottish businessman and prospector. A veteran of gold rushes in California and Australia, he became legendary among miners during the Queenstown gold rush for his luck at finding deposits of the sought after metal.

Gold deposits around the **SHOTOVER RIVER** were the centre of activity during the gold rush, earning it the nickname of "the richest river in the world".

While now ruins, the old mining station of **SEFFERSTOWN** was once home to miners' houses, as well as shops and a school.

Sefferstown

Shotover River

Take a detour to the top of **BEN LOMOND/ TE-TAUMATA-OHAKITEKURA** for 360-degree views of the area.

Ben Lomond

NEW ZEALAND

Finish

ARTHUR'S POINT was named after one of the lucky prospectors, Thomas Arthur, who found a large amount of gold here.

Eventually, the small town of Arthur's Point comes into view. It may be the end of the run, but there's still one last piece of gold rush history to discover. It was here, on a bend of the Shotover River, where plucky prospectors Thomas Arthur and Harry Redfern, gathered 113 g (4 oz) of gold in just three hours. This lucky strike was one of the first finds in this area – helping to set the gold rush in motion.

Start

SET OFF: *The route can be run in reverse, too. Take the bus (Line 2) from Queenstown to McChesney Road in Arthur's Point.*

0 ········ km ········ 1
0 ········ miles ········ 1

99

Abel Tasman Coast Track

ABEL TASMAN NATIONAL PARK, NEW ZEALAND

Following a section of one of New Zealand's best-loved hiking routes, this trail bathes joggers in staggering coastal scenery as it traces a line between rainforest and ocean.

11.7 KM (7.3 MILES)

213 M (698 FT)

TRAIL

214

Following the coastline from Mārahau to Anchorage, this section of the famous Abel Tasman Coastal Track is simply stunning. From the start, runners are immersed in lush native forest, with beech, Mānuka and Kānuka trees lining both sides of the well-maintained and signposted track. Breaks in the canopy bring glimpses of the sinuous coastline, kissed by the jewel-blue waters of Tasman Bay, and at points the trail opens out onto golden sand beaches. Wildlife can be seen in abundance here; the rocky foreshore is home to shags and oystercatchers, while offshore you might spot fur seals or pods of dolphins. Upon reaching the sandy crescent moon of Anchorage, there's a final treat in store: a water taxi back to Mārahau. Soak up the beauty of the Abel Tasman coast from a different perspective as you take a well-earned rest.

SET OFF: *Unlike the other parts of the Abel Tasman Coast Track, this route can be run at both high and low tide.*

A sheltered spot for boats – hence its name – **ANCHORAGE** has a large beach with some unusual rock formations.

Finish

ELEVATION PROFILE

200 m (656 ft)

0

0   11.7 km (7.3 miles)

ABEL TASMAN NATIONAL PARK

Stilwell Bay

Apple Tree Bay

Coquille Bay

COQUILLE BAY, a remote and tranquil strip of sandy beach, can only be reached on foot or by boat.

Start

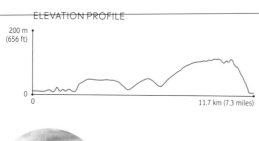

The Abel Tasman Coast Track is accessed from the village of **MĀRAHAU** via a causeway.

0 ···· km ···· 1
0 ···· miles ···· 1

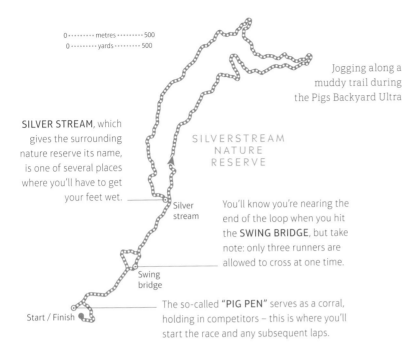

metres 500
yards 500

Jogging along a muddy trail during the Pigs Backyard Ultra

SILVER STREAM, which gives the surrounding nature reserve its name, is one of several places where you'll have to get your feet wet.

SILVERSTREAM NATURE RESERVE

Silver stream

You'll know you're nearing the end of the loop when you hit the **SWING BRIDGE**, but take note: only three runners are allowed to cross at one time.

Swing bridge

Start / Finish

The so-called **"PIG PEN"** serves as a corral, holding in competitors – this is where you'll start the race and any subsequent laps.

100
Pigs Backyard Ultra

SILVERSTREAM NATURE RESERVE, NEW ZEALAND

The wilds of the Dunedin countryside are the setting for this circular race, which can be either a one-time light-hearted dash or an extreme endurance event – it's entirely up to you.

Top Tip

Barbeque and coffee are provided, but there's no other food or drink supplied, so bring some with you.

VARIES VARIES TRAIL

Ever since Big Dog's *(p34)* was set up in 2012, backyard ultras – where runners tackle a roughly 6.8-km (4.2-mile) loop every hour until they drop – have been taking the world by storm. There are now over 290 of these events in 69 countries.

This one takes place in the pastoral surrounds of the Silverstream Nature Reserve, near Dunedin on the country's South Island. Runners speed through open countryside and conifer forest, keeping an eye out for the wild pigs that give the event its name. As the challenge is more about endurance than tricky terrain, the route is fairly flat – although there are some muddy sections and a couple of stream crossings to keep things interesting. There's a strong sense of community, despite the desire to be the last one standing: participants encourage each other around the course and bond over aching limbs and sleep deprivation. And, as runners gradually drop off, they cluster around the finish line to cheer those still going until the bitter end.

SIGN-UP: *The race takes place in February; register via* www.pigsbackyardultra.com.

ELEVATION PROFILE

250 m (820 ft)

0

0   6.7 km (4.2 miles)

Index

218

Acknowledgments

Dorling Kindersley would like to thank Adam Dennis, Vagisha Pushp, Stuti Tiwari Bhatia, Bharti Karakoti and Tanveer Zaidi, whose help and assistance contributed to the preparation of this book, plus the following authors for their words:

Sarah Baxter is a travel writer based in Bath. She works for many national newspapers and magazines, and is the author of *A History of the World in 500 Walks*. She can often be found running around the Cotswold hills.

Nancy Besharah has run trails and races around the world for decades – and doesn't plan to stop any time soon. When not running (or training for her next triathlon), she loves sharing inspiring stories, travelling with her family and walking her dogs.

David Bone is a run-coach and ultramarathon events director with Camino Ultra. An ultra-runner for over a decade, he has competed in 24 Hour World Championships and iconic races such as the Spartathlon (where he finished in the top 20 in 2021).

James Clark is a travel writer who loves being outside in nature. He can often be found meditating on a beach, hiking along a mountain path or running through a remote destination. For him, running is a great way to connect with life and disconnect from the mind.

Harri Davies is a multimedia storyteller. When it became clear that no amount of enthusiasm could counterbalance her lack of coordination, Harri realised that it might be better to find a sport without any teammates to disappoint. Today, she lives, writes and runs in Madrid, and will never stop finding it funny that the Spanish call jogging "footing".

Mark Dredge is a beer expert and the author of many books about beer. He's also an experienced runner, having completed many marathons and ultramarathons, and can most often be found running on the South Downs – usually with a pub as the finish. Find him at markdredge.com or on Twitter @MarkDredge.

Keith Drew is a freelance travel writer, editor and marathon runner. He writes about unusual places for *BBC Travel* and *The Telegraph*, among others, and is the co-founder of family travel website Lijoma.com, a curated selection of inspirational itineraries to more adventurous destinations like Iceland, Jordan, Sri Lanka and Japan.

Steph Dyson is a bilingual travel writer who writes about sustainable adventure travel for publications around the globe, including *CNN*, *South China Morning Post* and *The Independent*. She also runs the award-nominated website, Worldly Adventurer. You'll generally find her exploring the most obscure and hard-to-reach parts of a country.

Ally Head is *Marie Claire's* Health, Sustainability and Relationships Editor. She's also a keen runner, having completed countless half marathons and seven marathons, including London, which she ran in a Boston-qualifying time of 3 hours 26 minutes. It's a time she's looking to beat when she takes on the Chicago Marathon next.

Rachel Ifans is passionate about writing about women in sport: both those breaking boundaries in pursuit of equality and those everyday runners challenging themselves. She writes for publications like *Women's Running*, *The Independent*, *Glorious Sport* and *National Geographic*.

Heather Mayer Irvine is a US-based journalist and the former food and nutrition editor for *Runner's World*. Her work has appeared in national and international publications, and she's also the author of the *Runner's World Vegetarian Cookbook*. She has seven marathons under her belt, including the Boston Marathon, which she's run three times.

Mary Jennings is a writer and running coach from Ireland. She founded Forget The Gym, a coaching group that helps runners build confidence, whether they're a beginner or a marathon runner. She's also a regular columnist for *The Irish Times* on all things running related and the author of *Get Running*.

Stephen Keeling is an award-winning travel writer based in New York City. His favorite places to run (slowly) include the East River Greenway, the Stuyvesant Town Oval and along the Hudson River, especially in summer.

Warren King is an ex-lawyer and ex-banker who left the corporate world a few years ago to organize (and participate in) cool trail races in South Africa and around the world. He loves nothing more than running in the mountains with his dogs.

Lucja Leonard is an Aussie-British ultra runner living in the US. She loves getting out and exploring new trails on her travels, as well as competing in long-distance ultra events, such as the Marathon Des Sables and Ultra-Trail du Mont-Blanc.

Ben Lerwill is an award-winning freelance travel writer whose work appears in publications such as *National Geographic Traveller*, *BBC Countryfile Magazine* and *The Guardian*. He finished his first marathon in 2001 and has no plans to hang up his running shoes any time soon.

Mike MacEacheran is an award-winning freelance travel journalist who writes for publications such as *The Times*, *National Geographic*, *The Washington Post* and *Condé Nast Traveller*. He's reported from 115 countries and lives in Edinburgh.

Amy McPherson is a travel writer whose heart follows the wild outdoors, especially on a trail in the mountains. When not writing, she can be found running or cycling in search of nature, and never misses a chance to hit the trails on her travels.

Rebecca McVeigh is a writer and producer hailing from Northern Ireland, whose work has featured in international travel publications such as *BBC Travel*. Now residing with her family on the French Riviera, her favourite way to explore is by foot or on paddleboard.

Shafik Meghji is an award-winning travel writer, journalist and author of *Crossed off the Map: Travels in Bolivia*. Specializing in Latin America and South Asia, he has co-authored more than 40 guidebooks and writes for publications such as *BBC Travel* and *Wanderlust*. Find him at shafikmeghji.com or on Twitter and Instagram @ShafikMeghji.

Rachel Mills is a co-author of Rough Guides and DK Eyewitness travel guides to New Zealand, India, Canada, Ireland and Great Britain. An expert in sustainable, responsible tourism, she works part-time for flight-free travel company Byway and writes for *The Sunday Times*, *The Independent* and *The Telegraph*. Follow her on Instagram and Twitter @rachmillstravel.

Adrienne Murray Nielsen is a British journalist, writer and broadcaster. Before settling in Copenhagen with her family, she lived and worked in India and the US. Cross-country and fell-racing was a part of her youth, but these days a love of trails and city half-marathons keeps her on her toes.

Jabulile Ngwenya is a South African travel writer who has contributed to various international publications. She has visted 18 African countries and is passionate about changing the Africa travel narrative by telling unique stories abut its landscapes, history and people. Find her on Instagram @travelstoriesafrica and on YouTube at Travel Africa with Jabu.

Ashley Parsons is a wandering journalist, who likes to travel slowly by bicycle, horseback, trail running and hiking. Her works can be read in publications such as *Whetstone Magazine*, *Earth Island Journal* and *Sidetracked Magazine*. She can be found at theashleyparsons.com and on Instagram @ensellevoyage.

Alfie Pearce-Higgins is an enthusiastic amateur trail runner, overland adventurer and occasional writer. Currently based in London he has lived, worked, run and frequently lost his way across Africa, Asia and the Middle East.

Lucy Pearson is a freelance writer, award-winning book blogger and host of The Bondi Literary Salon. Originally from the UK, she's called Bali and Los Angeles home, and now lives in Bondi. While she's previously completed the London Marathon and several Royal Parks half marathons, her favourite track is now the coastal path from Bondi to Bronte Beach.

Kelsey Perrett is a freelance writer and editor specializing in travel and outdoor recreation. She is a co-author of Moon's *New England Hiking* and a senior contributing editor at GreatRuns.com. Her work has appeared in *Yankee Magazine*, *ROVA*, *Bluedot Living* and others.

Anna Richards is a writer, wine drinker, fancy dress aficionado and runner living in Lyon, France. Le Marathon International du Beaujolais is a happy marriage of her hobbies, and importantly, right on her doorstep. Her work has been featured in publications such as *SUITCASE*, *The Telegraph* and *The Independent*.

Michael Sheridan is a travel photographer and writer based in London with a love of trains, sport and travel. Work has taken him around the world, from the Alps to India and Sierra Leone, and he's been published in the likes of *National Geographic Traveller* and *The New York Times*.

Helen Sloan is an Irish writer and editor who has been living in Hong Kong for more than ten years. She spends her spare time running and hiking the city's hilly terrain, and has survived several of Hong Kong's ultra-marathon trail races.

Dan Stables is a travel writer based in England. He has authored or contributed to more than 30 travel books on destinations across Asia, Europe, and the Americas, and writes travel articles for many international publications. Find him on Twitter @DanStables, on Instagram @DanStabs, or at danielstables.co.uk.

Fiona Tapp is a former teacher who moved from the UK to Canada in 2006. Now an award-winning travel writer, her work has appeared in *The Guardian*, *Travel + Leisure*, *The Sunday Times* and other publications.

Michelle Tchea is the owner of Chefs Collective and a bestselling author specializing in gastronomy, travel and luxury hospitality. Her work can be found in national newspapers and travel magazines, including *Condé Nast Traveler* and *TIME Magazine*. She loves to run but is by no means a pro, although she does get to the finish line faster when there is pastry waiting for her at the end.

Peter Watson is a travel writer and founder of outdoor travel blog Atlas & Boots. A keen trekker and climber, he can usually be found on the trails of the Great Ranges. He's visited over 90 countries and is currently focused on climbing the seven summits – the highest mountain on every continent.

Whitney White grew up in Colorado's Rocky Mountains. Here, she developed a love of running that eventually led her to compete for her university's cross-country and tracks teams. Now working as a freelance writer in Spain, she spends her free time running Europe's countless trails.

Karolina Wiercigroch is a London-based photographer and writer who creates travel stories for a variety of magazines, including *National Geographic Traveller*, *Delicious Australia* and *Vogue*. Originally from Poland, she returns to run the forested trails of the Beskid Mountains at least once a year.

Matt Wisner is a writer and professional runner who lives in Eugene, Oregon. He was an All-American middle distance athlete in college and competed for the University of Oregon. Today, he has his own print magazine, *New Generation Track and Field Magazine*, which aims to characterize the fastest runners in the world.

The publisher would like to thank the following for their kind permission to reproduce their photographs:

(Key: a-above; b-below/bottom; c-centre; f-far; l-left; r-right; t-top)

Stock Photo Name: John Smith 200cr, 201tr; Jane Smith 150tr; John Smith 200cr, 201tr; Jane Smith 150tr; John Smith 200cr, 201tr; Jane Smith 150tr; John Smith

The publisher would like to thank the following for their kind permission to reproduce their photographs:

2 Shutterstock.com: EPA-EFE / Mohamed Hossam (c). **6 Getty: E+:** Pamela Joe McFarlane (c). **8 UTMB:** Frank Oddoux (bl). **9 Alamy Stock Photo:** dennKor (tr). **14 Pam Doyle:** (br). **Shutterstock.com:** Jay Yuan (tr). **15 Alamy Stock Photo:** doublespace-VIEW (cr). **Dreamstime.com:** Christopher Defalco (tl). **16 Alamy Stock Photo:** Edgar Bullon (br). **17 Alamy Stock Photo:** All Canada Photos (cb). **Getty Images:** Shaadi Fari (tl). **Shutterstock.com:** Josef Hanus (tr). **18 Len Wagg** (tc). **19 Getty Images:** Lance King (tl). **Joel Krahn** (c). **20 Alamy Stock Photo:** Alpha and Omega Collection (br). **Alamy Stock Photo:** Tom Grundy (tc). **Alamy Stock Photo:** Brian Green (cl). **21 Dreamstime.com:** Bnakano27 (br). **22 Kevin Morris** (br). **23 Getty Images:** Adam Springer (tl). **Shutterstock.com:** Christophe KLEBERT (tr). **24 Alamy Stock Photo:** Sundry Photography (tl). **25 Getty Images:** Brent Durand (cr). **Photo Courtesy of The Dipsea Race:** (bl). **Shutterstock.com:** Radoslaw Lecyk (tc). **26 ABQ Free Images** (br). **27 Alamy Stock Photo:** K.D. Leperi (tl); Efrain Padro (cr). **Getty Images:** Mark Newman (cl). **28 Alamy Stock Photo:** OntheRun photo (tr). **29 Alamy Stock Photo:** Theresa Scarbrough (bl). **Shutterstock.com:** Pat A Robinson / ZUMA Press Wire (cr). **30 Getty Images:** Kamil Krzyczynski (tc). **31 Alamy Stock Photo:** Peter Coombs (br). **Getty Images:** Jamie Sabau (tr). **32 Benjamin Weingart** (c). **33 Alamy Stock Photo:** Ian Dagnall (tr). **Getty Images:** Bryan Akers (bl). **34 Getty Images:** Kevin Liles / Sports Illustrated / Getty Images. **35 Getty Images:** Kevin Liles / Sports Illustrated / Getty Images (tc, bl). **36 Getty Images:** Maddie Malhotra (c). **38 Alamy Stock Photo:** Danita Delimont (cl). **Getty Images:** Kayana Szymczak (br). **39 Getty Images:** Boston Globe (tr); Maddie Malhotra (bl). **40 Alamy Stock Photo:** diversbelow (br). **Getty Images:** Steven Heap / EyeEm (c). **41 Getty Images:** Matt Anderson Photography (tl). **42-43 Dreamstime.com:** Demerzel21 (bl). **44 Getty Images:** fotog (bl). **45 Alamy Stock Photo:** Hemis

(tc); **Alamy Stock Photo:** Sipa US (cr). **Getty Images / iStock:** AlexPro9500 (cl). **46 Getty Images:** Ed Jones (br); David Madison (br). **Shutterstock.com:** A Katz (cr). **47 Getty Images:** Drew Levin (br). **48 4Corners:** VISTA / 4Corners (tl). **49 Alamy Stock Photo:** Verena Matthew (br). **Dreamstime.com:** Eq Roy (tr). **52 William Taylor** (tl). **53 Alamy Stock Photo:** robertharding (tr). **Shutterstock.com:** lindseywils1026 (crb). **54 RACINGTHEPLANET:** Thiago Diz (cr). **55 Alamy Stock Photo:** Giulio Ercolani (tr); **Alamy Stock Photo:** Steve Allen Travel Photography (bl). **Shutterstock.com:** Dmitry Chulov (cr). **56 Getty Images:** Pintai Suchachaisri (br). **57 Alamy Stock Photo:** Zoltan Bagosi (tr). **Shutterstock.com:** Christian Vinces (c). **58 Gabriel Pielke**

(c). **60 Dreamstime.com:** Meinzahn (cra). **Getty Images:** Ignacio Palacios (tl). **Shutterstock.com:** Ksenia Ragozina (bl). **61 Gabriel Pielke** (b). **62 Gabriel Pielke** (bl). **63 Gabriel Pielke** (c). **64 Gabriel Pielke** (tr). **Alamy Stock Photo:** imageBROKER (tr). **AWL Images:** Alex Robinson (cl). **Getty Images:** Anton Petrus (br). **65 Shutterstock.com:** A. Ricardo (tr). **66 Alamy Stock Photo:** blickwinkel (tr). **Getty Images:** Fyletto (cr). **67 Alamy Stock Photo:** Danita Delimont Creative (br); Dan Mammoser (bl). **68 Alamy Stock Photo:** Francisco Javier Ramos Rosellon (cr). **69 Alamy Stock Photo:** Carlos Aranguiz (cl); **Alamy Stock Photo:** Cannon Photography LLC (bc). **Getty Images:** Mlenny (tr). **70 Braulio Romero** (c). **71 Alamy Stock Photo:** Maria Jose Lou (cl). **Braulio Romero** (br). **Getty Images:** nertog (bl). **72 Antarctic Ice Marathon:** Mark Conlon (br). **73 Getty Images:** Rod Strachan (c). **Antarctic Ice Marathon:** Mark Conlon (tl). **76 David Altabev** (br). **77 Getty Images:** Daniel Solinger / EyeEm (cl); Anton Petrus (tc). **Richard Tilney-Bassett** (tr). **78 Visit North Iceland** (br). **79 Adrienne Murray Nielsen** (bc). **Getty Images:** Westend61 (cr). **80 Zoltan Tot** (bl). **81 Alamy Stock Photo:** Jacek Bakutis (cl); Rob Crandall (cr). **AWL Images:** Tom Mackie (tr). **82 Alamy Stock Photo:** David Lyons (cl). **Shutterstock.com:** Mike Shaw (tr). **83 FionaOutdoors** (tr). **84 Getty Images:** Handout (br). **85 Alamy Stock Photo:** Graham M. Lawrence (cr); **Alamy Stock Photo:** radnorimages (tr); **Alamy Stock Photo:** Athena Picture Agency LTD / D. Legakis (cl). **86 Getty Images:** Tolga Akmen. **88 Alamy Stock Photo:** Marcin Rogozinski (bl). **Getty Images:** Spotmatik (cr). **Shutterstock.com:** Pajor Pawel (tl). **89 Alamy Stock Photo:** Oliver Dixon (cl). **90 Alamy Stock Photo:** PA Images (br). **91 Getty Images:** Lillian King (cr). **Shutterstock.com:**

Brookgardener (cl). **92 Mary Jennings:** (cr). **93 Getty Images:** Craig Stennett (bl). **Shutterstock.com:** Wirestock Creators (c). **95 Getty Images:** Matthias Makarinus. **96 Getty Images:** Maja Hitij (bl). **97 Alamy Stock Photo:** Michael Brooks (tl). **AWL Images:** Jon Arnold (bc). **Shutterstock.com:** Sergey Kohl (cr). **98 Alamy Stock Photo:** Can Yelcin (tc). **PatitucciPhoto** (cl). **Shutterstock.com:** Kasakphoto (bc). **99 PatitucciPhoto** (c). **100 Alamy Stock Photo:** imageBROKER (bl); Panther Media GmbH (tl). **101 Getty Images:** Jan Hetfleisch / Stringer (tl). **102 Alamy Stock Photo:** Mauritius Images GmbH (bl). **Getty Images:** Monica Silva (tl). **103 Getty Images:** Avalon (br). **104 Alamy Stock Photo:** Rostislav Glinsky (cr); Andrey Khrobostov (bl). **105 Alamy Stock Photo:** Bob Gibbons (br). **106 Alamy Stock Photo:** Franck Chapolard (br). **107 Alamy Stock Photo:** Franck Chapolard (br); Jason Knott (tl); Hervé Lenain (cr). **109 UTMB:** Franck Dunouau (c). **110 Getty Images:** Jean-Pierre Clatot (tr). **Shutterstock.com:** Doris Rieder (tr); Simona Sirio (cl). **UTMB:** Frank Oddoux (br). **112 Getty Images:** Godong (bl). **113 Getty Images:** Olivier Chassignole (tc). **114 Golazo:** (br, bc); **Golazo** (tr). **116 Dreamstime.com:** Kornelija (cr). **Getty Images:** Alexander Spatari (tl). **117 CarlosLlerandi – LiqenStudio** (tl). **118 Getty Images:** Desiree Martin / Stringer (br). **119 Alamy Stock Photo:** agefotostock (tl); **Alamy Stock Photo:** Markus Lange / robertharding (br). **Shutterstock.com:** Yuri A / PeopleImages.com (c). **120 Shutterstock.com:** Manuel Fernandes (cr). **121 Alamy Stock Photo:** Loetscher Chlaus (cr); Dario (bl). **122 Alamy Stock Photo:** Imagebroker (cr); Alkis Konstantinidis / Reuters (bl). **Shutterstock.com:** Tatiana Popova (c). **123 Alamy Stock Photo:** Marios Lolos / Xinhua (br). **124 SPARTATHLON:** (bl). **125 SPARTATHLON:** (cr); Spartathlon: Robert Kulijewicz (tr). **126 Shutterstock.com:** A Daily Odyssey (cra). **127 Chudy Wawrzyniec:** Andrzej Olszanowski (tl, br). **128 Alamy Stock Photo:** Jeremy Graham (br). **129 Alamy Stock Photo:** Rudmer Zwerver (tl). **AWL Images:** Tom Mackie (br). **Shutterstock.com:** Haidamac (cb). **130 Transylvania 100:** Vlad Ionescu (c). **131 Alamy Stock Photo:** Sorin Colac (tl). **Dreamstime.com:** Porojnicu (cr). **Shutterstock.com:** Gaspar Janos (bl). **132 Transylvania 100:** Alexandra Tomulescu (tl). **133 Transylvania 100:** Adrian Crapciu (b). **134 4Corners:** Andrea Armellin (bc). **Dreamstime.com:** Silviu Matei (cr). **Getty Images:** Evgeni Dinev Photography (tr). **136 Salomon Cappadocia Ultra Trail:** Goshots (bc). **137 Getty Images:** Wissanu

223

224

Project Editors Rachel Laidler,
Elspeth Beidas
Senior Designer Ben Hinks
Senior Art Editor Vinita Venugopal
Illustrator Ben Spurrier
Proofreader Ben Ffrancon Davies
Indexer Helen Peters
Picture Researcher Adam Goff
Senior Cartographic Editor Casper Morris
Cartographer Ashif
Cartography Manager Suresh Kumar
Publishing Assistant Halima Mohammed
Jacket Designers Ben Hinks, Jordan Lambley
Jacket Picture Research Ben Hinks,
Adam Goff
Senior Production Editor Jason Little
Senior Production Controller
Samantha Cross
Managing Editor Hollie Teague
Managing Art Editors Sarah Snelling,
Priyanka Thakur
Art Director Maxine Pedliham
Publishing Director Georgina Dee

First published in Great Britain in 2023 by
Dorling Kindersley Limited
DK, One Embassy Gardens, 8 Viaduct Gardens,
London, SW11 7BW

The authorised representative in the EEA is
Dorling Kindersley Verlag GmbH. Arnulfstr. 124,
80636 Munich, Germany

Copyright © 2023 Dorling Kindersley Limited
A Penguin Random House Company
23 24 25 26 10 9 8 7 6 5 4 3 2
003-335311–April/2023

A CIP catalogue record for this book
is available from the British Library.
ISBN: 978-0-2416-1526-3

Printed and bound in Malaysia

For the curious
www.dk.com

MIX
Paper | Supporting
responsible forestry
FSC™ C018179

This book was made with Forest
Stewardship Council™ certified
paper – one small step in DK's
commitment to a sustainable future.
For more information go to
www.dk.com/our-green-pledge

The rapid rate at which the world is changing is constantly keeping the DK
Eyewitness team on our toes. While we've worked hard to ensure that this
edition of *Run* is accurate and up-to-date, we know that race routes and locations
are altered, trails can become impassable, and organized runs are sometimes
cancelled. So, if you notice we've got something wrong or something's changed,
we want to hear about it. Please get in touch at travelguides@dk.co.uk